BEING AND EDUCATION
An Essay in Existential Phenomenology

BEING AND EDUCATION

An Essay in Existential Phenomenology

DONALD VANDENBERG

Pennsylvania State University

PRENTICE-HALL, INC., Englewood Cliffs, New Jersey

To the memory of Martin Buber

C-13-074005-5
P-13-073999-5

Library of Congress Catalog Card Number 74-135405

Printed in the United States of America
Current printing (last digit):

10 9 8 7 6 5 4 3 2 1

PRENTICE-HALL INTERNATIONAL, INC., *London*
PRENTICE-HALL OF AUSTRALIA, PTY. LTD., *Sydney*
PRENTICE-HALL OF CANADA, LTD., *Toronto*
PRENTICE-HALL OF INDIA PRIVATE LIMITED, *New Delhi*
PRENTICE-HALL OF JAPAN, INC., *Tokyo*

Contents

9 Educating and the Power of Being   *131*

10 The Call to Being   *147*

11 Traditional Aims of Schooling   *164*

Preface

Seeking the basis of education in human existence, this essay employs existential phenomenology as a method to investigate major educational problems within the limitations and possibilities of being. I am deeply grateful to several European theorists for having shown the way, because previous work in the United States has not involved this method and approach. The educational thought of Romano Guardini, Martinus Langeveld, and Otto Bollnow, in fact, is made substantively available in English in Chapters Four, Five, and Ten, respectively, as the documentation acknowledges. If the indebtedness is not sufficiently clear in the text it is because of the greater debt owed them for opening the way to existential phenomenology of education and because of the greater debt shared with them to Martin Heidegger for his profound and originative way of raising the question of being.

Two-thirds of the chapters, but only one-third of the volume, have been previously published.

Chapter One appeared as "An Existential Perspective–Philosophy of Education in a Research-Oriented Environment," Proceedings of the Northwest Philosophy of Education Society, College of Education *Record*, University of Idaho, 7 (Fall-Winter 1967; Spring 1968), 22–30.

Chapter Two appeared under the same title in *Educational Theory*, 16 (January 1967), 60–66.

Chapter Four appeared as "Life-Phases and Values," *Educational Forum*, 32 (March 1968), 293–302.

Chapter Five appeared as "Existential Educating and Pedagogic Authority," *Philosophy of Education 1966*: Proceedings of the Twenty-second Annual Meeting of the Philosophy of Education Society (Edwardsville, Ill.: Studies in Philosophy and Education, 1966), pp. 106–11.

Chapter Eight appeared as "Educational Policy and Ideology," *Journal of Educational Thought*, 1 (April 1967), 38–50.

Chapter Nine appeared as "Non-Violent Power in Education," *Educational Theory*, 19 (Winter 1969), 49–57.

Chapter Ten appeared as "The Pedagogic Admonition in Existential Perspective," *Philosophy of Education 1969*: Proceedings of the Twenty-fifth Annual Meeting of the Philosophy of Education Society (Edwardsville, Ill.: Studies in Philosophy and Education, 1969), pp. 81–87.

These papers have been completely rewritten and expanded for this volume, and I would like to thank the editors and the secretary of P.E.S. for granting permission to reprint them in this way. More gratitude is due them and the review boards and program committees for allowing publication in the first instance, however; for that encouragement made this book possible. In this regard particular thanks go to Edward Kelly for the invitation to present the "position paper" on the 1967 N.W.P.E.S. conference theme that appears in a revised form as Chapter One immediately following.

DONALD VANDENBERG

BEING AND EDUCATION
An Essay in Existential Phenomenology

1
The Role of Philosophy of Education in a Research-Oriented Environment

Philosophy of education has many uses, but the most important of these is its role in teacher education. The college of education, however, much like the surrounding university and society, is becoming increasingly dominated by science and technology, and there often seems to be little need for philosophy of education. Much as the technological mentality in the surrounding culture has little use for "idle speculation" concerning the ends of human existence, the atmosphere of the college of education often serves, willingly or not, to dampen ardor for philosophical reflection concerning the means and ends of education. That teacher education occurs more and more in a research-oriented environment may very well be as it should be, but this nevertheless places the role of philosophy of education in question. What is the role of philosophy of education in a research-oriented environment?

This question can be understood in a variety of ways. The sociological, political, economic, and historiological ways of asking the question, however, are not of primary concern, for the obligations that the ensuing answers would place upon philosophy of education could not be fulfilled. A subsequent philosophical examination of the question would be necessary in order to see which obligations were philosophically legitimate. If perchance philosophy of education has served society well by assisting in the socialization of teacher candidates and the subsequent socialization of children; if it has served as a means to political power through the indoctrination of teacher candidates, and subsequently children, into particular value systems; if it has fostered the maintenance and expansion of the economic system through assisting in the centralization of the schools' programs upon vocational preparation; or if it has served these and other functions in the past, nevertheless these roles may have been thrust upon it from the outside, and may have distorted and obscured its genuine place in teacher education. This is neither to say that these are not proper functions of schooling nor that previous philosophy of education has been corrupted from its primordial innocence, diverted from its genuine possibilities through attempts to fulfill societal, political, and economic roles and obligations. It is to contend that a philosophical raising of the question is the necessary and prerequisite condition to the determination of how philosophy of education can be loyal to its own nature, to itself. A philosophical examination of the question may result in the conclusion that philosophy of education, like philosophy, "bakes no bread—i.e., yields no practical advice concerning how to get things done—but that this is precisely its virtue. Then to condemn it for "baking no bread" would merely reveal the technological-mindedness of the would-be condemner. Before it can be determined whether the societal, political, or economical "obligations" of philosophy of education are compatible with its own nature and can be fulfilled, it is necessary to be concerned in a philosophical way with the question, "What is the role of philosophy of education in the education of teacher candidates in a research-oriented environment?"

The question is not merely a "philosophical" question, however, for it belongs to a particular area of inquiry within philosophy, to ethics. It asks not what the role of philosophy of education is but what it should be. It cannot be asked, furthermore, as if it were an "academic" question, as if it were "abstract" and did not occur within human existence, as if it were not a matter in which the questioner's own being is in question. The ethical question of what the role of philosophy of education should be, then, can be articulated only within the context of a consideration of the possibilities and significance of human being, i.e., within a normative or philosophical anthropology. This context in turn is available only within the larger vista of ontology. The original question becomes an ontological question when it is asked with the greatest intensity, scope, and depth. When it is a genuine question, "What is the role of philosophy of education in a research-oriented environment?" merges indissolubly with the more fundamental questions, "What is the significance of my being?" "What is the significance of human being?" "What is the significance of being?" "What does it mean to be able to ask these kinds of questions?"

The questioning, however, has taken a formidable and unpopular turn. No question is more difficult and more unusual than the one concerning the meaning of being. The unpopularity of the being question, however, is relative to the societal dominance of scientific and technological thinking, the very reason for the original question. Because the prevalence of technological thinking has led the human race to a point where it is technologically possible to commit racial suicide, the infrequency of the being-question is in inverse proportion to its importance. Its unpopularity intensifies the questioning and implicates the further questioning of the ontological foundations of science. What is the being of science? Of scientific research? Of technology? If science is a human phenomenon, then what is it within human being that makes science possible?

The questioning now has taken an apparently perverse turn. In order to ascertain what the role of philosophy of education should be, it becomes necessary to question the role of *science* in the research-oriented environment. This questioning is concerned not to specify the goals of research but to seek for the necessary and sufficient grounds in human existence for the very being of science, to seek the existential presuppositions of scientific endeavor. What must be presupposed about human existence in order for science to be existentially possible? Only after this question has been explored can the original question be fully entertained.

ONTOLOGICAL PRESUPPOSITIONS OF SCIENCE

What must be presupposed about human existence for science to be? Awakeness and being there. Every scientist in any research area necessarily takes it for granted that he is awake and there. He never questions the most basic fact, not even if he is a psychologist, that he has a wakeful access to the world around him. Awakeness, simple being awake, is the hidden, obscure, and unnoticed foundation of all scientific research, and awakeness is strictly correlated with access to the world and with having a world—the wider awake one is, the more world there is.[1] Part of the significance of this most obvious datum appears in the realization that the mode of awakeness that accompanies scientific theorizing is not that which is most authentically human. Full wakefulness occurs in the working world and in complex sports, but not in scientific theorizing. In scientific theorizing with concepts that have been made logical, i.e., timeless, by the conscious intellectual manipulations of the scientist for the express purpose of theorizing, there is a modification of awakeness such that theorizing occurs in one of its deficient modes and therefore within a deficient mode of existence.[2] The behavioral scientist, moreover, also takes for granted the fact that the "object" of his inquiry is in fact a subject. For the behavioral scientist to take the subject's awakeness for granted is an oversight of enormous magnitude.

The ontological difference between being-awake and being-in-a-dream is not only apparent within almost everyone's own immediate experience (i.e., it is publicly verifiable), it is a greater degree of the difference between existing authentically and existing inauthentically. On the other hand, the difference is the proof that no naturalistic, objectivistic research comprehends or can comprehend the authentically human because of its initial methodological choice to omit human wakefulness and being there, i.e., to omit human being. Insofar as the objectivistic study of man in the behavioral sciences grasps real phenomena, and there is little doubt that it does, it grasps manifestations of alienation, for the lower the level of awakeness and the more the behavior is situationless, the more accessible it is to "objective" research.[3]

The ontological difference between being-in-a-dream and being-awake lies in the control the person has over "what happens." Dreaming is subjectively experienced as world taking over and everything that occurs happens to one. One's own initiative counts for nothing—precisely as if he is "in a dream." The dream is the ostensive definition of determinism, the example of what life would be like were behavior caused. Objectively, dreams are caused by on-going physiological processes that emerge into awareness. On the other hand, acting in wide-awakeness is subjectively experienced as originating solely from the center, the actor motivated wholly by what he is making happen within a shifting totality of relevancies, within the world. His own initiative counts for everything. Objectively, physiological processes are caused by acting, not its cause, or else scientific inquiry as one form of acting is not possible. The person, therefore, exists in the initiating and performance of intentional actions in wide-awakeness. If this is so, then what is omitted when human behavior is studied "objectively," what is overlooked when awakeness is presupposed, is precisely human existence, human being. The significance of this omission can be seen more clearly when the principal features of human being are in view.

Men exist authentically, i.e., they authentically exist, when they are acting in the world within full wide-awakeness. Man essentially is not an object, for his essence is his existence.[4] If man's most essential, most fundamental characteristic is his existence, if he is authentically or most characteristically human when he is most widely awake, then the essence of man, the human reality or human being, is as far from being a substance as possible. Man is not an object, a substance, because when engaged in wide-awake action he exists within the unity of his own temporality, i.e., when he is spatializing and futurizing from his own center, pastizing the present into having been and thus being authentically there in the present moment.[5] Because he exists in the ontological unity of the ekstatic structure of temporality, man is basically and essentially a subject, and an "objective" misinterpretation of a subjecticity is as "erroneous" as a subjective misinterpretation of an objectivity.[6] The "objective" constructs of the behavioral sciences, that is, omit the other person's awakeness, his subjecticity, and count it for nothing, when it is, rather, his human being. The omission means that the consideration of man through the "objective" constructs of the behavioral sciences is as *objectively* wrong as can be. The "objective" constructs enable one to look at another person "objectively" as if he were cut off from his world and not as an initiator of intentional actions, but the intentional action of the scientist's using the "objective" constructs to observe the other presupposes his own transcendence and being-in-the-world at the very instant that the other is objectified through the use of the constructs that presuppose that the observed person is not a transcendence having access to the world. The self-contradictory project of objectifying the other is thus not only objectively wrong (the other retains his subjecticity and what is most real about him has not been observed at all in spite of the illusion), it is an actual depersonalization of the other such that the use of naturalistic, objectivistic constructs in realms other than those in which they have their origin and legitimate meaning is an instance of, and contributes to, the alienation of men from themselves and from each other.

Because awakeness and being there are presupposed but not acknowledged, naturalism or objectivism in the human sciences is neither natural nor objective but naïvely unaware of itself. The objectivism of the behavioral sciences is a province of meaning that comes into being through the bracketing out of the being of human being. Because its methods parallel the bracketing of naïve, common-sense realism, it is easy to overlook the arbitrariness and effect of bracketing human existence out of the field of investigation by methods of inquiry that demand that the "data" be "scientific," i.e., by militant and ideological empiricism.[7] The bracketing out of the being of human being is nevertheless the methodological equivalent of murder and the bracketing out of the being of the investigator during the investigation is the methodological equivalent of suicide.[8] When it is taken for nothing, moreover, being erupts, thus "causing" the apparently irrational phenomena that the behavioral sciences "find." They do not correspond to its rationality, and so they are blind. When being erupts surreptitiously, without the guidance of thought, it emerges in a blind will to will; this will to will lies behind the calculative, manipulative thinking of the technological mentality that has its place only within very limited provinces of meaning.

The various provinces of meaning that are found in the constituted sciences are not equally provinces of being. They are not equally founded ontologically. Each province of meaning has ts own mode of awakeness, i.e., its own temporal structure, cognitive style, and sense of reality, and each has to be "entered" through a specific bracketing or "leap" from another mode of awakeness and province of meaning.[9] The cognitive styles of provinces of meaning are not interchangeable, and to bring the style or meanings from one province into another renders unavailable the meanings legitimate to the second province. If one brings the cognitive style and meanings of naïve, common-sense realism into the bracketing of the province of meaning of listening to a fairy tale or a joke, attending church, making love or conversation, watching a play or movie, and so on, he simply misses the meanings available within those provinces. If one does not suspend the naturalistic viewpoint when the curtain rises at the theater, he remains a spectator rather than becoming a participant in the drama because he is inauthentically there, alienated from the reality appropriate to theater. He sees actors in costumes playing roles (e.g., Olivier) rather than seeing the *personae* (e.g., Hamlet wearing his own clothes, being his brilliant, melancholic, indecisive self).

Analogously, the objectivistic bracketing of the research-oriented environment is a freely chosen, finite province of meaning which has a very incomplete cognitive style when considered from other provinces of meaning. To bring its constructs into other provinces, into other bracketings, results in the undesirable alteration and lack of availability of the meanings of the other provinces. If one sees an "ego" or "personality," weak or strong, when "encountering" another person he does not really encounter the other person but remains alienated from him through consciously bracketing out his being in a phenomenological "murder." He remains as distant from him as the spectator who sees Olivier remains alienated from Hamlet, and as the participant in the drama remains alienated from Olivier if he applauds Hamlet after curtain call, and he cannot understand the meaning of the other person. Likewise, the essential point that Carl Rogers made when he said that an objective diagnosis of a person does not help the person (or the therapeutic encounter) can be interpreted as signifying that the bracketing appropriate to diagnosis or to the construction of a theory of psychotherapy is totally inappropriate to the bracketing of the psychotherapeutic situation.[10] The objective diagnosis may be medically necessary, but psychotherapy, as distinguished from medical psychiatry, exists within a unique province of meaning attainable only through a leap into a unique bracketing in which diagnosis has no place.

Analogously, the bracketing appropriate to research within the research-oriented environment is totally inappropriate to the bracketing of the pedagogic relation. As the curtain at the theater rises, thus promoting the "leap" into the bracketing peculiar to dramatic participation, so the classroom door closes, bracketing the pedagogic relation from all outside or external meanings, including those of objectivistic research in the behavioral sciences. Insofar as the pedagogic relation and the educative process occurs, comes into being, as an existential encounter between two human beings, then insofar as the teacher brackets out the pupil's being-awake and being-there by structuring her perception of pupils through the use of "objective" constructs, she alienates herself from them and from their world and brackets the pedagogic relation out of existence. Insofar as the teacher's world is structured by the "objective," naturalistic constructs obtainable in the research-oriented environment in which philosophy of education finds itself, she is necessarily alienated from the pupil because she is in the wrong bracketing.[11] She is to some extent attempting to observe the pupils objectively when she should be relating to them with her whole being. Insofar as the constructs were developed within a cognitive style of pure theorizing, they were developed within a deficient mode of wakefulness, and the extent to which they structure the teacher's world is the extent to which she is prohibited from being wide-awake and authentically there in the classroom situation. Insofar as the teacher makes theoretical explanations of the pupil's behavior, she fails to understand the meaning of his words and actions because the particulars are lost by being subsumed within a general case. Insofar as the teacher then grasps a cross section of the pupil's being, what he is at a given moment, she cannot see him in his futuring, in his temporality, that is, as who he is becoming in his projection of being, and she cannot understand him.

If this be so, then part of an answer to the question concerning what the role of philosophy of education in a research-oriented environment should be is emerging. Further pursuit of the questions concerning the being of science, however, will prepare the way for the complete emergence of an answer to the original question. The province of meaning of the theoretical attitude of the social sciences has "objects" whose being is constituted by or within the bracketing, as the being of Cinderella is constituted by and within the bracketing of the "Once upon a time. . . ." The being of the "objects" constituted by the objective sciences of man is posited in "objective time," but they do not exist within the lived-time of wide-awakeness. Theorizing occurs outside of lived, social time such that the theorizer not only cannot grasp the living present as such nor the living person as a unity, he also cannot enter into social relations with other people: the "objective" theorizer is solitary. Scientific research into social relations and personality thus appear to be ontologically impossible. When the theoretical constructs of the social sciences are used outside of the theorizing bracketing of the social sciences, then, they are taken to represent something real, to have referents in the same way that common-sense realism ascribes referents to other words, and this unacknowledged hypostatization contributes to the alienation of men not only because the users make objects out of others' subjecticities but also because the words become so much free-floating, pseudo-sophisticated gossip that keeps people from meeting each other. Freudianism, for example, provided the where-withal for the free-floating reconstruction of the meanings of other people's words and actions in explanatory but arbitrary debunkings and arrogant *ad hominem* arguments. The permeation of the "culture," of the talk between people, by the constructs of the behavioral sciences more than a little contributes to the meaninglessness and alienation from the world, from one's self, and from others that prevail within the common historical situation.[12]

It may be presumed that the naïve objectivism of the behavioral sciences that tends to permeate the "research-oriented environment" is part of the global forgetfulness, loss, and oblivion of being that is conse-quent upon the dominance of calculative, manipulative, technological thinking on the planetary level, because it is above all the sciences that first and foremost are committed, in the interest of scientific disinterested-ness, to letting the object of inquiry be what it is, to letting what is be. Letting the subjects of inquiry be who they are, however, seems to be furthest from the minds of the "empiricists" in the "research-oriented environment" when they demand that the "data" be "scientific." It is the "empiricist" who first of all ought to accept the data as it is given. This is what a genuine empiricism ought to be, by definition, but to the contrary it is first of all the "empiricists" in the behavioral sciences who take a dogmatic stand toward eliminating subjecticity from the data.[13] The "empiricism" turns into an inverted rationalism that participates in the "apparent foundering of rationalism" because of its naïve objectivism and its externalization of reason. Reason becomes externalized when the "world" as constituted by the sciences, when a finite province of meaning, attainable only through a particular bracketing, becomes identified with the real, objective world as if it existed as such independently of the bracketing that enabled its constituting disclosure. This "rationalism," this mistaking of the rationalized world for the objective world, founders when the externalization is turned toward man and when it is maintained that man belongs to the world of objective facts *at the same time* that he is held to have purposes and aims such as the scientist's adherence to the norms of reason in order to ascertain what the objective facts are, thus being completely unable to account for his own intellectual life even and especially if he is a behavioral scientist.[14] The taking for granted of his own and others' wakefulness and access to the world by the behavioral scientist, in other words, is such an enormous oversight that it indicates the presence of a crisis in the social sciences. This crisis is due to, and can be characterized as, the forgetfulness of being.

The forgetfulness, loss, and oblivion of being is a phenomenon that permeates the planet in close relation to the dominance of manipulative, technological thinking, but it permeates the behavioral sciences as demonstrated by their overlooking man's being-awake and being-there, by their omission of human being. The manifestations of this forgetfulness appear everywhere in the supposedly research-oriented environment. There is no psychology of the child or youth that does not presuppose a psychology of maturity that presupposes an ontology,[15] yet child and adolescent psychologists are not noted for their ontological inquiries. There is no psychology of learning that does not begin with an existential analysis of the child's and youth's life-situation,[16] yet learning theorists are not noted for their ontological inquiries. There is no vocational guidance without a phenomenological description of existential working situations in the context of the working world,[17] yet guidance personnel are not noted for their ontological inquiries. There is no social psychology or sociology that does not take for granted the existence of the phenomena of communication and intersubjecticity,[18] yet neither social psychologists nor sociologists are noted for their ontological inquiries. There is no statistical analysis of data unless variables have been first of all grounded phenomenologically to insure their ontological independence,[19] yet empirical researchers are not noted for their ontological inquiries. If an ontological founding is necessary for an adequate stance in any of these areas, and if it is missing except by way of unconscious presupposition, then it is correct to say that the environment of teacher education, apparently dominated by a research orientation, is in fact dominated by "unconscious ontology" in an ideological way. It is also correct to say that insofar as schooling turns the child or youth over to the various specializations of the research-oriented environment, it turns them over to what are in effect special interest groups because of their forgetfulness of being. This is contrary to the well-being of children and youth. It is contrary to the public safety.[20]

Because of its necessary forgetfulness of being, moreover, no new or forthcoming scientific theory can be of direct assistance to a concrete pedagogy. It will necessarily be a reduction of, and an abstraction from, actual occurrences that omits the being of teachers, children, and youth.[21] Any and all attempts to "apply" scientific theory or finding to concrete human situations such as classrooms can be generated from, and only from, a stance that is in effect an *a priori* rationalism, because the "application" is a refusal to look at a living situation as such to see what it requires of one. This is a refusal to proceed "inductively" in favor of a method of imposition that is tantamount to *a priori* rationalism. The application of the behavioral sciences in education or elsewhere, that is, turns them into something else, into normative anthropology, because their application is tantamount to suggesting, advising, guiding, recommending, and/or dictating how life should be lived in the situations to which they are applied.[22] The result is that the legitimate domain of the behavioral sciences, the attempts to investigate and say what and how man and society is, becomes of secondary importance in their application, for what makes their application possible are accepted views of what man and society could be and should be. This application requires a mode of inquiry that is ontologically independent of the mode of inquiry of the behavioral sciences. An educational question of central importance concerns the kind of "personality structure" a certain "culture" will allow, for example, but this is neither a psychological nor sociological question but one of normative anthropology and cultural ideology. It is equally a question of the concrete educational situation wherein the pupil has something to say concerning who he will become if it is not to omit the being of the pupil.[23] It is at least partly a question of the concrete educational situation because the child or youth (like everyone else) *is* his future, and because it is the "structures" of the personal and societal futures that are of primary significance to this educational question.[24] No method available in the research-oriented environment, however, is able to study the future, i.e., the pupil's possibilities of being.

THE DUTY OF PHILOSOPHY OF EDUCATION

Philosophy of education in that environment, then, acquires the pedagogic obligation to waken awareness of these possibilities of being. Its pedagogic task is twofold: (a) to waken people who are becoming teachers to awareness of their own being, thence to enable them to choose who they will be in their subsequent encounters with pupils, and (b) to enable their pupils to choose for themselves who they will be. This is evident from the examination of the existential presuppositions of scientific inquiry and parallels the role of philosophy in the broader society. With the technologizing of the world it becomes the ontological function of the general philosopher to raise the question of being so that the limitations of scientific and technological thinking are seen for what they are. To omit the being of the investigator and the being of the investigated merits the appropriate technical philosophical designation: nihilism. The negating of being is a nihilistic undertaking. Then the encroachments of nihilism on the planetary scale thrust upon philosophy the duty of raising the question of being: What is the significance of being? Philosophy inherits the ontological function of asking the question of being, in the service of being, on behalf of being. Analogously, the technologizing of the world of the college of education thrusts upon philosophy of education the obligation to raise the question of the being of those who are to be educated, which is part of the broader question, "What is the significance of human being?" Whereas the philosopher raises this latter question as part of the questioning of being by his own being, the philosopher of education asks it as part of the questioning of being by those who are being educated. Whereas philosophical anthropology deals with what men can become and yields the decisive answer that they can become absolutely responsible for their own being and say for themselves who they are, the philosopher of education can say just as decisively that more determinate answers affecting educational problematics prevent pupils from finding out for themselves who they can become. That is to say that the acceptance of more determinate answers concerning who man is prevents the educative process from occurring. Then the philosophy of education has an ontological function because children and youth exist, because they are open to the world, have their being to be, and want to be someone themselves.

In the research-oriented environment of the college of education particularly, then, the role of philosophy of education should be to raise the question of the being of children and youth that they might respond to the call of being and become who they can authentically become.

If the original question was said to be an ethical question, then this statement concerning the obligation of philosophy of education merits specifically ethical articulation now that the ontological and normative anthropological justifications have been made. Philosophers of education and people who are becoming teachers should have some concern for becoming good themselves, for becoming more professional and more able to subscribe to a code of "professional ethics." The "ethics" of any profession, since Plato, become focused in the effort to make decisions for the good of the client, guided by the objective demands emanating from the situations of concrete practice. Because the objectivity of the pupil is his subjecticity, his existence, his being, the being of the pupil is the "absolute limit" and whoever surpasses this limit not only commits malpractice, he also impoverishes and destroys his own humanity.[25] Then the objective demands emerging from the situation in which educational thinking now finds itself emanate from the being of children and youth and their right to grow up authentically human. Then because immorality in educational thinking and practice, as elsewhere, is failure to be bound by objectivity, which in the case of one's fellow man is precisely his being,[26] educational thinking and practice ought to be bound by the objectivity of children and youth: their objectivity is precisely their future possibilites of being.

If all this be so, then the essential task of philosophy of education is to assist in the disclosure of these possibilities of being. It is the *essential* task because it pertains to the being of philosophy of education and is indicative of when philosophy of education is loyal to its own nature, when it exists authentically. If this has not been so clear in the past, then nothing but gratitude can be felt toward the increasing dominance of so-called empirical research in the orientation in the situation in which philosophy of education might find itself for its assisting in the disclosure of the fundamental orientation to the question: "What is the significance of the being of children and youth?"

2

On the Ground of Education

What is the significance of the being of children and youth? What is the significance of the being of man? What is the significance of my own being? What is the significance of being? What is the being of children, youth, myself, and man? What is the being of education? When does educating "have being"? How and when are pedagogic practices grounded in human being? Which ones are grounded in the being of the world? What is the being of the world? When and how does the world "have being"? What is being such that "there is" a world? Does the phenomenon of the world rest upon some hidden foundation or ultimate reality? What, in the last analysis, is real?

These questions, and more, are implicated by the question concerning the being of children and youth, for the latter signifies that pedagogic practice ought to be grounded in their existence, in their reality, if it is to be educational. To take the being of children and youth into account in pedagogy it is necessary to ascertain precisely what it is that is to be educated. What structural characteristic, feature, or aspect of the pupil, if any, receives the education? His mind? Personality? Self? Character? Spirit? His biological, organic body? Brain? Nervous system? Habits? Ear or larynx? What is it that is most real about the pupil such that its modification through pedagogy or otherwise counts as education? What such modification is constitutive of the educative process? What is the "ultimate" reality of the pupil? The question does not seek for constructs *about* the pupil but his being, his reality: What is the ground of education?

The preliminary replies of the previous chapter suffice to distinguish philosophy of education from other areas of inquiry but fail in the face of more intense metaphysical questioning, particularly in view of the unpopularity of metaphysics. Metaphysics is not only the most unpopular area of philosophy to the scientistic-technological mind, it is most vehemently "out of fashion" among philosophers themselves. Attempts to scrutinize reality and say what ultimately exists or what is the absolute foundation have been "repudiated" by the major trends of philosophy in this century.[1] The major trends, all beginning, taking root, and becoming established in the first two decades of the century, tend, in fact, to agree upon one thing: metaphysical speculation is done with, over, a thing of the past, for each of the major styles conceives of itself as "revolutionary" with respect to the style and substance of philosophizing.

The tendency of these major movements of thought to agree upon the elimination of metaphysics may, however, be merely symptomatic of the rootlessness and ungroundedness of life in the modern world. They may be manifestations of the general forgetfulness of being. At any rate, it requires metaphysical thinking to be able to decide for oneself whether the abandonment of metaphysics is a way of becoming more intellectually responsible or is a flight into irresponsibility. The impact of these so-called revolutions in philosophy upon educational theory, in turn, may be merely symptomatic of the groundlessness of modern education and may possibly be a flight into intellectual irresponsibility. This impact is revealed most clearly not in the "empiricism" of the "research-oriented" environment but in the numerous articles purporting to delineate the "proper" relation of educational philosophy to philosophy and to educational practice. The sheer volume of this material *about* the role and nature of philosophy of education (it swells to over one hundred articles and one anthology of reprints)[2] attests to the possibility of the groundlessness of contemporary educational theory. The customary approach tends to begin with some conception or preconception of the nature of philosophy, philosophy of education, or education to be promoted and/or destroyed. It may be to some advantage to approach the problematic from the other side, from the side of the educational problem involved, and ask: What if education is groundless?

This question no longer asks, What is the ground of education? The latter question might suggest that an answer was ready at hand and that the questioning was merely rhetorical. It is more important, however, to achieve an understanding of why the search for a ground is a significant inquiry. What if a teacher uses a method of teaching employing operant conditioning, but what if the reality of the child is his spirit? What if a teaching method attempts to foster the pupil's spiritual development, but what if the reality of the pupil is his brain and nervous system? What if education is groundless?

The question does not ask, What if educational *theory* is groundless? Asking this question would indicate that educational theory should seek grounding for itself, perhaps among those metaphysical theories that partly resulted in the modern trends to abandon and/or to abolish metaphysics, i.e., that a theory of the ground was at hand. The grounding of educational theory in some mistaken theory of the ground, however, would still leave education ungrounded except by chance. It is not the grounding of educational theory that is called for, but the grounding of education itself. An adequate grounding of educational theory can still leave education itself groundless, in spite of the possibility that the most appropriate way to ground education may be, perhaps, through the adequate grounding of educational theory.

By asking, What if education is groundless? the direction of inquiry is reversed. Instead of asking for a theory of the ground, of ultimate reality, then working out its implication for educational philosophy and then its implications for practice—involving thereby innumerable unsolved problems in the logic of implication—the question begins by asking about the significance of the being of children and youth, for it is in their being that the ground of education is to be sought. If education is a modification of that which is most real about them, and if ascertaining their reality becomes the task of philosophy of education, then the question of the ground concerns the implications of education for philosophy of education: What in the pupil's existence makes education possible? What exists education? If it is possible for pedagogic practice to be groundless, then it must be possible to ground pedagogic practice, to educate. Seeking for the *ground* of education, then, is seeking for the *nature* of education. The two questions are identical: "What is the ground of education?" "What is education?" The questions are identical because the only valid definition of education is a grounded one. If it is not so clear that there is a need for an adequate definition of education, the need for grounding pedagogic practice is somewhat clearer. The preceding chapter and these preliminary remarks may not be sufficient to indicate that education requires a ground or adequate founding in the being of the pupil, however; for it is not readily apparent even if the words are properly understood.

Three things make the need for grounding education somewhat obscure. First, education is frequently reduced to its most apparent and least common denominator: schooling, the transmission of factual information and skills, and the development of cognitive processes. The total process of education is reduced to its institutional and cognitive aspects. Second, *theory* of education is frequently reduced to theory of learning, cognition, or instruction. In either of these reductions something that may be central to education yet more limited than education itself is mistaken for education. Finally, it is only too obvious that teaching has something to do with imparting knowledge and ideas and with developing habits of thinking, and everyone already knows what these are. In any of these cases, some unconscious and unacknowledged metaphysics is held without question, dogmatically and ideologically, without a genuinely philosophical raising of the question of the basis of practice.

For this reason the need for grounding can be seen most readily from some direction other than the cognitive dimension. Without suggesting that the difficulties of cognitive education are any less than those of moral education, the latter seems obviously sufficiently problematic and prone to failure to make the need for grounding clear. What if moral education is groundless?

ON GROUNDING MORAL EDUCATION

The problem of moral education, in a sense, was solved long ago by Plato. If one knows the good, he will pursue the good. Simply teach the good to everyone, so that it is known, and they will be good; and the aim of moral education is achieved. Two apparently minor difficulties, however, remain: what is the good and how does one teach it so that the learner really knows it, i.e., so that his knowing results in the pursuit of the good? The explication of these difficulties will reveal the need for grounding moral education and hence education.

Plato himself had these difficulties. Rather than defining precisely what the good is, Plato wrote *The Republic* to specify the education deemed necessary to coming to *know* the good. He more or less evaded the problem of definition by imagining the education that would enable the educated person to see the good in a flash of intuition at the end of his education, itself a matter that would occupy the better part of fifty years. Even for Plato, in other words, there was great difficulty in defining the good in other terms so that one knew what was supposed to be taught when one set about to teach the good. Plato knew he had not solved the problem of moral education and things have not improved in subsequent years. They may at times have seemed to become easier, particularly when some system of values, some version of the good, was taken for granted, as in fact may appear to be the situation today. On the level of public school instruction, for example, there seems to be little difficulty in knowing the good. Regardless of the problems that philosophers of ethics and morals may have had in justifying and delineating the contents of morality or the good life (and regardless of societal conflicts over so-called values), there are large agreements concerning the specific details of morality and the good life: stealing is wrong, adultery is bad, cheating is not to be done, and so on. There are atypical cases and exceptional circumstances that are very interesting philosophically, and there are significant exceptions by certain important publics to any consensus, but on the general level of experiencing that is ordinary for pupils in the public schools there seems to be little difficulty in ascertaining the contents of moral education. There seems to be no problem in defining the good for educative purposes. The problems partially caused by more complex thinking and experiencing arise after leaving school and entrance into practical experience. The findings of cultural anthropology are supportive: with the exception of a few primitive societies, marriage in some form, with punishments to be administered for transgression of its bounds, is a universal phenomenon, as are both the rights of property and the expectations of honorable conduct, whatever forms these latter may take. This is not to argue that whatever is universal or cross-culturally "valid" is necessarily in accord with "human nature" and therefore good, but it does suggest that establishing the content of moral education seems to offer less difficulty if one is willing to generalize, at the price of a precision that may be inappropriate to the age level ordinarily associated with public schooling. Precision can be gained another way, by reducing the content of moral instruction to moral rules. If the content of moral instruction is "reduced" to moral rules there seems to be no problem of ascertaining the good for the purpose of universal public instruction.

The second difficulty, however, is not so easily handled, and the explication of the problem involved will indicate the fallaciousness of the preceding "resolution" of the first difficulty. Even when the content of morality is located in moral rules, the teaching of morality is not merely a matter of saying moral rules and having the pupils repeat them. It is not simply a matter of the "promulgation" of moral rules. If the pupil can state a rule ("Do unto others . . . ," "I shouldn't steal"), and particularly if he can give reasons for the rule, it is "promulgated," and of course the pupil is blameworthy if he breaks a rule that he understands (can, in his own words, say the reasons for the rule). But there are pupils who do in fact "break moral rules," even though they have been instructed in them and can give the reasons for them, and thereby demonstrate that they understand them. Because the aim of moral education is to promote moral conduct rather than simply to distribute an understanding of moral rules, or to allow those in authority to punish wrongdoers, it does not suffice to chastise the so-called rule-breakers. Such chastisement is as much an indication of inadequate instruction as it is a sign of blameworthiness. Because the aim of moral education is not to punish transgressors, even though punishment in some form may be inseparable from the teaching of moral rules and may be morally justifiable, its very use suggests that the word *knowing* requires a very special definition if knowing the good is to result in being good. If punishment is ever necessary or justified, not just any kind of knowing will suffice for the learning of the knowledge that leads automatically, as it were, to virtue, if in fact this is the aim of moral education. If being good is the aim of moral education, then regardless of the content of moral education and its justification, it is both necessary and important to consider methods of teaching and/or learning in respect to moral rules, or whatever the content may be, to promote the maximum achievement of the aim. It is necessary and important to ground moral education.

Another way to consider this second difficulty is to notice that, historically, ethics has tended to ignore or overlook the areas of human conduct that are the concern of "depth" psychology. With some exceptions, such as Kant with his notion of radical evil (man's tendency to use the words of morality as a camouflage for self-love), philosophers of morals have been somewhat naïve. Current ideas about moral education, discussion of moral rules, and value theory are not exceptions. There are two problems. One is the matter of taking "depth motivation" into account in moral judgment. Ascertaining the weight that should be given to human "irrationality" in the third-person judging of the morality of conduct is not being mooted here. The other problem is more relevant, for it is clear that the teaching of morality has no alternative than to be based upon an adequate and viable conception of human nature if it is to be effective; but what is an "adequate conception of human nature"? The fullness of the problem emerges when one probes into depth psychology, for one finds that depth psychologists are not only in disagreement but that they disagree most strongly precisely upon their conceptions of "human nature." Not only can one not find an accepted conception of "human nature" among the various depth psychologists, which consensus would establish the feeling if not the proof that their theories are valid, but one finds no grounds there for the selection of one theory of "human nature" rather than another. Apparently the views are equally "empirically grounded." In order to be able to select among the views in an intellectually responsible way, there must be a judgment concerning the relative groundedness of the various theories. Selection of the most adequately grounded theory involves a criterion of groundedness external to and independent of the theories involved. This is true in any case, i.e., even if the criteria of groundedness were not articulated but unconsciously presupposed. In order to be most fully responsible intellectually, the criteria of groundedness would have to be articulated in the context of a theory of the ground, i.e., in a self-conscious epistemology and metaphysics. Then, however, the psychological theory that was selected upon the criteria of groundedness in order to obtain an "adequate conception of human nature" to ground moral education would itself be nothing more than a detailed repetition of the theory of the ground. It would be a redundant explication of the theory of the ground expressed in psychological terminology, i.e., falling within the bracketing peculiar to the province of meaning of theoretical psychology and fallaciously appearing to be more concrete (cf. Whitehead's conception of the fallacy of misplaced concreteness). This repetition would fail to provide illumination to the person who comprehended the theory of the ground with sufficient adequacy to select the theory. Its usefulness is therefore unclear.

Depth psychologists, furthermore, sometimes employ unreflected-on "norms" in their theorizing such that one cannot fail to notice the normative appearance of much "psychology." The whole area of "mental hygiene," for a prime example, seems to be particularly riddled with the confusion of the "is" and the "ought," with *ad hoc* implicit moralizing, with the morally fallacious assumption that it is good to, that one ought to, and that one is able to pursue patterns of "behavior" conducive to "mental health," or promotive of what a particular "scientist" wishes to call "mental health" but which can very easily be a highly culture-bound conception of "good behavior."

On the one hand, moral philosophers and common-sense views of moral education have been too little aware of the "psychology" they presuppose and have consequently presupposed a simplistic psychological view. On the other hand, "psychologists" have been too little aware of the ethics and normative view of man that they presuppose and have consequently presupposed a simplistic moral view. And on the third hand, teachers are hardly to blame if they increase the confusion by operating in general upon a quasi-psychological, quasi-moralistic basis, particularly in the areas of "motivation," "interest," "discipline," and so on, i.e., in whatever has to do with the way of life within schools. They are not particularly blameworthy if rules necessary *but not sufficient* to accomplish the tasks of instruction ("Assignments shall be completed on time," "Speak to the entire class if you have something to say") take on psychological and moralistic overtones in the life of the school when "commands" fail to accomplish their purpose and when the teacher tries to understand the failure with the help of whatever ideas or constructs she has available. Nor are teachers blameworthy if there is further confusion of "scholastic achievement" with "moral worth," when, that is, evaluation of "scholastic achievement" is accompanied by moral evaluation as happens when not doing school work (or doing it poorly) is assumed to be "wrong" or "bad" and when the "good student" is perceived as, or judged to be, the "good" person; when, that is, "scholastic achievement" in effect becomes equated with "moral worth." Nor are teachers at fault when "concepts" from "mental hygiene" receive moral connotations within school life when pupils appear to be "unhealthy," when, for example, the attribution of an "inferiority complex," a "neurosis," of "maladjustment," "withdrawal," and so on, are used by the teacher to justify an emotional, quasi-moralistic negative or positive reaction to a pupil allegedly so afflicted. Teachers are not to blame in all these cases insofar as philosophers of morals have been somewhat innocent of their "psychology" and psychologists have been less than innocent of their "ethics." Teachers are not guilty when they share the confusions of the "best qualified experts."

The difficulty of moral education that arises from the attempt to discover the kind of knowing that is "really knowing," so that those who learn the good also know it and will in fact pursue it, is not so much a matter of theory of knowing as it is a matter of restoring to ethical theory insofar as it is related to instruction the tension that was originally found in Plato when he accompanied the principle of knowledge of the good with the Socratic (or Delphic) principle of self-knowledge: know thyself. This principle or imperative essentially restores the connection between moral rules (if and when they are the content of moral instruction) and depth psychology. The Socratic imperative retains the original tension because it is based upon an "adequate conception of human nature," upon a view of man as a self-conscious being, and thereby grounds moral education. Invocation of the Socratic imperative, moreover, may be particularly desirable in establishing a connection between the teaching of moral rules and depth psychology if other ways lead to an arbitrary choosing among "psychological theories" or to promoting the illusion that teaching is akin to some form of psychotherapy. Knowing the good seems necessarily related to some form of knowing oneself, at any rate, if one is to learn the good in such a way that it entails pursuit of the good because of the "irrational" or "depth" components of human being. The exploration of the second difficulty of the problematic of moral education has then transposed the original question, "What if moral education is groundless?" into the question, "How can one found moral education in 'human nature' in order to maintain the tension between knowing the good and knowing oneself?"

When a moral rule is "learned" so that knowing it entails living in the way it describes, it can be said to be part of one's very being. To say that it is "part of one's very being" is merely to use the most general terms available. Were one to refer to acquiring a "habit" of following the rule, or to a "disposition" or "tendency" to act according to the rule, or to an "ability" to do what the rule indicates, the unnecessary specification of "habit," "disposition," and so on results in reification, i.e., in making an object out of a self-aware process. It mistakes a construct about a phenomenon for the phenomenon itself. It results in alienating oneself from the matter of inquiry, or in reasoning from effect to cause, which is fallacious reasoning, particularly when subsequent citation of the inferred cause purports to explain the effect. It results in another forgetfulness of being.

If what is most concrete is man in the world, if the human reality is wide-awake action in the world, then references to "habit," "disposition," etc., are an unnecessary, superfluous multiplication of entities that leads into the bracketing and province of meaning of psychology. They result in psychologism, in psychologizing the phenomenon away by doing philosophy with theoretical "constructs" borrowed from theoretical psychology and injected into one's metaphysics. It is precisely this error that has to be avoided if moral education is to be grounded, for the ontological status of "habit," "disposition," and so on is far from settled, and it is not *theory about* but *visibility of* the phenomenon that is essential to the grounding of moral education. Because the ontological status or the reality of "habits," etc., is not settled, the more specific designations for acting in accordance with a moral rule are more vague and more misleading than the expression "part of one's being." In spite of the prevalence of the usage "habit," for example, no one ever experienced a habit or observed one. It may, after all, be an unnecessary hypostatization, a groundless construct, a fiction useful for certain kinds of theory construction but nonetheless an arbitrary fiction.

To say that when a moral rule is learned so that knowing it entails living in the way it describes it becomes part of one's very being, on the other hand, not only utilizes the most general available conceptualization to refer to the full concreteness involved, but also parallels the ordinary usage, "That's the way I am," and, "You know me," when these are given as the reason or excuse for having done something. That one can do something because that is the way he is depends upon his being and upon his being himself. It depends upon acting in characteristic or stylized ways in varying circumstances, and the self-justificational excuses depend, obviously, upon self-knowledge as well. If this is so, it makes sense to ask three questions: "What is this being that can incorporate a moral rule into itself (or, better, excorporate itself knowingly into the space described by a moral rule)?" "What is this being that can be or not be itself?" "What is this being that is aware when it is and when it is not itself?" These questions merely require rephrasing to put the locus of questioning squarely into ontology: What is the being of man? What is human being?

The foundation of moral education thus lies in a phenomenological ontology to discover the sort of knowing of the good that entails being good, for this is the philosophical area that inquires into these questions. It also lies in an existential ethic to maintain the Socratic imperative and rapport with the "depth" dimensions of "personality," for this is the area of philosophy that inquires into the question of self-knowledge and self-understanding. Both of these claims are true by definition. It has been the work of this chapter to indicate that merely a proper grasp of the problem of moral education shows that its roots are to be investigated in existential, phenomenological ontology if it is to be grounded. The analysis of the educational problem into its root questions indicated that the proper resources for the formulation of educational problematics and educational theory are those of existential phenomenology. For moral education to be successful, it is necessary for moral rules (if and when they are the content of moral education) to acquire some status in the pupil's being, that is, to acquire ontological status. To assist in developing methods of moral education, there ought to be inquiry into the matter of the ontological status of moral rules, into how they acquire it and whether they require it to control, direct, guide, or suggest conduct. Methods of promoting the "internalization" of moral rules, or, better, of promoting the externalization of conduct into the space specifiable by moral rules, have to be compared with methods of moral instruction utilizing "intelligence," "reflection," "insight," and so on, if moral education is to be grounded. Such inquiry is ontological inquiry no matter who does it, unless one remains content with free-floating theoretical constructs. But then moral education is not grounded.

On the other hand, such inquiry can be pursued with the phenomenological method, which would have several merits. First, it is thoroughly modern in that its use as a method of philosophizing dominates the philosophical scene on the European continent, for it constitutes one of the aforementioned revolutions in philosophy in this century.

Secondly, it is a method that is "publicly verifiable" in intent, on principle, and in practice and could conceivably bid fair for a consensus (at least to the extent that any verification principle can, among those who use the specified method properly).

Third, phenomenological method attempts to get down underneath "perceived phenomena," that is, beneath "phenomena" as they are seen through highly structured perception (that is, through concepts and constructs that are more or less forced upon the phenomena from outside), in order to confront the phenomena in question directly, and in this sense it is purely descriptive and nonemotional.

Fourth, it is rigorous in its following its own rules of thought, such as "Never let a received construct such as 'habit' get in the way of seeing what is there to see," and this rigor lends itself to the attainment of the aforementioned intersubjectively valid results.

Fifth, it is a method that is absolutely disjunctive with any of the methods of the "research-oriented environment," thus allowing philosophy of education to make its own contribution to the study of education irrespective of the validity of the points made in these two chapters.

Sixth, the previous merits are not only desirable but probably demanded of any thinking about the *public* education of other people's children, of any thinking about the public schools, in order to avoid partisanship and the political and social exploitation of children and youth.

Finally, phenomenological ontology is highly compatible with existential ethics and the existential perspective is required by the problem of moral education by definition.

THE FOUNDATION OF EDUCATION

The phenomenological, ontological (i.e., existential) inquiry into methods of instruction of moral rules, and into the comparison of moral education *via media* moral rules to methods utilizing the pupil's intelligence, insight, etc., *sans* rules, would take its primary direction from the educational problem to ground instruction in moral rules. Whether instruction via moral rules is the most "appropriate," "efficient," or "desirable" mode of moral instruction, however, may be open to considerable doubt.

The difficulties respecting "character training" or the inculcation of "moral and spiritual values" in public schools in a pluralistic society are simply insurmountable. Too many life-styles compete for recognition; too many interpretations and versions of "moral and spiritual values" contend for accommodation. As suggested, a body of moral rules could make a fair bid for acceptance. More important, any school requires rules and regulations respecting attendance, behavioral expectations, etc., merely for its efficient operation, or, rather, merely for its operation. These rules that are necessary for the functioning of the school as a going concern do not demand public agreement. They are decided administratively. But these are also *moral* rules, in effect, insofar as they define right and wrong conduct within schooling. These institutionalized *moral* rules are ordinarily enforced by teachers in some way or other regardless of other efforts at moral education in the classroom. On the one hand, moral rules are easier for ordinary teachers to handle than, for instance, "moral and spiritual values," even if agreement on the latter were presumed, as in the case of some private schools. On the other hand, even if a universal practice of direct moral instruction in "moral and spiritual values" or in "character training" were established where the aim is approached directly, as in released-time programs or courses in morals or ethics, or even if instruction were reduced to "cognitive learning" and "skills," nevertheless teachers would still be confronted with the expectation of enforcing the institutionalized rules and regulations as they applied to their area of concern, and they could do their job well or badly in this respect.

Two areas of endeavor and inquiry thus open up. In the *ontological foundation of moral education*, moral education is pursued directly, as in a course with that name or intent, or indirectly, as in the teaching of the humanities or social sciences when one of the explicit objectives, sometimes the primary objective, is "character formation," "personality development," or specified "changes in attitudes." When this endeavor is investigated so as to be grounded in human being, the inquiry is within the area of the ontological foundation of moral education. In the *moral foundation of education*, "character" or "personality" is "formed" by "pressure" to "conform" to the institutionalized way of life focused in the rules and regulations by becoming defined therein. In this area of endeavor a teacher may be primarily concerned with the "transmission" of "cognitive knowledge" and "skills," but she becomes involved in moral education in the "concomitant" learnings that occur whenever her enforcement (or lack of enforcement) of the institutionalized rules is conducive to the development of right and/or wrong conduct within the schooling "process." When this endeavor is to be ontologically grounded, the area of inquiry can be designated as the *ontological foundation of the moral foundation of education*. Because all founding is necessarily ontological, the two areas of inquiry can be designated as the foundation of moral education and the moral foundation of education. Because the "institutional press" to conform to schooling rules may be as strong an influence as attempts to engage in moral education directly, because the moral foundation of education may be as effective in respect to promoting changes in conduct as moral education, the distinction between these two areas of endeavor and inquiry breaks down. The distinction is "theoretical" and not ontologically grounded, because the effects of the moral foundation of education and moral education intermingle with each other and with the effects of extra-schooling and extra-pedagogic forms of influence on the pupil's existence. Further explication of the lack of grounding of the theoretical distinction between moral education and the moral foundation of education will lead the present discussion back to the point of inquiry of which the examination of moral education was only an illustration: What if education is groundless?

Ever since Plato (and since Herbart, Dewey, Childs, and Stanley, to include the contemporary tradition),[3] there has been an awareness that all education is perforce a moral undertaking. Pupils expect to be "better" and to live "better" lives for having gone to school. Parents, teachers, and the public expect the school to have something to do with helping pupils live "better lives" as a result of schooling. No matter how schooling is conducted, it has some impact upon the pupil's existence that affects the quality of his later life for "better" or for "worse." Every educational and pedagogic choice, from those that occur by the dozen during an hour of class to those that *appear* to be of much greater magnitude on the level of school board policy, affects the later life of the pupil in some small measure, for better or for worse, so that it can be argued that all schooling and pedagogical decisions are ultimately moral in nature. Without being moralistic, it can be said that this is what it is all about. All this has been said before by the people cited; the point is that since it is probably beyond the capacity of empirical research to ascertain whether the moral foundations of education or directly pursued moral education has greater effect upon the pupils, it is equally legitimate to refer to the general area of inquiry opened up as the ontological foundation of moral education or the grounding of moral education, even when one is attempting to ground the moral dimension of cognitive education, that is, when one is attempting to ground the enforcement of the rules and regulations of schooling that are necessary to maintain the process of instruction, regardless of the content. If all education has moral bearings and a moral dimension, and if all education affects conduct in some way, and if all conduct has a moral aspect, then an effort to ground moral education has to search not only for the ground of something clearly identifiable as moral instruction, but also for the general moral foundation of any and all education.

It is possible for schooling to result in *im*morality, in other words, through emphasizing some things rather than others, through having things done one way rather than another. If any and all education has moral bearings, then schooling as a total process can have a total moral or immoral impact on its pupils: if the process of schooling is based upon an inadequate conception of "human nature," the "products" might have "warped personalities" or "faulty characters" and thus might be said to have had an immoral education. There is no such thing as amoral education, or education that is neutral with respect to conduct, if by definition it all affects the pupil's existence, his very being. It is ontologically impossible for anything educational to be morally neutral.

The preceding discussion has been vague and general in its intentional effort to avoid defining the good, but three kinds of "moral education" that need grounding have been uncovered: (1) direct moral instruction in moral rules, (2) enforcement of school rules and regulations as these impinge upon and as they structure apparently non-moral instruction, and (3) apparently non-moral instruction as it yields school outcomes that affect life outcomes. It has been pointed out that the first and second of these rest upon an artificial theoretical distinction, for their relative influences upon the pupil are indistinguishable. It remains to indicate that the distinction between the second and third is also an artificially maintained theoretical distinction. Simply, there is no pure acquisition of knowledge or skill learning that occurs in the abstract, apart from the pupil's existence. This is merely a respecification of the idea that all education has moral consequences. Then the only legitimate use of the phrase "moral education" is to denote that education which deserves approbation and commendation, as in the parallel usage, "a moral person." The phrase "moral education" is actually redundant, because all education is moral and there is no reason to say "educative education." What the phrase "moral education" points out when it is used to commend a given program is that the program is in fact educative, rather than miseducative or noneducative. This use presupposes a normative view or model of education, presumably a grounded view. This in turn suggests that education is not that which occurs in schools, but something that happens to a person, in or out of school. It happens in school when schooling becomes educative by being grounded in the being of the pupil, which then means that education cannot be reduced to the "acquisition of knowledge" (of the good or any other kind), and that the "acquisition of knowledge" has to be grounded in personal being to include the moral dimension to be adequately grounded. Then, as the distinction between the foundation of moral education and the moral foundation of education breaks down because of their indistinguishability within the existential matrix of schooling, so does the distinction between moral education and education break down, because they too cannot be distinguished within the existential matrix of schooling. As the former distinction had to be made as a preliminary step in the understanding of the complexity of the problem of moral education and to indicate the need for grounding the teaching of the good (for not just any teaching will accomplish the aim, which is to promote moral conduct after the pupil leaves school), so too did the latter distinction have to be made as a preliminary step in the understanding of the problem of education and to indicate the need for grounding teaching, for not just any teaching will accomplish educating. Not just any teaching affects the pupil in his whole being, in his very being. As the need for founding moral education in the pupil's being was indicated through suggesting that the notion of "habit," "disposition," "attitude," "ability," "character," "personality," etc., are groundless hypostatizations, and that attempts to teach as if they were substantial entities leaves moral education groundless (and to no avail), so too are any notions of what or who it is that is educated unfounded and to no avail unless grounded in human being, and so too is any schooling based on groundless constructs unfounded. What if education is groundless?

To conduct inquiries concerning the ground of education so that schooling might have something to do with the being of those who are being educated, then, is what philosophy of education is called upon to do. Thus the existence of children and youth can be taken into account, and this is the significance of their being for the philosophy of education.

Then the questions asked at the beginning of the chapter delimit the area of inquiry appropriate to the philosophy of education when considered from the viewpoint of education itself. What if education is without a ground? What is the significance of the being of children and youth for education?

3

The Philosophical, Historical, and Societal Context

In order to ground education, the being of children and youth has to be taken into account in the practical situation of the classroom. This is ontologically impossible if the teacher's consciousness of the pupil is reduced, limited, and structured by the theoretical constructs of the behavioral sciences, for then she makes an object out of the pupil inasmuch as the pupil as a wide-awake, self-conscious being who is open to the world can neither be seen nor experienced nor encountered by a so-called objective observer (Chapter One). An attempt to take the human reality of the people who come to school into account in the classroom necessarily becomes involved in existential inquiry, for asking the question concerning the being of children, youth, education, and the world plunges one directly into ontology (Chapter Two). Asking the questions concerning the nature of philosophy of education and the nature of education situated the present inquiry in its institutional and educational context and the separate lines of questioning converged upon the conclusion that the appropriate resources for philosophy of education are those of existential phenomenology. The inquiry can now be situated in its philosophical, historical, and societal context.

EXISTENTIAL PHENOMENOLOGY

Existential phenomenology can be defined "operationally" as the kind of philosophizing, predominant among French- and German-speaking philosophers on the European continent, that traces its origin backwards through Sartre and Merleau-Ponty to Heidegger's *Being and Time* (1927). This work stands central to the existential, phenomenological movement because of Heidegger's originary cross-fertilization of the problems and substance of "existentialism" obtained from Kierkegaard and Nietzsche with the method of phenomenology derived with modification from Husserl.[1]

The phenomenological method as developed by Husserl in the first decades of the century was his attempt to ground cognition in the actual structures or processes of consciousness. There was a crisis in the theory of knowledge that Marxist-Leninists were coming to grips with through the sociology of knowledge, that John Dewey in the United States was attempting to resolve through his formulation of an experimental logic, that Bertrand Russell and Alfred North Whitehead were attempting to resolve through investigations in the foundations of mathematics and symbolic logic, and that Husserl attempted to resolve through development of the phenomenological method. Like Russell and Whitehead, he came to philosophy from mathematics, but like Dewey he undertook to investigate and ascertain the kind of conscious experience that was necessary to obtain valid knowledge. Whereas Dewey attempted to describe the experience necessary to obtain valid knowledge with objectivistic language (even borrowing terms from the natural sciences), when he was not doing a quasi-transcendental deduction by indicating what experience had to be in order to obtain warranted knowledge, Husserl developed the phenomenological method in order to gain direct access to the various strata and acts of consciousness and to be able to describe them "purely," i.e., without imposing any philosophical abstractions on them.

In the phenomenological method of research the philosopher modifies his own consciousness in order to gain access to the precognitive, preintellectual levels of awareness in order to be able to describe how consciousness builds up, or constitutes, the objects of which it is aware. Ordinary, everyday consciousness of things "leaps over" the "subliminal" constitutive functions of consciousness without noticing them in its haste, in its naïve and dogmatic assumption that perceived objects actually exist in reality prior to perception in the same form and structure as they are perceived, as if perception of them contributed in no way to the constitution of their forms. This common-sense realism and its naturalistic metaphysics is bracketed, put into parentheses or out of play (but not denied in any objective sense as it is for subjective idealism) in the initial phenomenological bracketing, in order to gain access to the stream of consciousness as such. The practicing phenomenologist "pretends" that the objects of consciousness do not exist—precisely so he can see them better as the phenomena that they are, for consciousness as they appear to consciousness, thereby gaining access to the processes and activities of consciousness.[2]

The movement into the phenomenological bracketing is not too unlike the bracketing involved in the transition between various realms of meaning: The suspension of the thesis of the existence of the "objects" of consciousness within the phenomenological bracketing is analogous to the abandonment of the naturalistic thesis when the curtain rises at the theater if one intends to participate in the drama and to become conscious of Hamlet, e.g., rather than Olivier. As the actor's existence is held in suspension in the modification of the consciousness of the theatergoer that is constitutive of the dramatic personae and the play, so too is the existence of the "objects" of consciousness put into parentheses, bracketed, by the modification of consciousness that enables the philosopher to describe the phenomena that appear to consciousness as they appear. Explorations and descriptions can then be made at a number of different levels. The phenomenologist can describe phenomena as they appear, the process or activity by which their appearing is brought about (i.e., the constitutive activities of consciousness), both poles of the subject/object relation together, or the relation between the constituting subject and the phenomenon. These different focuses of phenomenological description are established by various bracketings subsequent to the major phenomenological reduction, and there are more bracketings than mentioned. In any case, however, the phenomenologist attempts to describe purely (i.e., without preconception, prejudice, or ideological bias) what he sees because he is endeavoring to get to the beginnings of the activities of consciousness: he is, indeed, *researching* the data of consciousness as he attempts to explicate and elucidate the processes whereby the phenomena that he sees make their appearance to and within consciousness. He attempts to be loyal to the data of consciousness in his effort to establish the foundation for valid cognition.

This brief exposition of Husserl's program for phenomenology is noncontroversial in the sense that it presents the kinds of things with which almost any philosopher who regards himself as doing phenomenology in the Husserlian sense would agree. As such, Husserlian phenomenology is very different from two things that might seem, at first, very similar: phenomenological psychology and introspection. Husserl attempted to lay the foundation for the "first science," to establish the universal and absolute basis for cognition, by discovering the "operative laws" and valid norms of consciousness. His attempt to describe the operations of consciousness and to formulate the norms that would ground cognition differs markedly from the work of American psychologists who are known as phenomenologists but who are actually *phenomenalists* in their method, for they remain within the naturalistic viewpoint even though they point to the significance of the phenomenal field as the determinant of behavior.

They do not try to describe the phenomenal field from within, but rather attempt to gather data *about* it from without in order to explain (but not describe or make visible) human behavior by means of theoretical constructs *about* the phenomenal field.[3] By attempting to formulate an "empirically grounded" explanatory theory, what is called phenomenology in psychology in the United States is actually a practicing phenomenalism even though it calls attention to the significance of the phenomenological, i.e., to the activities of consciousness. Nor is phenomenological method a sophisticated form of introspection, although it might seem to warrant that emotionally laden term in the circles of educational psychology that are objectivistically oriented. Nothing could be further from the truth than to charge phenomenology with introspection, for the phenomenologist's consciousness, like everyone else's, is thrown outward toward the phenomenon of which he is conscious: "extrospection" would be as fitting as "introspection," but no more so. It is indeed a description of first-person experience in general terms, but the attempt to be loyal to the data of consciousness, "presuppositionless," and self-critical distinguishes phenomenological description from the "looking within" that historically has been designated by the technical term *introspection*. The attainment of intersubjectively valid results, at any rate, overcomes the legitimate charges frequently made against introspection.

Perhaps the most significant of these results, a central finding of Husserl accepted by subsequent phenomenologists, is the intentionality of consciousness, of all acts of consciousness. There is strict correlation between consciousness and the phenomenon of which one is conscious. Being conscious of something is an aspect, the central aspect, of all types, modes, forms, and acts of consciousness.[4] This is so true that the use of the noun *consciousness* is phenomenologically inaccurate, insofar as it tends to hypostatize an activity: a consciousness as a substantial entity is never revealed as such to "consciousness." Whether perceiving, imagining, feeling, or reflecting, conciousness always intends an object in the world and is wholly occupied by that object. "Consciousness" is always conscious of something—it is indeed consciousness, which is to be conscious, which is to be conscious of _____ (whatever).

The significance of the intentionality of consciousness will be pointed out after a few critical observations are made. The attempt of pure phenomenology to establish a science of pure transcendental consciousness may be ontologically impossible because of difficulties readily apparent in the initial phenomenological bracketing: it is doubtful if the being of the phenomenon can stay bracketed, for as the "object" is transformed into a phenomenon for consciousness, it is precisely in its being that it then appears. It is the being of the object that is overlooked in the naturalistic bracketing and that is disclosed precisely through suspension of its existence. Analogously, it is doubtful if the being of the consciousness of the phenomenologist himself can stay bracketed, for it is precisely his own being that appears as his consciousness expands itself to include the ordinarily dark, preconceptual levels of awareness. These reservations about the phenomenological reduction, of course, do not question the methodological legitimacy of the bracketing: they question what *really happens* within it. If in some sense the being of the phenomenon or of consciousness (which may be the same thing because of intentionality) cannot be fully bracketed or will not stay bracketed, then pure phenomenology's attempt to describe pure transcendental subjectivity is ontologically impossible. The bracketing is not what it at first appears to itself to be. Within the phenomenological bracketing the phenomenon is, rather, the world within experience; the subjective correlate of the world within experience is no longer consciousness but, rather, human existence. It is subjecticity rather than subjectivity.[5] If consciousness is always of something, and if on the one hand that consciousness is always an existing subject and on the other hand that something it is conscious of is always the world as it exists for a particular consciousness at a particular time, then *human existence is open to the world and finds itself in the world already.* If consciousness has to be conscious of something in order to be, furthermore, then *it is always transcending to the world in order to achieve its own being as consciousness by becoming conscious of things* in a temporal and temporalizing activity; and if *consciousness is human existence, or human being,* then *human being is continuously transcending activity.*

The significance of the intentionality of consciousness as articulated by Husserl and accepted by other phenomenologists appears in its being ontologized, particularly in the emphasized statements, which state the modifications of Husserlian phenomenology that have been made by Heidegger and Sartre, respectively. They also state the central claims of Heidegger and Sartre as well as of the broader movement of existential phenomenology. They point to the endeavor, scope, and realm of existential phenomenology, which is a phenomenology in that it remains within the phenomenological reduction to dig down into successively deeper layers of conscious existence. Instead of attempting to ground cognition in consciousness, it might undertake, as one of its projects, to disclose the existential presuppositions of knowledge and science: What must be presupposed about human existence in order for science to be? Awakeness and being there? It also attempts to elucidate other facets of human existence to grasp human being in its totality insofar as this is humanly and philosophically possible.[6]

Existential phenomenology as the method of philosophizing of the present inquiry, then, is the attempt to describe the phenomena of education within the conditions of human existence. There is little attempt herein to achieve original descriptions of the latter; they are accepted from general philosophy so that the focus coincides with the concern for educational problems. The *modus operandi* is to articulate problems of education within human existence to the extent that these are disclosed phenomenologically and are amenable to purified description. The approach has been utilized, illustrated, and justified in the first two chapters; it is now stated explicitly to establish the philosophical context of the inquiry.

TWENTIETH-CENTURY EDUCATIONAL THOUGHT

The technique of focusing upon educational problems and of using the resources of philosophy to articulate, intensify, illuminate, and resolve them is preferred to that of beginning with received conclusions of "existentialism" as if it were an ideology or *Weltanschauung* and forcing its "doctrine" upon a context to which they may be foreign. This approach is not original with this volume. Both the pragmatist John Dewey and the Neo-Aristotelian Harry S. Broudy stated that their approach was to begin with an educational problem and to utilize philosophy as it became necessary. Dewey did not "apply" pragmatism to education; on the contrary, he denied that philosophy could be applied to educational practice in that way. He insisted that philosophy of education was merely the formulation of educational problems that would allow education to assist in the development of the intellectual and moral characteristics necessary to solve current societal problems.[7] Broudy did not "apply' his "classical realism" to education, but merely formulated educational problems to reveal their metaphysical, epistemological, and axiological roots, and dealt with them at that level within the framework that made most sense to him.[8]

The present approach falls between Dewey's and Broudy's. With the advantage of hindsight, it can be seen that Dewey's rejection of the standard problem areas of philosophy was not only premature, due perhaps to his overcommitment to (and overdefense of) scientific method, it was also false to himself. He did not really reject metaphysics, for instance, but rejected one *kind* of metaphysics in favor of another, in favor of the grounding of knowledge and values in experiential reality. On the other hand, the revival of classical realism by Broudy probably did not adequately take into account the validity of Dewey's instrumentalist critique of the traditional concept of the truth of knowledge by correspondence.[9] To remain between Dewey and Broudy, then, the present inquiry will deal with educational problems within a classical area of philosophy, e.g., ontology, but without utilizing the language or conclusions of any view established prior to the various revolutions in philosophy in this century.

This is necessary because Dewey's participation in one of the revolutions in philosophy resulted in his revolutionizing, or reconstructing, the philosophy of education. Analogously to the way that one cannot accept a pre-Kantian metaphysics after Kant, or a pre-Marxian social philosophy after Marx, or Newtonian physics after Einstein, a pre-Deweyan philosophy of education simply cannot be "revived" after Dewey. One exposes himself to certain valid criticisms that he already knows about in choosing a less tenable view to oppose a more tenable view when the latter has already shown the more doubtful tenability of the former. Because Dewey's philosophy of education is the most significant contribution to education that has been made within any of the revolutions in philosophy, it is necessary, if one wishes to be modern, to be post-Deweyan. Philosophy of education has to be post-Deweyan to be situated in its historical context.

The historical context of twentieth-century educational thought, however, can be considered at two levels: in the trends of the intellectual climate of the colleges of education and in the more technical realm of philosophy of education as an academic discipline. Some data concerning ideas that were advocated by leaders in education who were not necessarily professional philosophers of education are summarized in the following chart:

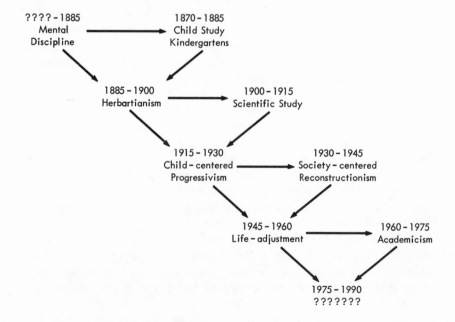

The "data" are arranged on fifteen-year intervals (using round figures) according to the Hegelian dialectic in order to be able to say something meaningful about almost a century of educational thought in a few paragraphs. Theories of mental discipline based upon faculty psychology dominated pedagogical thinking at the schooling level from the Renaissance until 1890, when Herbartianism took firm hold and spread across the United States as quickly as educational television (and probably for similar reasons). This was replaced by child-centered education, which in turn was replaced by some form of life-adjustment theory under the slogan advocating educating all the children of all the people. This summary of the main trends indicated by the chart, however, is much too rapid a survey even for philosophy.

The theory of mental discipline held that the mind consisted of various faculties, e.g., memory, observation, etc., that could be developed and trained through exercise. The major faculties were those of reason, feeling, and will, and it is interesting to note their similarity to the cognitive, affective, and psychomotor domains in the Bloom taxonomy of educational objectives. At the end of the nineteenth century, however, faculty psychology was "dead" and the thesis of mental discipline generated its antithesis in the child-study movement. People who were training to become teachers in normal schools simply studied real, live, whole children. The intent was to develop a sympathetic and loving regard for children and nothing more. Mental discipline and child study then became synthesized, so to speak, in Herbartianism. Herbartianism was teacher-centered, to be sure, but it was based upon an idea of the developmental stages of the child and furnished a considerably "softer" pedagogy than did the idea of formal discipline. Herbartianism then became a new thesis, as it were, which generated its own opposite in the scientific study of education. The latter rejected the *a priori* derivation of developmental stages according to the cultural epoch theory that Herbartianism adhered to, and it leaned heavily upon developments in experimental psychology and tests and measurements. These in turn can be said to have been synthesized in child-centered progressive education, for the early years of the scientific study of education removed some vestiges of mental discipline from the schools (while re-instituting others, e.g., drill went out with Herbartianism but came back in under S/R learning theory), and Herbartianism did advocate beginning each lesson with the child's interests. Pupil interest in Herbartianism was teacher-generated and involved the imposition of the teacher's ideas of what children allegedly were "naturally" interested in at certain ages, but there nevertheless was concern for the child's interest. It was simply necessary to remove the mystique of the cultural epoch theory, which the scientific study of education did, and begin each lesson with the child's felt, expressed interests to give birth to child-centered progressive education.

The "synthesis" of child-centered education became a new thesis, so to speak, which then generated its own opposite in the Depression and World War II years when the need for societal awareness and social reconstruction could no longer be evaded, even in colleges of education. These two then became "synthesized" within life-adjustment theory as there was a swing back toward "child-centeredness" with the discovery that social reconstruction could not proceed independent of the individual's personal adjustment to society. Because life-adjustment theory advocated the desirability of the accomplishment of psycho-social developmental tasks and preparation for societal roles to the neglect of "academic" learning, it prepared the way for its own opposite, the return to emphasis upon academic, college preparatory subjects and intellectual excellence that is associated with the passage into the space age. If the arrangement of the data on the chart has any heuristic power, then a new synthesis of life-adjustment and academic discipline should be emerging soon. This volume attempts to be situated historically by aiming toward that synthesis.

No metaphysical or cognitive claim is asserted about the Hegelian dialectic that is used in the chart and its explanation: it is not claimed that "history is on our side." Some perspective, however, is needed in an area of human endeavor that knows only too many "fads" and "pendulum swings" from one extreme to another. The "syntheses"—mental discipline, Herbartianism, child-centered progressive education, and life-adjustment—represent mainstream educational thinking because they encompassed insights contained in earlier points of view within the framework of new emphases. The "antitheses"—child study, the scientific movement, reconstructionism, academic excellence—represent oppositional points of view that have been important and fruitful by way of stimulating controversy and remembering facets of schooling that were forgotten or neglected by overcommitted adherents to mainstream views, but remain tangential to education as a cumulative field of study because of their lack of capacity to build on what has gone before. For the most part, adherents to the "antithetical" views were oppositional, but they were not the loyal opposition that is able to remain within a communalized dialogue about education. Advocates of the academic disciplines and academic excellence in the late fifties and sixties, for example, found it more convenient to scoff at life-adjustment theory than to come to grips with its partial truth. Although they served a useful function in reminding others of the necessity of intellectual development in schooling, which indeed was forgotten by some (but only some) of the advocates of life-adjustment theory, they nevertheless remain peripheral because of their own forgetfulness of the fact that even college preparation and college and university education help students to adjust to life *in some sense*, or they are not only beside the point but destructive in nature. The schema of the chart, then, presents some major educational trends in this century to indicate the attempt to maintain perspective by locating the present volume in respect to what has gone before.

The second level of grounding the inquiry in historical context is somewhat disjunctive with the first, for the chart does not represent major trends in technical philosophy of education. If it is granted that the period of Dewey's most widespread and significant influence began with the publication of *Democracy and Education* in 1916, then the influence of the first and second "generations" of pragmatists coincides, roughly, with the child-centered and society-centered progressive educational theories of the 1915–1945 period as listed on the chart.[10] If it can be hazarded that the pragmatic tradition began losing its influence in philosophy of education, and in the field of education at large, at approximately the time that some of its leading spokesmen were unsuccessfully trying to persuade the Progressive Education Association to adopt policy supporting social reconstruction, 1947–1954, it can also be ventured that philosophy of education in any form began losing its influence in the broader field of education shortly thereafter. If the third generation of pragmatists were frustrated by the phenomena of the McCarthy era and the onset of the Cold War,[11] the fourth and fifth generations of pragmatists in philosophy of education seem to have been frustrated by the increasing intensity of the Cold War and the onset of the space age and all the collateral phenomena.

Most of the nonpragmatic philosophers of education who followed Dewey actually wrote in order to oppose Dewey and the other progressive thinkers. As such they were merely advocates of what he opposed and failed to be post-Deweyan. Philosophers of education ordinarily classified as "perennialist" or "essentialist" more or less rationalized their opposition to Dewey in the educational arena with philosophical positions that were pre-Deweyan and pre-twentieth century and thus did not generate new contributions to the cumulative discipline of philosophy of education. If they do not belong to the mainstream, they are ahistorical and irrelevant to the task of becoming historically situated. The reason for this is not simply undue adulation of Dewey. Both in his educational philosophy and in the philosophical support for the educational recommendations, Dewey achieved syntheses of the individual and society, the individual and the world, the child and the curriculum, work and play, the school and society, mind and body, and so on. Irrespective of Dewey's particular syntheses of these dualisms or polarities, it is clear that any subsequent philosophy of education has to achieve comparable syntheses to avoid an untenable one-sided emphasis. An equitable balance has to be achieved between the individual and society in educational practice, for example, to avoid the twin dangers of under- and over-socialization, and educational philosophy has to be similarly balanced toward the concreteness of the individual and the significance of the social or it is anthropologically inadequate. The same argument applies *mutatis mutandis* in respect to the other syntheses, which is why revivals of pre-Deweyan educational ideas cannot be considered to be contemporary and why it is no overstatement to say that no post-Deweyan philosophy of education has appeared. Instead, there have been extensions of his views in various directions and revivals of pre-Deweyan views. Most of the reason for this seems due to the greatness of his genius as displayed in the comprehensiveness of his grasp of philosophical, societal, and educational problems.

THE SOCIAL CRISIS

If Dewey saw the task of philosophy of education as one of formulating educational problems so that the intellectual and moral traits necessary for the solution of societal problems could be developed through education, then indicating how the present volume stands with respect to his attempt to situate theory of education in its social context and with respect to two modifications of his view will situate the present inquiry in the history of technical philosophy of education and simultaneously in its societal-historical context.

To be able to generalize adequately about societal problems and take into account major difficulties, Dewey looked for long, slow changes in the fabric of society that might generate basic disharmonies. He found that three major changes had occurred in the previous centuries: the Industrial Revolution, the development of scientific methods of inquiry, and the democratization of society. Because these changes did not occur in harmony with one another and did not affect the way people formed values, many serious social problems developed. If people would acquire habits of scientific, experimental problem-solving in schooling, including the learning of values through group problem-solving, then they would have the flexibility, capacity, knowledge, sympathy, and desire to modify social institutions as necessary in order to alleviate societal difficulties.

Repeating Dewey's analysis at mid-century, William O. Stanley suggested that social problems persisted because there was no widely accepted method for coming to grips with them and no encompassing frame of reference within which the different parties to disputes could communicate with each other.[12] This appears to be in essential agreement with Dewey, but Stanley brought the thesis up to date by suggesting that the breakdown of the nineteenth century community and the transition to a multigroup mass society created a situation wherein people identified with the aims and goals of particular interest or pressure groups at the expense of an identification with the broader community. The loss of community resulted in the societal prevalence of noncommunalized conflicts, i.e., conflicts that do not occur within some commonly accepted frame of reference, which then remain insoluble until they are communalized. To restore community and communication, Stanley recommended intensive study of societal problems in school using the method of "practical intelligence," which he insisted was a legitimate extension of Dewey's problem-solving method. The important difference was that rather than using the pupil's own, or the student group's own, long-range goals to solve social problems, the basic principles of the American Creed were to serve as criteria or norms. This substitution was to serve to communalize cultural conflict by bringing it within the scope of democratic ideals, to which most Americans profess allegiance, and the practice of researching for the facts about a societal problem and then discussing the facts in conjunction with different projected solutions and with democratic ideals was to develop the methodological skills necessary to alleviate societal difficulties.

Institutionalization of Stanley's proposals, however, presupposes the existence of that community which he claims has been lost. It presupposes a prior agreement to the resolution of societal problems by means of free and open discussion and public debate, that is, that the groups that have the most socioeconomic and political power—and the most to lose through the resolution of social problems—will agree to allow, and to participate in, public discussion of societal problems in public schools. They are supposed to be inclined to do so out of a higher loyalty to democratic ideals and procedures. Implementation of Stanley's proposal would be allowed by a society that does not need it, not by one that does. The prior community of persuasion necessary to carry out his program would lessen the urgency, and perhaps validity, of his proposals. These few critical remarks should not be understood as attempting to refute Stanley's thesis that the social crisis can best be understood as a loss of community. On the contrary, it may be more pronounced and decisive than he estimated.

Stanley's proposal incorporates the substance of an earlier book on the methodology of policy-making, *The Improvement of Practical Intelligence*.[13] In the early sixties one of the book's co-authors, Kenneth Benne, suggested that a major fault of the progressive, pragmatic tradition in the philosophy of education of the twenties and thirties was that it was "liberal-optimistic."[14] It was somewhat naïve concerning its underlying conception of human nature and regarding the possibilities of genuine social progress, particularly as might be achieved through public schooling. His point of criticism has peculiar force because he speaks from within that tradition and seems not to merely reassert a conservative thesis. Like

Dewey's view, the whole experimentalist tradition in educational thought has been premised upon a faith in human intelligence, in ordinary people, in education, in democracy. Faith, in this tradition as elsewhere, not only exceeds the evidence but manages to survive in spite of evidence to the contrary. Philosophy, however, follows wherever evidence and argument lead. It is no more necessary to be pessimistic than optimistic: both are superfluous theses. It is necessary to base education upon an adequate conception of human nature, to be able to account for the misery, frustration, and sorrow that accompanies human living, i.e., upon human being as in question in its being; and this the pragmatic tradition, except for William James, seems not to encompass.

This volume situates itself in the societal context by attempting to come to grips with the problem of the loss of community. It also accepts Benne's claim that the social reconstructionism that Stanley recommends and that he himself formerly advocated omits the "quest for identity," which is interrelated with the "quest for community." The loss of community *and* the loss of identity can easily be shown to be the origin of societal difficulties if the validity of Dewey's and Stanley's interpretations is granted.

Groups of people do not exist as groups apart from the individual people who compose the "group." *Group* is a theoretical construct that has no ontological reference. It is used legitimately for sociological explanations wherever certain forms of alienation occur: individual people can and sometimes do attempt to gain their personal identity by identification with a "group," but this is in despair over being themselves and is a loss of personal identity. If in one's own eyes he seems to gain his own identity by letting his own individual existence become subsumed within a role in a group, he becomes aware of other people who belong to his own and to other groups not as individual people but as members of that group: members of other groups no longer exist as individual people within the awareness of a person who mistakenly attempts to solve the problem of finding out who he is by taking over the answers of other people as they have become consolidated in group norms. To restore community it is not necessary to find ways of getting groups to communalize their intergroup conflicts within some larger frame of reference; it is necessary for "group members" to become aware of the people belonging to other "groups" as the individual, existing people they are. For this it is necessary to become aware of oneself as an individually existing person who is ultimately not subsumable to the "groups" with which he shares interests and goals because *these* "groups" are just other people too. Then if Stanley is right about the loss of community, the major social difficulties can be alleviated by the educational development of people who are neither alienated from themselves nor others: schooling should promote the quest for identity or authentic existence and the quest for community or authentic coexistence. Philosophy of education, then, fulfills its societal function when it attempts to disclose how education can promote authentic existence and authentic coexistence.

The conclusion concerning its societal function converges with the previous raising of the question of the being of children and youth in educational context (Chapter Two), and in the context of the institutional preparation of teachers (Chapter One). If philosophy of education attempts to fulfill its ontological function within the disciplined study of education (Chapter One), and if it also attempts to fulfill its heuristic function by seeking for the ground of education (Chapter Two), it simultaneously fulfills its societal function of formulating the theory concerned with the educational development of the kinds of persons who are able to cope with contemporary societal difficulties insofar as these are ultimately reducible to an alienation from oneself, from others, from the world, and from being. What is the loss of identity other than the loss of being? And what is the loss of community other than the dominance of the technological mentality and the global forgetfulness of being?

The lines of questioning also converge in indicating that the appropriate resources for philosophizing about education are those of existential phenomenology. The point, however, can be arrived at independent of the particular articulation of these chapters. On the one hand, Heidegger has suggested that philosophy is phenomenological ontology. Because he correctly continues to insist upon the primacy of the analysis of human existence in spite of allegations of reversals in his mode of thought, it is legitimate to amend his claim to say that philosophy is existential phenomenology. On the other hand, Dewey, because he perceived the societal function of philosophy, suggested that philosophy is philosophy of education. If one grants both Heidegger's and Dewey's claims simultaneously, then philosophy is the existential phenomenology of education.

These introductory chapters have not merely situated the inquiry in its institutional, educational, philosophical, historical, and societal contexts. The major problems in these contexts are reducible to, because they are manifestations of, the oblivion of being. They are one with the planetary forgetfulness of being that exists the societal crisis. Only man, situated between the animals and the gods, between earth and sky, can have a crisis. If this is the source of his tragedy, it is also the source of his glory.

The crisis in "society," convenient, nonexisting scapegoat, is a crisis in human being: because man exists the critical position, it is the very crisis in humanity that enables him to raise the question of the meaning of being on behalf of being. Only because his being is in question in its being can man raise the question of being: Why is there being rather than nothing? Why is there the being of man? What is the significance of the being of man? What is the significance of the being of children? Why are there children?

4

Education, Life-Phases, and Values

What is the meaning of the being of children and youth? Why do they exist? Is it merely to become adults? Is existing as an adult inherently superior to existing as a child or youth? Would an affirmative reply imply that it is better to have children than to be a child? Is it better to be adult than to be young? The pertinence of these questions derives from the attempt to ascertain the significance of the life-phase in which education occurs in respect to the whole of a human life. Is its significance to be found in the phase in which it occurs, in subsequent phases, or in respect to the whole? How does the earlier question concerning the significance of the being of children and youth for education relate to the question concerning the significance of education for the being of children and youth? Is the significance of education for their being dependent upon the significance of childhood and youth in the whole of human existence? Why are there children? Merely so that they may be educated *out* of childhood into adulthood? Is it better to be as an adult than to be as a child?

The questioning concerns the meaning of human being, but with respect to the relationship of the parts or phases to each other and to the whole and with respect to the relationship of education to the phases and to the whole. A formulation of the whole, its various phases, and the authentic values of each phase as part of the whole is therefore necessary to ground education in the being of the child and the youth. This chapter will explicate various stages in the context of a whole life in order to obtain the values appropriate to each life-phase. The brevity of the treatment of the phases of primary concern will be balanced by the following three chapters, which concentrate on education within these phases after the context of each is established.

CRITICAL EVENTS

There can be general phases of life only if there are commonly experienced turning points to distinguish the phases from each other and to give each phase a form of its own. Particularly important to distinguish phases would be decisive events in which the person reflected upon his life and gained a new awareness of the "past" in a reorientation to the "past" and "future" as they appear to him at that time. This reorientation to the "past" and "future" as they appear to one, of course, is nothing other than a reorientation of oneself to one's self. This includes a reorientation of the temporal structure, among other things, because the "larger amount" of the "past" that is there from which one has to exist futuringly yields an accordingly distinctive way of being able to experience the present moment. Differing ways of experiencing the present moment in different life-phases establish forms of existence peculiar to particular life-phases: experiencing the present moment in the way appropriate to a particular life-phase is existing authentically within that life-phase. The values realized in the authentic temporalizing of the present moment (i.e., in the mode appropriate to the life-phase) are the authentic values, the authentically human values, or the values of authentic existence within a life-phase. In other words, there can be general phases of life if there are general crises that people go through such that their authentic mode of existence, their mode of being most wide-awake, changes because of the crisis and its resolution. The distinctive feature of the differing forms is the temporal structure of existing that is peculiar to each life-phase.

General phases of life, of course, would be relative to general forms of life available in a society, but since the present concern is with education in a post-civilized society there is some generalization possible in a "cross-cultural" sense—relevant wherever there is instituitionalized schooling beyond puberty. Wherever there are secondary schools, the following critical events and life-phases may be distinguished:

Decisive event	*Life-phase*
conception	prenatal life
birth	childhood
pubescence	youth

Decisive event (cont.)	*Life-phase (cont.)*
societal entrance	young adulthood
leveling off	mature adulthood
retirement	old age
dependence	senility
death	

Note: The schema is based upon Romano Guardini's formulation in *Die Lebensalter; Ihre Ethische und Pädagogische Bedeutung*, number six in the series, *Weltbild und Erziehung*, 5th ed. (Würzburg: Werkbund-Verlag, 1959).

There may be other critical events that set off minor phases, such as learning to walk or beginning to go to school and infancy and early and late childhood, but to consider all possible modulations would obscure the general picture with detail.[1]

The decisive events, furthermore, are not alleged to be traumatic experiences in any universal sense, for in the paradigmatic or normative cases they are not. They are transitional periods of variable abruptness, and although they partly happen to one (rather than resulting from one's own action), they cannot be considered as limiting or conditioning or determining factors. Birth, for example, when considered objectively is a separation from the mother that is determinative for one's whole life, but this is not understandable subjectively. Subjectively, one exists as born. Birth is neither determinative nor indeterminative of anything else. It has always already happened. The same argument, *mutatis mutandis*, applies to the other crises. The only difference is that there may be more consciousness of the crisis as such on either or both sides of it. This changes nothing, however, because none of the crises can be fully understood on the hither side. Then they happen, then the rebirth, then they always have already occurred, as factical and inescapable as the primary birth but neither determinative nor indeterminative of anything, subjectively considered.

The crises may be considered as part of the conditions of human existence wherever there are secondary schools. The life-phases, on the other hand, are completely distinguishable only theoretically: the whole is always present in each. Each phase, even those that have not yet occurred objectively, exists in dialectical interplay with the others. (E.g., I am the child I once was, I am the old man who once wrote this book, and I am both of these, but not primarily, while I am now writing it.) For the life-phases to exist in dialectical relation, however, they have to exist to some extent independently of each other in their own forms, separated by decisive events.

CHILDHOOD

Insofar as prenatal life approximates sleeping rather than being awake, it is more unconscious than conscious existence.[2] Suffice it to say that whatever is done to insure that this phase of life is lived authentically or fully belongs within the realm of medical science, governed by medical ethics. If the "fetus" is to "live" the fetal period "fully" and if this requires a healthy, well-nourished mother, then the values to be realized at this stage are seemingly dependent upon whatever enables the mother to obtain adequate nutrition and medical care. Insofar as this phase has to be lived fully in order for subsequent phases to be lived fully, it would seem that society, through the exigencies of societal bookkeeping, ought not to permit the existence of unhealthy, ill-nourished mothers.

From the child's point of view, phenomenologically, that is, childhood begins in an unfamiliar, doubtful, hostile world. To the extent that his questions about this strange world are answered affirmatively, the child explores it. The problem of ethics is the same as in any other phase, but relative to the temporal structure of childhood.[3] The child has to realize the good, but this is severely limited to the kinds of values that can be realized within the limited time-span of his present. Because he cannot include much of the past or future in the present as he temporalizes its presence, he cannot prepare for adult life, for adolescence, for next year, and hardly for next week. The child can neither see that far ahead of himself nor project into the "future" in that way. To live fully as a child, consequently, is to live for this hour, this day, being lost in the present moment. Because the ethical problem is for him to realize intrinsic value in all he does, he ought to play. Playing brings a fullness to the child's being that is otherwise lacking and forms the fundamental world that will afterwards be taken for granted. In childhood play the fundamental and primordial relation to being is formed and remains rooted, except for subsequent major therapy or its equivalent. After childhood one sees no more of the world than he saw as a child: all clarity, unity, distinction, relation, and quality that are later distinguished are based upon the childhood exploration of the world, because the child experiences everything with his whole being, with an intensity and depth never likely to be regained.[4] Playing in calm safety establishes the child in the world and in being. He not only has to play, he ought to play because play constitutes his being as a child: play exists childhood.

The child has to play if he is to enter youth full of confidence in the world, if he is to "survive" the "crisis" of pubescence and be able to live the life-phase of youth fully. The more fully childhood is lived, the less of a crisis pubescence will be, because of the greater anchorage in the world and the consequent greater confidence in it.[5] Conversely, the less the child is able to explore the world in play, the more alienated from the world he becomes and remains—and the greater will be the crisis of pubescence and the less fully will youth as a life-phase be lived.

YOUTH

Whereas childhood is basically exploratory of concrete possibilities of the world in play, youth is fundamentally adventurous because the two "defining characteristics" of postpubescent youth are tremendous energy and enthusiasm, and lack of experience in the social-historical world. If childhood has been lived fully, then with the ascending of life's curve the youth becomes increasingly aware of his personal power and vitality and the opening up of numberless possibilities.[6] The deepening reflective consciousness can become dissociated from the pre-reflective consciousness of things and the dissociation enables thoughts concerning who one will be and what one will accomplish to run on extravagantly, unchecked by practical experience of what is possible within the social-historical world. The ideas, ideals, and convictions of youth thereby become unconditional, opinions become absolutistic, and conduct becomes uncompromising. The power of ideas and character become overrated because youth lacks both the concrete involvement and the disinterestedness that are requisite to the formation of adequate value judgments. Greatness of ideas and unconditionality of sentiments are readily confused with the power and conditions necessary to realize them. They are confused with what is possible within the world.[7] These are the general conditions for venture and heroism because choices can be entertained, chosen, and pursued that would not be considered to be possible alternatives later on: youth is adventurous.

Youth is the time to make life-decisions, such as vocation and marriage, that establish, at one stroke, one's whole future being. These require a reasonable view of the world and of personal qualifications, however, that is necessarily lacking as long as the person is in school. Guidance can be too "realistic" and frustrate the courageous, heroic choices that ought to be made in this phase, and it can be too "idealistic" and prey upon youth's vulnerability. Youth as a life-phase is vulnerable to self-abnegation, to seduction by "noble causes," to use, misuse, and abuse by politicians, religious leaders, organizations with public relations men, and by whoever else is willing to appeal to youthful idealism and promise that the golden era will be ushered in as soon as youth support the cause.[8] His state of ignorance of what is factically possible is needed for the great life-decisions to be made with forthrightness and conviction, but this opens youth to the danger of being misled into supporting someone else's cause because it so readily believes that all ideals that sound good not only are good but are realizable. The more fully the childhood was lived, the more confidence the youth has in his venturings and the more he believes in ideals of some sort. The less grounded he is in the world because of the inadequacy of his childhood play, the more vulnerable the youth is to propaganda, force, and suggestion.

In either case, however, youth as a life-phase is idealistic. The secondary school interposes a somewhat artificial, if necessary, period in which young people are diverted from exploring the societal-historical world that is the ordinary extension or natural consequence of their childhood explorations of the social-physical world. They are diverted into exploring the intellectual-historical world, i.e., the background of the social-historical world. The experienced vitality urges them into their own future in the societal-historical world, but they are directed in their schooling to go into the past instead. The flight of their consciousness into the future continues, however, as an "extra-curricular activity," necessarily disharmonious with any curriculum that can confront them in school. Youth is necessarily idealistic because its values are formed apart from the only context that could give them meaningful validation. In spite of appearances to the contrary among some segments of youth that seem to be thoroughly "modern" and quite "realistic," "skeptical," and/or "cynical," youth is idealistic because even these values are largely based upon intellectualistic conceptions and opinions and not upon practical experience.[9] These are also idealistic when they are self-deceptions for fear of getting one's hands dirty in the societal-historical context. The youth cannot know that good sometimes fails in the world, that there is evil in the world, or that evil sometimes succeeds where good fails because no one can know these things unless he himself has failed in the social-historical world *because* he himself was good. Because the youth, therefore, cannot know it in the right way, as an outcome of his own practical experience in concrete, historical, societal events and in everyday behavior, he cannot be truly cynical or realistic. Apparent skepticism is a posture. The ideals it conceals are readily apparent and it soars above existence. The values of youth are floating, formed out of conjunction with the conditions of human existence, because of the way youth experiences the world where there is secondary schooling. This idealism is neither good nor bad: it characterizes youth because the temporal structure is future-oriented and future-laden.

Because of his strong orientation toward the future, preparation for that future in terms of acquiring skills and knowledge, the ordinary basis of competency and power, seems relatively unnecessary to the youth. He overrates the power of ideals and character and really has no idea of what he can do, of what others are able to do, or of what in general can be done. He lacks awareness of the tenacity of the facticity of being, of the factuality that inheres in the human condition, because he sincerely believes that "society" is eagerly waiting for him to come and make his contribution. He implicitly imagines "society" as just beginning when he enters it; he lacks the comprehension that the societal-historical world in which he will find himself has been "going on" for quite some time. He lives for the future as he sees it, in rather narrow perspective, exuberantly, and overexpectantly.

The problem of ethics is again to realize the good, but under the conditions of youthfulness: with the enlarging awareness of himself as a person, of his own responsibility, opinions, vitality, and power, the greatest danger to which youth is exposed is that of the peer group. To lose himself in the peer group is to fall into mass existence, into anonymous, everyday, inauthentic existence wherein he lets the collectivity take over the responsibility for his own existence. As the child gradually becomes more of an ethical problem for himself, so too does this increasing responsibility and individuation continue in youth: the youth ought to become more self-reliant, to be thinking more and more for himself, and to be acquiring a healthy mistrust of the opinions of others.[10] He ought to be doing this in order to live the life-phase fully and to be able to weather the crisis of practical experience by achieving at that time an adequate reassessment of his adolescent ideals.

ADULTHOOD

When the youth leaves school and enters society, confrontation with the factors of practical experience presents the young adult with the critical phenomenon of the singular inappropriateness of his ideals to what can actually be done in the societal-historical world. In addition, he finds that he lacks ability and preparation to do much of what he had formerly thought possible and that what he actually can do is neither especially interesting, revolutionary, nor significant.[11] In the working world he finds that other people, including the older, better established persons who formerly helped him but with whom he now has to work and to compete, also have initiative, convictions, and ideas that are as good as but at odds with his own and that they are hardly ready to allow him to exercise his initiative. He finds that societal-historical problems that he previously had all solved are in fact very complicated and controversial and that his simple norms are hardly applicable. He learns that the principles he had been adhering to absolutistically are most unreal and that he has to compromise, "sell out," or become corrupt in order to survive.[12]

He recognizes that one of these, or a similar course, has to be chosen if any of the ideals he retains are to be realized in the actuality of the societal, political, and economic life about him: he learns the meaning of *Pollyanna*.

The crisis of practical experience introduces the young adult to the meaning of *Pollyanna*. He has been a Pollyanna and now recognizes it. The crisis of practical experience creates an awareness of youthful naïveté as the young adult begins to see how the right things are seen, the right things are said, but nothing happens to realize them. Instead, what appear to be hypocrisy, stupidity, self-seekingness, and aimlessness govern everywhere, especially within himself, for what he formerly thought to be right gives him very little guidance in action. Yet the words still seem right: he discovers he has been in a false ethical position of great words. He comes to understand that it is very difficult to win virtue within the existential, societal matrix, much more difficult than having the right convictions and principles and adhering to them intellectually; and that it is very difficult to achieve character in the face of the discouraging and demoralizing effects of the misery and wretchedness that are progressively exposed. As the young adult discovers facticity—that much of what does not have to be nevertheless *is*, and continues to be with a great, massive persistence—he discovers for himself that the inescapable condition of all realization is great patience and endurance.[13] This discovery, however, can be made only by the young adult who reassesses his ideals in the right way after the crisis of practical experience. The crisis is the falsification of the ideals of youth by the world and the accompanying awareness of this falsification and of a need for reassessment. An adequate reassessment involves a willingness to enter into the responsibility of maturity; an inadequate reassessment attempts to flee this responsibility in either of two ways. The first way is simply to fail to reassess adolescent ideals, that is, to reassert them without significant change in spite of (and because of) their falsification by experience. In this failure the ideals are reasserted with all the more vigor after the person evidences the gap between them and the societal-historical reality. The person becomes either (a) doctrinaire, absolutistic, and fanatical; (b) revolutionary, bringing nothing new because of lack of contact with the present, and possessing only a fantasy of success; or (c) critical, but in a scornful way, empty of affirmation. By holding fast to youthful ideals, he holds fast to youth as a form of existence, as a life-phase, and remains isolated from the societal-historical situation even if he appears much on the scene.[14] Because there is nevertheless an awareness that the ideals are falsified in the crisis, this holding fast constitutes an alienation from the historical situation.

The second way the reassessment can fail is through complete abandonment of ideals, convictions, and principles in a regression to the average mode of existence to be found in a society: the reassessment is evaded through flight from personal responsibility into average everyday existence, anonymity, and depersonalization. This route pursues the allegedly useful and obviously pleasurable under the guise of "realism": "One has to be realistic." This is, however, a refusal to overcome one's own adolescence, for it continues the mode of existence of youth who fall into the peer group and do not flee the present into the future they have to become: it carries the false hedonism of the adolescent peer group on into adulthood.[15]

The young adult who revaluates his adolescent ideals adequately avoids falling into fanaticism or hedonism, establishes what he is able to do, resolves to do it, and does it. To other people he appears to develop character, but this is the self-conscious consolidation of his physiological, emotional, and intellectual resources, of his whole being. He gradually develops an inner strength to endure whatever is necessary to do what he has decided to do. This is not the same as the stubbornness or obstinancy of fanaticism, because it is a resolve to do what one can and is relative to situations. It retains something of the adolescent ideals formulated anew in the context of their realization, and authentic in the sense that they correspond to one's feelings and thoughts, to one's inner and outer being, because the reassessment is not merely of the ideals but of oneself, of the situation, and of what one is able to do in the situation considered in a global sense. The consolidation is a reunification of one's fragmented and distracted being and the consequent inner strength is merely the courage to be. It is the courage to be as oneself in a less than wholly supportive environment.

The ethical problem of this life-phase is wholly one's own: part of the crisis of practical experience is the realization of responsibility for one's own existence. The revaluation of ideals is indeed a rebirth, of which one is aware as such and which has to be made by oneself in order to be adequate by resulting in the acceptance of this responsibility. If the two previous life-phases were lived fully, however, then the recognition of the instability of human affairs in the crisis of practical experience prompts the establishment of certain values in one's own existence: reliability in what one undertakes, keeping the word that one gives, remaining true to the trust invested in one, maintaining a sense of honor and acquiring the capacity to distinguish in words and deeds between the just and the unjust, the noble and the common, the genuine and the counterfeit.[16] Before the reassessment, for example, the genuine and the counterfeit were hardly distinguishable in oneself: the professed ideals were sincerely believed in and the conviction that they ought to be practiced was real, but that, too, was a conviction. The ideals were largely inauthentic, because they were intellectualistic matters of conviction and belief rather than operative, functional guides for action to begin with. They were not framed to guide action because youth is denied the possibility of genuine action. Of course they were inappropriate to the context of historical action. The increased clarity over one's own existence that is established within the adequate re-evaluation of youthful ideals as one becomes situated in the historical context enables one to distinguish more clearly between the genuine and spurious in others, and so on for the other values belonging to young adulthood. The young adult, in other words, amidst the "storms" of societal, economic, and political life, chooses to realize in his own life the values that he himself finds to be worth repeating. These will be the so-called enduring values if the person has lived the previous life-phases fully, for then he has the confidence in the world that enables him to choose to repeat those values precisely because they do not seem to be enduring. His realizes that, whatever else, he can still decide who he himself will be. That one has to realize his values in his own existence is understood concomitantly with the realization that little success is achieved in anything if one begins wholly anew—there is only building on what has gone before.[17]

The next turning point comes with the leveling off of one's vitality, drive, ambition, industry, and striving, when he has finally secured a comfortable, stable and relatively permanent place within established society. As the successful revaluation of youthful ideals proceeded through to the integration of one's resources, the subsequent utilization of these consolidated powers proceeds through until one experiences the limitations of his personal strength. The crisis of experiencing the limits is a becoming aware of the limited nature of one's personal energy, of one's finitude. This critical event is less clearly definable than the others and it may not be a generally distributed, distinct event, for mature adulthood may be related to young adulthood as late childhood is to early childhood, differing chiefly in that it is founded upon the previous phase. If young adulthood and mature adulthood are considered as one phase of life, adulthood can be distinguished into subphases, for somewhere toward the onset of what is ordinarily called "middle age" one realizes that there can be an excess to work, to battle, and to the responsibilities that can be undertaken. Despite one's best intentions, the work accumulates and then piles up, the demands upon his time become increasingly greater, and what there is to be done becomes so overwhelming that he finally becomes satisfied with making a home, etc. This "leveling off" differs from the flight to hedonism that is an incorrect resolution of the earlier crisis because it succeeds the correct revaluation and is its result: reaching the limits of one's power can occur only upon the foundation of the integration of one's resources. It involves, therefore, the loss of all illusions, including any to be found in hedonism and those remaining after the adequate re-valuation of the ideals of youth. Then one always had new undertakings to plunge into, but now one sees that things are much more wretched than he had thought and that the accomplishment of whatever he can do will not help very much. As young adulthood deepens into mature adulthood, more and more wretchedness is disclosed "behind the scenes," until there is complete disenchantment and realization that as a matter of fact the world is already there. Life goes on, but it becomes more tedious. One sees the same impulsive acts with the same miserable consequences committed over and over. One sees deeper and trusts fewer people as it becomes clearer that promises will usually not be kept. Personal security does not make up for the disenchantment and one may proceed to live out of mechanical necessity, living it through rather dully, or out of a superficial optimism. The disenchanted adult may become skeptical, scorn-ful, silly, or playful, and may engage in political action or financial specula-tion to relieve the dreary monotony; and through these idlings he may slowly gain a new feeling for the worth of existence.[18] In respect to ethics, mature adulthood implicates the same values as before, to realize the good through the same inwardness of ethical concern, acceptance of responsi-bility for his own being, and an even deeper fulfilling of the self-imposed obligation to help and to try to regulate in spite of all failure, but it is accompanied by an increased intensity of the awareness that the meaning of duty lies within oneself. To others the person who is a "mature adult" because he evaluated the situation adequately in the crisis of adolescence and is now living his present life-phase fully appears to be a very strong character with great self-discipline—Schweitzer, Gandhi. To himself there is of course considerable self-discipline but also great renunciation, par-ticularly of the distractions and entertainments that so readily occupy the people who are in despair over becoming themselves. It involves not so much courage to be as resoluteness. Because the disenchanted person has no more illusions of great victories, however, he is precisely able to engage in the activities that have their accumulative effect. He thus achieves what matters and endures. He is the stuff that great statesmen, doctors, and teachers are made of.[19]

Then with the decline of vitality comes retirement and old age and wisdom. As the whole symphony is there in the last movement, so the whole of an authentic life is there in old age, and this is what makes possi-ble the wisdom of the elder statesman or the sage.[20] Then decay and deterioration until the decisive dependence of senility. There may be no particular crisis preceding senility, but if not the declining of vigor proceeds until dependency upon others occurs. Then gradual acceptance of the end and death.

THE TEMPORALIZING OF BEING

The differences between the "forms" of existence in the various life-phases can be seen most clearly through the shifting structure of the person's temporality. The child lives in the present moment and can encompass little of the past or future within his present. The future that he is does not extend beyond a few hours or days ahead. If he attempts to project further or all the way to adulthood, this "projection" is merely a vague presentiment with extremely large gaps of "in between" now and then that are utterly empty: he really can project no further than next week. The future dimension of the present stretches out as the child grows older, however, so that by late childhood and the onset of pubescence he is beginning to be mostly future-oriented. Throughout the youthful period he becomes increasingly oriented to the future that he intends to conquer. Youth plans to conquer the future and tends to live in that future, for what living in the present he does that is not overbalanced by the future is a carryover of childhood, symptomatic of not having lived childhood fully. The future into which youth projects, however, or rather the future he projects in front of him, will never be brought into being because there are still gaps of "in between" that cannot be bridged on principle—"then" is purely imaginary because youth projects into a dream future. The crisis of practical experience awakens youth from this dream, and the adequate reassessment of youthful ideals restructures his temporality from projecting across the present in its haste to get to the future to projecting into the present as the means to get to that future. Temporality continues to shift throughout young adulthood to focus more and more upon the present as one gradually surrenders waiting for something to happen in the future (i.e., for the future to happen) and instead projects authentically into the concrete possibilities present to one (i.e., into the immediate future that these possibilities of the present are), doing what he can to make that future happen by futurizing into it. The temporal structure of old age is largely retrospective, and that of senility is focused on the present, as in childhood but lacking the tone of expectancy and beginningness that belongs to the child's present.[21]

The shifting of the temporal structure, of how one experiences his time, of course, has its authentic and inauthentic modes in each phase. The brief summary concentrates upon the authentic modes, e.g., retrospection should not dominate until retirement, or, when retrospection dominates, the person has existentially, if not in fact, retired. The focus upon the changing temporal structure, furthermore, is an effort to let the analysis of the life-phases disclose the movement into authentic existence in such a way that it neither seems fantastically difficult to achieve nor contrary to prephilosophical common sense.

Throughout young adulthood the individual who has lived his childhood and youth fully and has revaluated his adolescent ideals adequately is moving into authentically human existence as existentialistic philosophers are wont to describe it. The mature adult is authentically there in the historical situation co-historicizing in and with his generation in the open anticipatory resolve that characterizes authentic existence.[22] The attestation that this is an adequate conception of authentic existence comes from the prephilosophical understanding of the movement into authentic existence. The person who exists authentically may not understand philosophical conceptions of existence, but if he exists authentically he lives each life-phase fully and discovers throughout young adulthood that each year passes more quickly. This is the surrender of the waiting for the future and the taking up of the projecting into the living concrete possibilities. There is also prephilosophical understanding of the kind of "remembering" and "foresight" belonging to different life-phases, and these are nothing other than ontic manifestations of the "past" and "future" as they are lived. How the "remembering" and "foresight" affect the ekstatic temporal unity of the so-called present defines the authentic mode of existence in each phase. If the fanatical and hedonic resolutions of the crisis of practical experience are failures in reassessment of oneself, it is because the temporal structure becomes falsified therein: the fanatic or doctrinaire essentially eliminates the present by projecting the past upon it, for in lieu of making choices in situations, he *remembers* a previous decision, calls it a conviction or principle, and lives mechanistically from the past, without foresight into the consequences of his actions, without responsibility for the consequences of his actions, without responsibility for his own being. The hedonist essentially glorifies the present by cutting it loose from both past and future in his opportunistic concern for the pleasure of the moment, irrespective of what it was he intended to accomplish in the world and of the consequences of his actions. He neither remembers nor foresees and his life has no continuity; he is not a person because he has not accepted responsibility for his own futural project of being.

All this can be illuminated by casting the point in Kierkegaard's terminology. The fanatical resolution of the crisis of practical experience is the ethical stage of existence; the hedonic resolution is the esthetic stage; the adequate resolution is the teleological suspension of the ethical. The kind of striving that is necessary in order to become oneself, an existing individual person, is predicated upon the suspension of the ethical. Although Kierkegaard seems to have conceived of the esthetic, the ethical, and the teleological suspension of the ethical as three moments of existence that one phases in and out of, it is equally illuminating to cast them into chronological pattern: childhood as a phase of existence is the esthetic phase; youth, the ethical phase; adulthood, a synthesis of both previous phases. The erroneous solutions to the crisis of practical experience, then, are in reality covert decisions to remain on the childhood (hedonic, or esthetic) plane of existence or the youthful (fanatical, or ethical) plane of existence. To promote the adequate resolution of the crisis of practical experience, i.e., to promote authentic existence and authentic coexistence, it is then necessary to live childhood, i.e., the esthetic, and youth, i.e., the ethical, fully. It is not necessary to "practice" authentic adult existence in school, to learn its values by habit, drill, or training; it is necessary to exist authentically *as* a child and *as* a youth in order to prevent later regressions to the forms of existence quite appropriate and authentic to the life-phases that occur before the critical events of puberty and societal entrance respectively.

The educational significance of the phenomenological descriptions of the life-phases should now be clear, as should the significance of the being of children and youth for education. In any literal sense, the child and youth cannot prepare for adulthood because of their limited foresight. In the broad sense, they can best prepare for adulthood by living their present life-phase fully, by being themselves as children and youth. This follows from the nature of the life-phases of childhood and youth, but it also follows from the relativity of values to life-phases: to superimpose the values appropriate to adult existence on childhood is to contribute to the alienation of the child from the world, himself, and others, and to defeat the realization of the values imposed. That is, to conceive of schooling as preparation for society alienates the child from the world, himself, others, the school, and society, and necessarily fails to be preparatory. More specifically, repeated requests from special interest groups for emphasis in schools upon what they often call "moral and spiritual values" are self-defeating. What they want are the kind of people who are able to embody "enduring" values in their own lives in adult society, that is, the kinds of people who are able to resolve the crisis of practical experience adequately. But human existence is not linear, and to try to promote values appropriate to adult existence in childhood existence is to engage in a self-defeating and self-destructive project and simply the effect of an inadequate resolution of ideals after the crisis of practical experience. To advocate inculcation of "moral and spiritual values" in school, in other words, is a fanatical abuse of children. Analogously for the more general point: to advocate schooling as preparation overlooks the significance of the being of children and youth as such because it is not better to be adult than to be a child; each phase is an irreplaceable part of the whole and the whole is not just the linear sum of its parts. Children do not exist in order to become youths, nor youths, adults. Within each person's life, each hour, each day, each year, each life-phase, comes only once. Each moment is irreplaceable and worth the whole. This is not a value judgment but a factical claim. The whole is present in the present moment and nowhere else. It follows that not only must the child be able to play to exist fully as a child, i.e., to live each moment in its irreplaceability by realizing its values, he *has* to do this as a child to be able to exist fully as an adult.

In other words, the restoration of the consideration of the child as a person in his own right that was associated with progressive education seems to be the prerequisite to the realization of authentic values within adult society, for this respect for the child is necessary to enable him to live the phase of life that he finds himself in fully, and this is necessary to living the next phase fully, and so on. This is the significance of the being of children and youth for education.

5

Educating in Childhood and Authority

The search for the ground of education in the being of children and youth is paradoxical. The closer the ground is approached, the further it recedes from view. When childhood and youth are lived fully, with the whole being, education is grounded, but this removes the ground from the process of educating by another person. Does not living childhood fully mean playing and therewith total freedom from adult domination and control? Does not the freedom required to ground educa*tion* remove the ground from educa*ting*? What can be done to influence the development of the child or youth that is not an alienating imposition, that is not restrictive of the pupil's living his present life authentically? What is the significance of educating for the being of children and youth?

The paradoxical element in the search for the ground of education is that this search restores the respect for the child and the youth that is associated with and constitutive of progressive education, but at the same time it thereby "restores" the authority-crisis that is also associated with, and perhaps constitutive of, progressive education. With the restoration of this respect the pupil's *education to* freedom becomes an *educating through* freedom, but once the pupil's freedom to be himself is granted, whence educating? The questions concerning the significance of the being of children and youth for education and the significance of educating for the being of children and youth coalesce in the question concerning the

58

ground of pedagogic authority. The ground of educating does indeed slip away precisely when it seems to be grasped in the concept of living each life-phase authentically, but perhaps this is the most fundamental way of putting the question concerning the ground of educating, i.e., the question concerning the ontological basis of pedagogic authority. To disclose the place of pedagogic authority within the pupil's choosings in his living his present life-phase fully, i.e., within the pupil's being, becomes the way to ground educating.

The authority-crisis generated by the progressive education movement was the obverse side of its respect for the child as a person in his own right. Adherents professed a strong anti-authoritarian bias that often seemed silly to outsiders, who wondered why the exponents of freedom in education "forgot" their responsibilities toward educating the young people within their care. The actual authority-crisis emerged, however, in the doubt generated by the progressive education movement and in the difficulty of being able to render a definitive and justifiable statement of the nature of pedagogic authority in response to, or as a refutation of, the claims for the dignity of the child as a person that were extended by progressive educational theorists. They extended a challenge that basically has remained unanswered. The "anti-authoritarianism" of progressive education, on the other hand, proves unsatisfactory because it is an over-statement and partial truth to begin with. It is claimed that good teachers do not have to resort to the use of authority to gain pupil cooperation. This truism, however, easily and quite erroneously becomes converted to a belief that whoever says he is nonauthoritarian is a good teacher: it can become a slogan by which individuals who repeat the incantation convince themselves they are good teachers. It also led, historically, to the "empirical" study of "authoritarianism" and "non-authoritarianism" insofar as these could be operationally and observationally defined, but never has it led to a development of the distinction between authentic and inauthentic pedagogic authority. In what is now the classic work on nonauthoritarian authority, Kenneth Benne held that pedagogic authority belongs to the social office of teaching: the teacher represents and embodies the authority of the community, perhaps the extended community, over the young.[1] Other attempts have located authority in the teacher's expertise, in the kind of person the teacher is, and in the content or method of instruction, while others have ignored the problem by outright claim. These fail to ground education, however, for they can all be granted and operative and educating can still be ungrounded. The teacher can be acknowledged to possess the authority of the parents, the community, her expertise in the scholarly world and in pedagogic methodology, and nevertheless lack it in the eyes of the child—the only place it counts toward grounding educating. To locate pedagogic authority within the child's world, i.e., from the child's point of view, is to disclose how pedagogic authority exists itself in the lived-world of the child and to ground educating.

THE CHILD IN
THE PRIMARY WORLD

The lived-world of the child, the mode of being-in-the-world that is characteristic of childhood, is such that the child lives in a world that invites exploration. He exists within purified reflection wherein the prereflective realm is clear of the subterfuges and bad faith of the realm of reflection. He is, consequently, authentically there in the world. He lives directly into the world, prior to the development of the subject/object split, prior to the alienation from the immediate world. The child's open communion with the world in his play, in fact, is not merely the place wherein the individual's relationship to being is formed, it is the primordial and originary relation to being. As Heidegger tried to reach the primordial relation to being by returning to the philosophical sources of the pre-Socratic Greek world prior to the alienation of philosophy, from the world and from itself, that it suffered in the hands of Plato and Aristotle when being became Being, an object of thought, so might he have tried doing a phenomenology of childhood to get back to the primordial sources or originary relation to being. The child lives in open communion with his world, standing out directly into it, existing his world. His world invites exploration, therefore, because within his "awareness" of the world no "objects" of thought intervene between his prereflective awareness of things and himself. Their qualities are experienced as so many little demands or values that invite him to have something to do with them. At least the small child lives directly into the world.

Before he discovers speech, the child is one with his world. The mother's nipple, or reasonable facsimile thereof, for example, is that which demands a rapid movement (of the head) and seizure and pulling on, regardless of the "cause" of the initial "learning." The nipple *is* that which demands thus and thus. It has its being as nipple in demanding something: it exists in the world of the infant as exerting this demand, this ought, even though he has not yet heard of ethics or mastered moral language. Whatever "need" or "drive" or "reflex" may be said to underlie the action by those who are adept by explaining the seen by the unseen, the conscious experiencing by the baby is that the nipple exists-to-be-grabbed as soon as it comes into view.[2] The nipple is a lived-fact, an existential, permeated-with-value fact in the infant's world. It is not a scientific but a world-fact. It is disclosed authentically as such to the child. Similarly and generally, living directly into the world discloses things authentically to the child and they invite him to play with them.

Upon this background of authentic disclosure of world, in this non-thematic projection into concrete possibilities in living directly into the world, the event of language occurs. There follows the distancing from the world best expressed as the subject/object cleavage. The acquisition of speech gradually levels the "objective" world off or down to a uniform and orderly unity on the one side, and a subjective "I" becomes complex and independent of the world on the other. The child's primary, nonverbal but conscious discourse with the world gradually becomes articulated in the language that has surrounded him since birth, and this articulation of his world gradually transfixes objects corresponding to the "referents" of the ordinary language, of the vocabulary, of his parents and other teachers. The "entities" within his world become established, i.e., constituted, as "objects" that are present at hand by the human voices he hears.[3] This, however, is a gradual happening that requires the whole of childhood. Only after pubescence with the increasing power of reflection (and maturation of the brain) is it possible to lose the primary relationship with the world completely, i.e., to be completely alienated from the world. The gradual distancing from the world, however, actually precedes the acquisition of language. It begins, in fact, with the acquisition of the world, for to be one with the world requires its dialectical opposite in order to be. To-be-at-one-with the world and to-be-other-than the world are two aspects of the relation to the world. The world, the "other," invites exploration very early, and as it is explored it increasingly constitutes itself more as the world.[4] The world (i.e., "entities" in the "focus" of directed awareness and the ground of their appearance) beckons to the child; the child explores. The more he explores, the more the world beckons and the more world there is (for him). The more world there is in positional consciousness, however, the greater is the nonpositional consciousness of the other-than-the-world, i.e., of himself. Again, the more world there is, the more consciousness there is; the more consciousness, the more there is "something" other than the world as its correlate. The primal distancing from the world begins to occur within the child's "open communion" with the world before the event of language inasmuch as his discourse with the world, his action, precedes his dealings with language and establishes meanings that words help him to articulate.

Because his discourse with the world is separable from his use of language, occurring at least partly before language is acquired, the play and exploration of the world of sound, color, taste, odor, shape, magnitude, weight, etc., is wondrously "confused": his experiencing occurs "through" all the "senses" simultaneously and in "confusion" because of the open communion with the world and the intensity of his experiencing.[5] "That music is so good I could eat it." This intensity is experienced as the intensity of the world, and it is the strong, vivid colors, spectacular shapes, surprising surfaces, etc., that fascinate the child. The intensity of the world pulls the child into it; it invites, even demands, his exploration. It is the things in the world and the world itself that are fascinating, contagious, and alluring to the child. By the time the child's world is developed enough so that it can be properly said to "invite" him, there has been sufficient articulation of the world in the child's exploration of it to establish a preferential area, or "interest." He is "interested" in what invites him. To respond to or to accept the invitation by exploring some preferential area, however, involves thematization of the quest, i.e., some intellectualization. This can result in the "acquisition of knowledge," etc., that is, in the further articulation and stabilization of the child's world. After the world attracts the child and pulls him into it so that he can and does explore it, the child turns toward the world and goes to the world.[6] That he can later go to the world and take it home to himself is dependent upon the earlier attraction it has for him.

Things in the attracting, inviting world are what they appear to be. The child crawls across the living room floor near his mother's house slipper: What is this thing? It can be an "unnoticeable" that is merely passed over; a fuzzy blob to slobber on, or pure sensuous datum; a cradle to put a doll into, or a toy; a "Mother's slipper" if it reminds the child of his parent, i.e., a sign of something else; a gift to take to Father; a hammer to play with, or instrumentality; or a slipper if he recognizes it, i.e., a commodity and article of apparel.[7] It, the thing, in this case a house slipper, can be a great many things in the world of the child: things are what they appear to be, and his world is still sufficiently open to let them appear in their being. If he is to live this life-phase fully, his task as a child is not to learn what things are to adults, but to let them be. It is to play with them and let them disclose themselves in their original glory. Things have a marvelous, glorious appearance to the child in his wonder. In his world they *are* marvelous and they challenge him to let them disclose themselves.[8]

The turning of the child to the world to go to it in play that occurs after the "open communion" in which things appear in their glory requires the "open communion" as its basis. To be able to go to the world, one must have a world already there to go to. One must be able to recognize things in order to explore the world. The place of toys is crucial, for it lies between the primary attraction of the world and going to it in exploration. In first play, the ball entices the child to roll it, the stacked blocks urge him to stack them higher or knock them over, the empty box wants filling and the full box demands emptying, what is open requires poking into or crawling through, what can be climbed upon asks for it, the puddle exerts an ought-to-be-splashed-in, and so on.[9] Toys, like things in the attractive world, are experienced directly in their qualities, in their values, and this experiencing of their values entices further play that results in further disclosures of the qualities of things, which results in further play, and so on. Which objects make good toys for the child, furthermore, does not depend upon his parents' opinions: because the place of toys lies "between" the primary attraction of the world and going to it to explore it, everything encountered in this phase is a toy to the child. He plays with all the things he encounters in order to realize their qualities. By handling them, by repeating what is familiar again and again, he realizes their values in his own being again and again, for this repetition is not the dull, habitual movement it might seem, but continues to be exploratory and consummatory. The seeming repetition involved in the child's play is exploratory because whatever the toy, it becomes part of his world, part of him, as he excorporates himself into its space through these manipulations as the "toys" play back with him. From his point of view, it is the toy that does the unexpected, not his own hand that lacks coordination, and these unexpected things that toys do entice him to further play, further exploration of the toy-thing, and further extension of his lived-space. Thus playing is an existentially serious affair, for it is the child's essential business, that which he ought to be about.[10] Play exists childhood because childhood as a life-phase is becoming at home in the world.

THE SAFETY OF THE WORLD
AND PEDAGOGIC HELP

Play is possible, however, only in a secure world where all possibilities of being are open. A precarious, unstable, threatening, and hostile world does not invite exploration, nor does it encourage him to go to it, nor do things beg to be played with. The safeness of the world, however, is a factor beyond the child's control. There is no way for him to establish the relative danger or safety of his world and there is no point in thinking he can have courage or not, because he is too simple: he will explore his world if it is safe and not if not. Part of the attraction of the world in the beginning, that is, is precisely related to its inherent safety. But how can the safety/danger dimension of his world vary? With this question the ground of educating begins to appear. The "elements" of the child's world may be classified as organic factors, helplessness, safety, and exploration.[11] The organic or "bodily" factors are insufficiently developed for independent existence in the world, and the child is mostly helpless but in need of less and less help as he grows. If he is helped sufficiently, his world becomes safe and he explores. If his helplessness is not sufficiently ministered to, the world does not become safe enough and he does not explore it. This can happen in a variety of ways. Feeding the child and supplying food for him to feed himself, for example, are ways of helping him. If he does not get enough to eat, the child is not only hungry but he lives in a world that does not give him enough to eat: he lives in a world in which there is not enough food. In either case the world is unsafe and does not invite playful explorations. Because the safety of the world stands between his helplessness and his explorations, the child's access to the world exists through the help that others give him in establishing the safety of his world: he is cut off from his world unless he is helped. Authentic expansion of the child's world depends upon the adults who are responsible for him, for if they engineer the safety of the world in proportion to his helplessness, they free him to explore an inviting world. Adult help liberates the child for his own possibilities in the world of play. Through participation in his being, they let the child be.

The valence of the child's world, in other words, depends upon his helplessness and the ministration thereto by adults. If help is proportional to helplessness, if it is authentic solicitude, the child is freed to lose himself in the inviting world in play and to become the world. He becomes his world because his wandering into its new, inexhaustible richness is the disclosure of possibilities and these possibilities belong both to the world and to the child: ball bouncing, for example, belongs to the world and to the child simultaneously. When totally engrossed in bouncing it, the child is the ball. Its possibilities are his possibilities. The child has enormous possibilities of development because the world's possibilities are virtually inexhaustible. Part of the inexhaustibility of the world is its bigness. Chairs that adults sit down in have to be climbed up into; adults are giants, tremendously loud, strong, and unpredictable. The large world itself is unpredictable because its laws (things fall) are unknown, and the unexpected is continuously expected.[12] The child's explorations are limited, therefore, even when he is adequately helped. He is limited by his body, which gets tired and requires food and rest, by the factuality of the world as it helps and hinders his projects, by his "past," as it begins to circumscribe his world and his developing possibilities all too soon, by his limited power, with which he has to reckon, and by other people, particularly the adults upon whom he depends, with whom he also has to reckon.[13]

These limitations, particularly the last two, furnish the basis for the possibility of educating through the pedagogic relation and for disclosure of the world through speech. When the infant first hears speech, it is in the air around him, in regard to him, and directed to him. He begins to understand it as being about the world and revelatory of it;

as concerning himself; and as being directed to him, establishing relations between others and himself. These are three ways in which "language" constitutes his being. The first is the major pedagogic area; the third the pedagogic arena. The talk that is directed to the child is the "preformed" pedagogic arena, the place where all subsequent talk in teaching occurs, which may not seem to be very illuminating except when one considers that it is the vicinity of the ground of educating.[14] Birth is the acquisition of bodily independence and represents how physical and moral independence are intertwined, because a foster mother will often do as well as if not better than the real mother. This bodily independence, however, permits the pedagogic relation, because all the help and care that the mother gives the child can be considered as part of the pedagogic undertaking: to free the pupil (baby) from the teacher (mother) so that he can be someone himself.[15] Within all the talk that is addressed to the infant by the mother, that which assists his wanting-to-be-someone-himself is *ipso facto* pedagogic. It is not pedagogic if it helps insufficiently or if it prolongs dependence. In either of these cases the solicitude of the mother is deficient. By the same token, authentic solicitude on the part of the mother helps the child precisely so that he can gradually come to do without help. A glance at the totality of the pedagogic task might clarify this. The unborn child is totally dependent on the parent; the adult is totally independent, if he survives the crisis of practical experience in the adequate reassessment of his adolescent ideals. Whatever helps the movement from the total dependence of prenatal life to the independence of mature adult existence is pedagogic if its source is other people. The *actual* purposes in pedagogy at the classroom and lesson level may quite appropriately be very specific, but the real aim behind these purposes is the development of a person who no longer requires pedagogic assistance. The total independence of adult existence can be, and has been, stated in a great variety of ways, but however it is stated, the aim of educating is to let the pupil live his life as an individual, independent being who recognizes the uniqueness of others, i.e., who accepts responsibility for his own being and his being with others. Because being-adult signifies these things, pedagogy is only helping another person to become adult.[16]

This is neither the imposition of adult values upon childhood nor the use of childhood and youth to prepare for being-adult as if that were radically different: the child already wants to be independently—if he is authentically there in his world as a child, which he will be if his world is safe. In the safe, inviting world the child is authentically there in the world, transcending to the world from his own origin, guided by possibilities in the world. This guidance by the possibilities of the world, however, has to occur within his perspective of them for there to be world-facts.

There is a bond, so to speak, between the child and his world resulting from his living directly into the world that resists its displacement by domination of the child by other people: the invitingness of the world to be explored can be restated as the child's wanting-to-be-independently. The hyphenation is essential to indicate the presence of a unitary phenomenon: insofar as the world invites the child, i.e., insofar as the child is in the grip of the attracting world and of the fascinating things in it, he wants to be, and this desire to be is manifested in his playing. Why does the child play? Because he wants to be, and being as a child is playing. Insofar as the freedom of action that is definitive of playing can be said to inhere in the playing itself, he wants to be independently: the doing of the play activity is playful only if it is independent of external guidance in the at-oneness of the child with the toy, etc. A structuration of the child's being, in other words, is his wanting-to-be-independently, and this underlying "motivation" keeps pedagogy from alienating the child from himself when it restricts itself to helping the child become an "adult," when it remains within authentic solicitude. The child's wanting-to-be-independently, his wanting to project into his own possibilities, can be restated as his wanting-to-be-someone-himself to supply the attestation of prephilosophical understanding. Ordinary language has a distinction between being a nobody and being somebody, between a person who is a "nonentity" (i.e., indistinguishable) and a person who is someone (i.e., a "V.I.P."). This distinction was captured in the blues lyric, "You're nobody until somebody loves you." The suggestion in the last line of the song to find somebody to love implies that it is more desirable to be a somebody than a nobody. The song's popularity signifies that the wanting-to-be-somebody was latent in the "consumers" of the popular song.

The wanting-to-be-someone-oneself, moreover, is also a restatement of Heidegger's, Sartre's, and others' formulation of the basic human motivating force as the desire to achieve being, or having one's being to be. Neither the wanting-to-be-independently or wanting-to-be-someone-himself should be considered as the verbal expression of a value or as an ideal that is consciously held by the child: they are underlying structurations of being-child. With his whole being, the child wants to be someone himself: he wants to respond to the existential imperative of having his being to be. This does not mean that he knows what or who he wants to be or that he knows precisely what this entails in various situations, nor does it mean that the child or youth knows what he wants in each situation. Neither does it mean that the child is responsible for maintaining the motivation of wanting-to-be-someone-himself.[17] It is not aimed at by the child because it is part of the lateral structuration of his forward projection into concrete possibilities in the world; the necessary condition of the wanting-to-be-someone-himself is not supplied by the child because the condition is receiving adequate help, or having a safe world established by that help. Within the scope of temporality, help is not something one does to or for a child but what one does with him. Its real aim is not so much to help in this or that circumstance but to be able to stop helping in general by increasing the independence of the child from the source of help. But the child accepts help in the wrong way if his wanting-to-be-independently is not maintained, if he does not continue to want to be someone himself. If he wants to be someone himself, he will explore the world vigorously and require distinctly pedagogic help. The pedagogic arena develops out of the talk of the parents to the child; this talk becomes distinctly pedagogic when the child explores the world with such intensity he knows he requires help to continue, for then he asks for help and the responsive talk about the world will be revelatory of the world that he has been exploring, and he will ascribe authoritativeness to what is said in the talk. The help given each time it is requested enables the child to be independently at that time, and this is the significance of educating for his being. The cumulative effect is to enable the growing person to be an independently existing adult.

AUTHORITY IN THE WORLD OF THE CHILD

Thus there are three presuppositions of educating: helplessness, room for development, and the pupil's striving to be someone himself.[18] If pedagogy is merely helping the child or pupil to become an adult, pedagogical striving depends upon the pupil's wanting-to-be-someone-himself and the exploration of the world prompted by the striving-to-be-independently, for by helping under these conditions—that is, by disclosing possibilities in the world that the child is exploring—pedagogical striving inserts itself between the child's helplessness and his striving to be someone himself. It inserts itself within the pupil's project of being and grounds itself. The child dwelling in a safe world is aware of help when he needs it in his explorations, and in accepting whatever help he requires in order to be someone himself, he grounds educating.[19] The acceptance of such help, then, is the ontological ground of pedagogic authority. It is when educating has significance for his being.

The talk directed to the child is the preformed pedagogic arena. When what is said helps the child, it is accepted. Because such help is fully accepted only when it is fully asked for, the child constitutes the authority of the teacher: he ascribes authoritativeness to the words of the parent or teacher when the words disclose possibilities in the world contributory to his explorations of the world. For the child, pedagogic authority originates in the relation with the parent when the parent helps him to be someone himself. Even in a safe, inviting world, the child encounters difficulties with which he needs help. When the parent's help is indispensable, the child "submits" to "superior judgment" without reflectively choosing whether or not to follow adult direction.[20] This mode of helping is the disclosure of a possibility of being into which the child throws himself immediately because he was already trying to find the opening into the darkness that surrounds him that the parent disclosed. The bright and attractive world in which the child plays has a limited horizon with many dark areas inside as well as beyond. In this world, language has a revelatory and constitutive function. The child is open to the qualities of objects but does not know what they are: names create objects out of diffuse phenomena. When the child relates the name "slipper" to the object, it first becomes primarily a slipper for him in his world. Unless he has witnessed its instrumental function earlier in an impressive way, he begins to know it as a slipper because it is a slipper in his world after he "learns its name," i.e., what it is. For prereflective, prescientific consciousness, "naming an object is causing it to exist or changing it."[21] The child is an Aristotelian realist, so to speak, for when he asks what a thing is he wants to know what it is, its essence, not what its name is or what people call it. For the child's awareness, the name or word bears a meaning that is imposed on the phenomenon, which transforms it into the "object" referred to by the name: once named it is this and no other. Because language is in possession of the world into which the child is born, his learning the language as he learns to speak with others pulls him into the common world that is encompassed by the basic vocabulary of his "native" tongue and expands, stretches out, and levels off his own world to the common world of everyday speech. In this ordinary language the child finds that he is not the sole constitutive founder of the world and that all those whose speech he hears help constitute the common world of cultural objects.[22]

The transformation of the child's own world to the common world that occurs through his acquisition of language might seem to be alienating and depersonalizing. Such is not actually the case, for four reasons: (1) the alternative to learning the common language is more alienating; (2) the very simplicity of ordinary language suits the relative simplicity of the child's world; (3) the common language discloses genuine possibilities of the world (if not the only ones); and (4) the common words provide for an identification of child and parent, or child and teacher. This identification comes about through the disclosure the parent makes to the child when the child asks for help, and this disclosure, occurring actually as a co-disclosure, reveals objects and possibilities of being.

The co-disclosure of a possibility of being occurs in an "identification" of parent and child in some concrete possibility. The child has a question and needs help. He asks the question. As the parent listens to the question and understands it, the focus of his awareness becomes directed to the dark place in the child's world. If he hears the child, he to a certain extent *becomes* the child, situated in the child's situation, facing the same situation; he spatializes and temporalizes into the world the child has been spatializing and temporalizing into. In reply, the parent spatializes and temporalizes into a concrete possibility, existing into it, bringing it into being in his being. As the child is listening and looking for that particular possibility, he, too, spatializes and temporalizes into it as he sees (understands) it, existing into it and bringing it into being in his being. "Where's the door?" "There." Such disclosure is genuinely a co-disclosure because of the simultaneity of the projection into the "same" possibility of being. Parent and child co-exist in the disclosure: there is an identification of parent and child in the opening into the world that exists the revealed possibility. To the degree that the parent reveals authentic possibilities, he has authority in the eyes of the child that is grounded in their spatializing and temporalizing together. If the co-disclosure occurs in response to the child's questions about the difficulties he has in the exploration of his world, the parent's authority is simultaneously grounded in the child's project of being, in the coexistence of the parent and child, and in the possibilities of being in the world.

Educating rests upon the authoritative relation between parents and children. The authority relation between adults, as in a power structure on a job or in community law enforcement, are not models for the existential pedagogic relation. The parent–child relation and the authority therein is also an inadequate model for schooling, moreover, because educating within schooling occurs afterwards, on the basis of parental help, with larger children, and in the presence of other children. The legal and moral authority that the parent has for the child is also an inadequate model for educating, but its consideration is instructive. As the parent is legally and morally responsible for the child until he becomes of age, so the teacher is at least morally responsible for the well-being of the child during the time the child is within her care, and, more importantly, she is responsible for the development of the child's world. It may be that the responsibility for the development of the child's world is primarily the parents', and that formal schooling serves the parents in fulfilling their responsibility; but, regardless, the whole child comes to school. Once there is schooling the teacher is legally and morally responsible for the development of the child's world while he is within her care. This responsibility necessarily entails the authority to develop the world of the child. This responsibility and authority for the child accompanies the responsibility and authority to the child that develops within the parental relation in the co-disclosure of possibilities of being.

The responsibility and authority that the teacher has for the child is extremely significant existentially, for the child who has grown into a safe world through an existentially adequate relation with his parents takes a great deal on trust and confidence in them. This trust in the parents colors the appearance of his teachers, who have his confidence with or without meriting it through the coexistence of the co-disclosing of possibilities of being. This makes the teacher morally responsible for the child in yet another sense: the child is very susceptible to seduction, to having his being for others rather than for himself, no matter what he does. Learning the alphabet, learning how to print, whatever, can be done as part of the child's exploration of the world, i.e., for its own sake, or for the teacher because the teacher wants it done. Learning to print, say, can be authentic if it is done playfully, if the pencil plays with the blank page, and it can be inauthentic, or done solely within the conflict of being-for-others, if it is done to please the teacher for the child's own ulterior purposes. Learning how to print a particular letter for its own sake and then showing it to the teacher to share the joy can be distinguished from learning to print the letter in order to avoid punishment and/or to derive joy from showing it to the teacher. The latter illustrates the seductiveness of the teacher that the child is open to and for which the teacher is morally responsible. On the one hand, the child's trust has to be obtained and maintained as part of the authoritative, co-disclosing, coexisting pedagogic relation for educating to have significance for his being. On the other hand, the pupil wants to be someone himself and this wanting-to-be-independently has to be kept alive, for it is the mainspring of pedagogic endeavor: if he is dominated the pupil does not explore his world and does not need help, there is no co-disclosure of possibilities of being, and educating is groundless and insignificant. The teacher, in other words, can abuse the child's trust and try to develop "hangers on" and "pets," but she will not do this if she is clear about the ground of educating in the being of the child, for then she will be aware that the child's wanting-to-be-someone-himself is the means of educating and accordingly allow room for disobedience.

Room for disobedience is the safeguard against encroachments of the inauthentic use of authority that occur when the teacher lets herself fall away from herself in her being as a teacher. If she is capable of abusing childish trust, she is capable of using her acquired authoritativeness inauthentically, in ways that are inauthentically pedagogic because they are little conducive to educating as the co-disclosure of possibilities of being and incompatible with the conditions of authentic coexistence. By allowing room for disobedience, the teacher prevents herself from taking advantage of the pupils, for she allows room for the pupil to be someone himself and thereby also makes room for genuine obedience. The paradoxical element in the grounding of educating is that the child has to be free to disobey in order to genuinely obey. *Room for disobedience grounds educating in the pupil's being!* **The being of educating is grounded in the maintenance of the possibility of its nonbeing.** If the possibility of the nonbeing of educating is removed from educating, if room for disobedience is not allowed, the possibility of educating is removed because the pupil's trust will be abused, he will fall into having his being for others, no longer wanting to be someone himself, and there will be no disclosure of possibilities of being, i.e., no learning that is grounded in his project of being.

Allowing room for disobedience, of course, is allowing room for the pupil's freedom: what is freedom from the viewpoint of authority except the possibility of disobedience? To suggest that there has to be room for disobedience, then, places freedom in dialectical relation rather than in opposition to pedagogic authority. The child has to be free to be someone himself to explore the world to require and to receive help as the disclosure of possibilities to ascribe authoritativeness to what the teacher says: he has to be free if he is to be able to ascribe authoritativeness to what the teacher says to ground educating. To allow room for disobedience in the classroom, although dangerous, is no fearsome ordeal, however, for the child who has lived his childhood fully goes to school full of great expectations, wanting to explore and to do whatever is done there. There is little likelihood of a genuine authority-crisis occurring before puberty. After puberty there may be such a complete distancing from the world that the "I" is developed sufficiently to make a genuine authority-crisis possible, but before this there is not likely to be one. Appearances to the contrary are most likely to be manifestations of the pupil's hunger to experience his freedom, as developed from his wanting-to-be-independently, that are quite compatible with a readiness to acknowledge a need for help on other occasions. They are not symptomatic of a general crisis of authority.

FREEDOM IN
THE WORLD OF THE CHILD

Within the child's awareness, the wanting-to-be-independently or wanting-to-be-someone-himself, his being, is experienced as freedom. The experience of freedom is the concomitant of being the sole originator of one's wide-awake actions, of actually existing independently rather than being dominated by someone else in the conflict of having his being for others. The experience of freedom is that of doing things freely. There are differing phases or stages in the development of experienced freedom that are essentially "subphases" in the development of the life-phase of childhood: their explication will indicate subphases in the development of pedagogic authority and articulate what it means to let room for disobedience in order to ground educating.[23] The phases in the experience of freedom are increases in the complexity of experiencing the self and world, a deepening of conscious existence, and the gradual opening of the subject/object difference. The child is first aware of objects, then of his own project among objects, then of alternative projects among the world of objects, then of his own projects among the projects of other people, then of the world or total context in which these various projects occur.

When the infant is simply aware of objects, about all he can do is grasp, fondle, and manipulate them one at a time. His awareness flits from object to object as the child's being becomes satiated first with this, then with that. There is hardly any temporal span to awareness, and all movements are virtually "capricious," justified by the values to be realized in the particular object of the moment irrespective of connections with other objects, the context, or consequences. The freedom experienced at this phase is the freedom of caprice, for action follows the "whim" of the moment. This is entirely appropriate for this life-phase because of the extremely simple and limited structure of temporality. As the exploration of the world continues, however, remembrance and familiarity lead the infant to expect to experience certain qualities if he reaches for this object, crawls over for that one. As he builds up memories, he becomes able to futurize, and in this temporalization he becomes aware of his own projection toward objects and of individual projects among things in his world: he can decide to reach for them. This is the experience of the freedom of initiative, in which the freedom of caprice becomes transformed by an inward awareness of itself.

The third level of experienced freedom is reached when the awareness of initiative becomes correlated with objects and projects such that the infant actually makes a decision: he decides between the bottle and the ball. That is, he is aware of alternative projects or actions and can choose between them. Since they involve some effort and there is now some duration tied into the temporal structure, there is an awareness of short range consequences and the results of effort. The freedom experienced is the freedom of power. He can be aware that the choice is to crawl across the room after the ball that has just rolled away or pick up the bottle again that is still close at hand, then go crawling for the ball and rejoice when victorious. He has decided and then found the action to be worth the effort. This is the transformation of the freedoms of caprice and initiative into the freedom of power and accomplishment through the inward awareness of itself. Freedom of conquest initially begins, however, when the child's consciousness has deepened sufficiently to be able to hold *one* project in mind at a time and decide if it is worth the effort. When he is able to choose among two projects and decide which is more worth while, he develops freedom of choice. This involves considerable distancing from the world with considerable mediation of meanings between the child and the world. His world has to have developed into a referential totality that in this stage becomes more coherent and interrelated as the values of the world begin to arrange themselves hierarchically on his preferences as established in his choices in his project of being.

Freedom of choice, however, is not yet the highest and most complex stage of experienced freedom. Consciousness deepens further, so that the child not only is able to choose which of alternative projects is worth more effort, or is more worth while, but is able to see the whole context in which his projects occur and to compare his own projects with those of other people. This is the stage of moral freedom. Ideally, the parents would have helped him develop to the stage of moral freedom by the time the child comes to school, for most of the development toward this stage occurs through his ordinary exploration of toys in a safe world. The additional "pedagogy" needed involves the child's learning, after he has reached the level of awareness involved in freedom of choice, that there are things that he is permitted to do and things he is not permitted to do. When this distinction is possible, the child is able to enter into a pedagogic relation freely and of his own accord.[24] Before this he accepts help as a matter of course; after this he can choose to accept or reject help.

In the phases of freedom of caprice and freedom of initiative, the child is exploring his world, answering its provocative summons, responding to the qualities of things that seem to demand something of him. The child's being is expanding into the world in responsiveness to these experienced values; it is also adapting itself to things as they are experienced. If he is prohibited in these expansive movements, his exercise of freedom of caprice and initiative *seems* to be the freedom of revolt and refusal. The "negativism" associated with phases of childhood when considered phenomenologically is the irrepressibility of the experience of freedom—of being independently. When the child's consciousness has not yet deepened sufficiently to make freedom of conquest or choice possible, he has to be independently anyway. He does this, if necessary, by positing a world of refusal. He can rebel, repudiate, break and smash, for he is the originary "rebel without a cause," the cause being the only one anyone ever has, the need to experience his freedom, i.e., to be himself, i.e., to be. When his consciousness has deepened so that this infantile freedom of caprice and initiative can be transformed into the freedom of conquest, it will be, providing that the world the child explores is safe enough. Then as he develops into the stage of freedom of choice, he is able to begin to take other people's projects into account. When he can do this, then if he is told that some things are permitted and others are not, he gradually becomes able to distinguish between what he wants to do and what he is permitted to do. When he can make this distinction, regardless of what he does about it, the appearance of authority changes. Otherwise he could not really choose to do what he wanted to do instead of what he was permitted to do: there would only be a clash of wills, of choosing between what he wanted or what his parent wanted, and this choosing would remain on the level of freedom of caprice. "Obedience" at this stage is submission or repression of one's own being, but not obedience. Only when what the parent or teacher wants can be distinguished in the child's awareness from what is permitted and what is not can the child freely disagree with the parent and disobey, and only then can he fully obey and experience the fullness of the authority he freely ascribes to the parent. To allow room for disobedience, then, is to allow room for freedom of conquest and choice and moral freedom. It does not allow room for freedom of caprice and revolt, for part of the pedagogic task is to create the conditions for the transformation of these freedoms into those that are the necessary conditions for the exploration of the world.

When the child is able to distinguish in his parent's or teacher's speech what is permitted from what they want, when what is permitted becomes separable from the person of the parent, he is able to distinguish in himself what he wants from what is permitted. Then he is free to ascribe authoritativeness for his conduct to values experienced in the social world. Then he is in the same kind of relation to these values that he is in respect to the values in the attracting world, but these values pull him into the social world. That is, when the child distinguishes what he wants from what is permitted, the ontological foundation is an overdistancing from the world, for "what he wants" is experienced as given internally, in isolation from the world and from "what is permitted," which is given externally. Being able to make the distinction is a manifestation of partial alienation from the world, but the alienation is overcome if the child chooses to do what is permitted, if he chooses "obedience," because if this is a free choice the child has then let the values implicated therein be and exert their demand upon him, much as he earlier splashed in the puddle upon its demand of him. This can happen, however, only if the norms or values in "what is permitted" actually are able to exert their obligatory nature upon the child independently of the person of the parent or teacher. Through the ontological trust developed in the coexistence with the parents in authentic co-disclosures when help was needed, the child trusts doing "what is permitted," i.e., lets the values implicated therein be. He does what is expected of him, for the most part, when he is able to, i.e., when he can freely choose to do so and still be someone himself, and when he also sees the validity of the values therein.

The authoritativeness that can be ascribed to the values in what is permitted differs from any previously granted authority. There are three stages: before he learns to talk, after learning to talk, and after distinguishing what he wants from what is permitted. Although there is full co-disclosure of possibilities of being and coexistence in all three levels, only in the last can there be genuine obedience, because only then can there be freedom of moral choice and genuine disobedience. Only in the fourth year of life, approximately, is the distancing from the world complete enough for the occurrence, in simple ways, of the distinction between what he wants from what is permitted. Then through the fifth year the distinction develops gradually, if the parents teach him that there are things that are and that are not permitted, until it is quite a clear distinction by the time schooling begins. The importance of being able to make this distinction and the having things to do that are and are not permitted in order to develop conscious existence in its light cannot be overstated. Without it there can be freedom of choice, but never moral choice, i.e., never the transformation of the experience of freedom, of one's being, into the moral realm of coexistence, because there can never be the experience of moral value as something independent of what particular persons want, as something demanded by the situation. Paradoxically, the possibility of "obedience" to the demands of situations, to "what is permitted," to value, develops simultaneously with the child's discovery that he can want. How else? Authority develops concomitantly with freedom; the teacher maintains the pupil's moral freedom by letting room for him to disobey precisely so that he might be able to come to authentic obedience to the norms and values incorporated into the teacher's way of existing, i.e., of her world, and nevertheless continue to be someone himself. Room for disobedience maintains the tension between pedagogic authority and the pupil's freedom, between the pressure exerted on the pupil's existence by the norms present in the person of the teacher to whom he freely ascribes authority and his wanting-to-be-someone-himself.

This tension is constitutive of the pedagogic relation, for it manifests that the pupil's wanting-to-be-someone-himself is maintained and that the teacher's presence is exerting norms of some kind. It manifests that the pupil is exploring the world with such intensity that he requires help; that he is in a sufficiently secure world that he is able to accept what help he requires; that such help comes to him in the form of disclosure of possibilities of being that is governed by the teacher's authentic solicitude that discloses the pupil's possibilities with rather than for him, so that educating might be grounded in his project of being, i.e., in his being, but that nevertheless requires something of the pupil because it comes into his being only through his futural projection into it. The tension belongs to educating because the pedagogic relation is one that is entered into with an awareness on both sides that its object is to destroy itself in the pupil's no longer needing help, yet with an awareness that within its limits there is a genuine and authentically human coexistence to be obtained precisely when one member of it ascribes authoritativeness to the other and the other ascribes freedom to the first.

The significance of educating for the being of the child and the youth is that—through the responsibility of the teacher for the development of the pupil's world that becomes effective through the norms embodied in the teacher's being when the pupil freely ascribes authority for his conduct to them and authoritativeness to what she says for his understanding—there occurs a gradual transformation of the world of his exploration from the physical world of play to the intellectual-historical world that he has to explore in order to become situated in the social-historical world as an authentically existing adult. The significance of educating for the being of the pupil is that it establishes him in the world, in being, but only through allowing the room for disobedience that takes into account the significance of his being for educating. Educating establishes, or grounds, the pupil in being to the exact extent that it is established, or grounded, in his being, that is, to the extent to which educating constitutes itself as the co-disclosure of possibilities of being. When teacher and pupil participate in such co-disclosure, educating is grounded, but this is not the final ground of educating.

In the authentic pedagogic co-disclosure, what occurs is something that far exceeds cultural transmission, instruction in subject matter, acquisition of knowledge, or skill formation. What occurs within genuinely pedagogic authority is authentic co-historicizing. If Heidegger was right when he said that it is being-in-the-world that historicizes,[25] then the co-historicizing of educating constitutes being.

Educating establishes being. It establishes the teacher's being, the pupil's being, and in the co-historicizing of their being-in-the-world it establishes the being of the world. The being of the world is its worlding, and in the worlding of the world being comes to be. Then pedagogic authority resides in the teacher as a guardian of being.

When the teacher is a guardian of being, she lets being be her guardian, and then educating becomes the site wherein being comes into being. Then not only is educating grounded in being, but being is established by educating. When being exists educating, educating exists being.

6

Educating in Youth and the Truth of Being

To ground educating in the being of children and youth, a phenomenology of the child's world has been necessary in order to ascertain the conditions under which a child will freely ascribe authoritativeness to what is said by others. The phenomenology was descriptive, but similar results might have been obtained through a transcendental deduction. There is educating, no doubt about that. This educating presupposes that authority is freely ascribed to what the teacher says. This in turn presupposes the child's being-in-the-world, his wanting-to-be-someone-himself, his going to the world in exploration, his requiring help in disclosure of world in order to be independently, his experiencing freedom of moral choice in a transformation of the pure spontaneity of freedom of caprice in order to be responsive to the values embodied in the personal existence of the teacher, the possibility of disobedience, disclosure of possibilities of being through speaking, being there with others, understanding, and so on. There is educating; human being must be structured this way to make educating possible. Or, the aim of education is authentic being. This presupposes that it is also the means of educating, that is, that the pupil's wanting-to-be-someone-himself is maintained, that as his project of being it motivates his exploration of the world, and that he will accept help in this exploration in the form of authentic disclosures. Educating presupposes that the pupil is authentically there in the world. It also presupposes that the teacher is authentically there helping the pupil to liberate himself for his ownmost possibilities. When these conditions prevail there can be educating and authentically pedagogic authority because they make it existentially possible. If not, then not; and this is the significance of the being of children for educating.

It may not be the significance of the being of youth for educating, however. If pedagogic authority is coextensive with educating and if there can be an authority-crisis any time after puberty, then the conditions under which it can be taken for granted that the pupil will come to trust the teacher and ascribe authoritativeness to her words diminish with the onset of youth as a life-phase. The being of youth may not have been adequately taken into account in the considerations of how pedagogic authority appears in the child's world. What is the significance of the being of youth for educating? What is the meaning of educating for youth?

These questions are more difficult to approach than their counterparts concerning children. Children would starve, take sick, and die were it not for pedagogic assistance and authority; youths are hardier, especially considering that, as a life-phase, youth includes all post-pubescents who are still in schools and who have not yet undergone the crisis of practical experience on their own; it includes college and university students. A great deal of hardly testable "pop" psychology, sociology, and moralizing, furthermore, gluts the media and market whenever the authority-crisis in youth is widespread, making youth as a distinctive life-phase difficult to envisage in an unemotional, unbiased way.

Youth is a "subject" upon which everyone has strong opinions already, and politicians ever draw near. There is difficulty in posing the question of the significance of the being of youth in a sufficiently radical manner, in a way that gets to the roots—to the very being—of youth as a life-phase.

THE RETURN TO
THE ORIGIN OF BEING

In an attempt to gain perspective an existential interpretation of a very dead historical phenomenon will be repeated as a "case study." Empirical researchers sometimes use the case study method to examine phenomena in their context in the real world. Clinical psychologists, e.g., employ it to generate understandings and generalizations of a certain kind of validity. Likewise is the "field study" beginning to be used to investigate problems of schooling from the viewpoint of the administrator.[1] The following "case study" of the German Youth Movement at the beginning of the century illustrates in a paradigmatic way the authority-crisis that may occur in youth as it has been manifested at large scale in the

United States in the lost generation after the First World War, then in the beat generation after the Second World War, then in the hippie-yippie generation during the Vietnam War, etc., etc. It also concerns related phenomena such as student unrest, disinterestedness in schooling, and the "drop-out" predicament, which are at bottom an alienation from schooling and what it stands for. The remoteness in time and place might assist in yielding balanced perspective on the significance of the being of youth for educating and the significance of the being of education for youth; the reality of the occurrence might assist in the grounding of education within the conditions of human being.

In the German Youth Movement the school boys in a college preparatory high school, a *gymnasium*, in Steglitz near Berlin, left their school and homes and tramped around Europe. They were soon followed by youth from elsewhere, until the abandonment of school and home became a general societal phenomenon. Why did they leave opportunities that, since they were the academic elite, might seem very enviable? *What did they leave?* To describe their situation from their point of view without interpreting it or judging it moralistically one has to use words that are moralistic, in the way the youth were moralistic, to convey their mooded understanding. Why did they themselves think they were leaving?

In their own minds the German youth fled the increasing drabness resulting from the industrialization of the city in protest against the mendacity and materialism of the age. They left to protest a tradition that seemed pretentious and lifeless and that interfered with their orientation to the future. The whole tradition and way of life "forced" upon them in school and at home seemed torpid, ungenuine, and uncreative. They fled what seemed to be a rigid life-order to seek genuineness, unobligatedness, and continuous becoming. By fleeing the overorganized "traditional" school at its best, they fled what seemed to be an over-structured milieu: neither the structured knowledge, daily assignments, nor school and community mores gave them room for their desires, interests, purposes, and goals. They fled a stifling atmosphere in order to breathe and consciously sought the precise opposite of what they fled. As they wandered around Europe, they had in mind to seek the new, far, and distant, but their actions revealed their true "goal," that of goallessness. They had no goals in mind, for they went nowhere. They did not go to Paris or to Rome, but wandered through the Black Forest, through the pines. Their wandering, in other words, had no aim but itself, to move around the landscape aimlessly.[2]

The wandering was the manifestation of a quest for a primordial way of living, a mode of being, that corresponded to the wanderer's own aimlessness. That it was an expression of the wanderer's simple having to be (for himself) can be seen through the shifts in the youth's temporal structure and concomitant shifts in the underlying moods or states-of-being. The temporal structure of the youth had become very bound in school. The organizing of their lives by the hours and days of schooling was not "natural," i.e., authentic, but was to great extent imposed upon their existence. The routine bound the youth's temporalizings into the anonymous pattern of schooling, "capturing" them so that the future was the next examination, etc., that impinged upon the individual, rather than promoting a free futurizing movement into which the youth might expand freely. The wandering freed the youth's temporal structure (and his temporalizings) from its bindings, from its being bound into public time with its objective past and future. The freeing of the present from its bonds to the earlier and the later made the experiencing of the present "timeless," and the disclosure of the world that occurred within that present became unique: as the present became loosened from the public time of schooling, it became worth while in its own right. The availability of the possibilities therein restored the youth to the childlike trust in the possibilities of the present. It restored his trust in present being. Each hour and each day became worth while in and for itself; each tomorrow became an inviting place to enter, acquiring an aura of holiness. In this progressive development of the sacredness of the present and the morrow, the world became open, bright, and promising. The *world* became an inviting place to enter because the disclosure of the world gradually came to occur within the wanderer's mood of high-spiritedness.[3]

All disclosure of world occurs through mooded understanding, through an understanding that is enveloped in a "mood" or state-of-being. The state-of-being, moreover, is primary in determining how the world is disclosed to one: to be in a constricted mood reveals a limited and limiting world, whereas to be in an expansive mood reveals an expanding, open world. This simply means that all disclosure occurs to existing people, i.e., to human existence, and human being is such that it is always in some state-of-being that is felt by the individual: the taste and smell of one's being is always present as part of one's self-conscious being. Everything, including the disclosure of world, happens within a state-of-being. Even the colorless, disinterested "lack of mood" appropriate to theoretical or scientific understanding is precisely a mood. It is a mood approaching a satiation with being wherein the world disclosed is a dull place and being is almost a burden.[4] As the youth wandered through the landscape, they underwent a gradual shifting of moods, or states-of-being, and with this shifting the mode of the disclosure of the world gradually shifted as well. This is most noticeable in the experiencing of time because the form of the temporal structure is the state-of-being: each mood has its own temporal structure; the temporal structure forced on the youth in home and school forced a state-of-being, or mood, of boredom upon them. As they wandered, the freeing from the public time of the schools was accompanied by a freeing from the state-of-being it induced. Therewith occurred, gradually, the childlike disclosure of world wherein the present possibilities became of great value.

The gradual shifting of the youth's state-of-being constitutes the anthropological significance of the wandering movement because of the accompanying changes in the general quality or valence of the world disclosed. The youth experienced extremely high spirits with the initial escape from schooling; this became a general elation as equanimity began to be restored. This became joy with the further restoral of equanimity, and this in turn gradually became the more primordial optimism of the child in his open communion with the world. The anthropological function of wandering was its return to the primary optimism of the child at play in a safe world.[5] It was in the basal joy of wandering that was attained after the overly exuberant elation had subsided that the present moment became unbound from the "urgent future" and "dragging past" in an existential freeing from externally imposed learnings and goals. Then in the sheer joy of abandonment to the wandering itself the apprehensiveness of the past and future slid away and disappeared. Rather than tradition or external obligations covering over the present moment, the "instant" stretched itself out and became not a place to be passed over quickly but one in which to dwell. In this stretching out of the present moment in which the moment became livable, the past and future simply foundered.[6]

Through wandering, the youth were freed to spatialize and temporalize from their own centers, i.e., for authentic existence. Then in the accompanying joy they could trust "nature," which became more open to them because of the trust, which increased the joy of wandering, which enabled the youth to become more and more open to the landscape as such. They became able to abandon themselves with confidence to the continuous movement of "nature," to drift along the stream of life therein. They identified with flowing brooks and streams, with the endless revolutions of days, months, and years, with mornings and springs, and these moments became expressed in song and lyric poetry.[7] They identified, i.e., had a personal I-Thou relationship, an immediate at-oneness, with things encountered in nature analogous to the unification of the child with his toys. This relationship was extended to plants, animals, and natural phenomena, even to the ordinarily repelling aspects of "nature." Even violent storms, for example, raised the wanderer's spirits because their own kind of greatness was experienced: the being of the wanderer opened to encompass the spatiality of the storm, rather than retreating from it in the more customary oppressiveness experienced of storms.[8] In this gradual union with the things of "nature," the youth came to dwell more and more in the landscape as such in the completely open communion with it that belongs to the earliest phase of childhood existence. They gradually became the landscape.

The aimlessness of the wandering and the shifts of the states-of-being through which the world was disclosed made the disclosure of the landscape quite different from the world disclosed to a farmer, woodsman, sportsman, or scientist, because the provinces of meaning in which *their* disclosures occur cause them to look at and objectify the landscape and things therein. Instead of observing the landscape, the wanderers experienced it, for the landscape presented itself to them. It cannot present itself within the other provinces of meaning because their bracketing constitutes a distancing that landscape has difficulty breaking through. The shifts in their state-of-being, in other words, were initiated as much by the landscape they were experiencing as it was by their own wandering movement. In the state of primary optimism and open communion with "nature," the landscape presented itself and enabled the experiencing in depth.[9]

The anthropological function of wandering was its return to nature, but if "nature" is given the interpretation of thinkers of the Romantic Movement, e.g., Rousseau, Wordsworth, or Emerson, it is interpreted sentimentally, youthfully, falsely. Rather than being a return to nature, the wandering of the youth movement represents a return to the origin, to the source. It was *a return to the ground of being.* Through the changes in the state-of-being, the wanderer's being opened to landscape and the landscape opened to the wanderer. The landscape, however, was not "nature"; it was being, simple being in itself. It was being qua being. Then what happened in the return to the origin when the wanderer's being opened to the landscape's being and the landscape's being opened to the wanderer's being was the movement whereby *being cleared a space for itself.* This worlding of the world, the truth of being, could not occur while the boys were in school because of the obstructiveness of the between-world of constructs that developed within the bracketing of the public time-structure of schooling and of the provinces of meaning of the academic disciplines studied therein. Although the anthropological function of the wandering was the return to an unconditional relation to being, its non-anthropocentric function was to allow being to clear a space for itself. What happened in the wandering was not merely a return to the ground of being, but a return of being. It occurred through joy because the matter of returning to the origin of one's being, the homecoming, is the originary joy.[10]

THE RECOVERY OF BEING

The wanderer sought a primordial life of continuous becoming and found it in the movement of the streams, the days, and the seasons in the life of nature wherein his world could world itself. As critic of the civilized, "bourgeois" world, he sought to return to the original source of being, to obtain the originary relation to being, to confront being without the interposition of someone else's constructs. He sought being and found himself because he found the conditions under which one can be at home with himself. Through the gradual change in his basic state-of-being, the negativism that had been oriented toward him, denying his being in its external imposition of a whole way of life, and against which he generated his own equal and opposite negativism in order to be someone himself—against which he posited a world of refusal in the experience of the freedom of revolt—became replaced by an affirming, life-supporting, positive world. The wanderers were enabled to become as affirmative as what they encountered. The wandering changed nay-saying into yea-saying because its return to the origin allowed for originary thanking, the response of their own being to the recovery of being by being.[11] It generated grounds for authentic gratitude and the positing of a world of acceptance. Precisely because children and youth are not independently functioning adults, they often find it difficult to be grateful and to express gratitude, particularly in the affluent and post-affluent segments of society. They do not know what to be grateful for, and it seems to them that the world owes them (and the nonaffluent as well) a living until they enter society as independently functioning adults. No matter how much they are given, from their viewpoint it is only their due; and they are right, having no standard of comparison. The only thing they, or anyone else, can be grateful for is simply that they are allowed to be, and if they are not allowed to exist authentically as youth within the confines of schooling, then some form of return to the origin of being is necessary if they are to become affirmative toward being in order to be capable of authentic gratitude and to be in the truth of being. The return to the origin in the wandering movement, therefore, is illuminating insofar as its extreme form discloses the phenomena involved in *the recovery of being*.

The recovery of being that occurred in the return to the origin of being in the wandering movement was prepared for by sacrifice. The youth sacrificed the goals and rewards of schooling, the good opinions, well-wishings, financial and other support of their families, and the place in organized, civilized, bourgeois society that would have been the chief "reward" for having been among the academic elite in a highly selective, competitive schooling system. It was prepared for by their readiness for nothingness, i.e., for what the burghers might have referred to as nothingness, or nonbeing, had they been ontologically sophisticated. This readiness to go into "nothingness," this sacrifice of themselves defined as the successful sons of the successful bourgeoisie, was precisely the sacrifice necessary in order for them to recover their own being for themselves. Because they did recover their own being, however, they fled from rather than to their own nonbeing, and they fled toward rather than from their own being. They fled the schools, then, in order to preserve the truth of their own being.

The German youth had to flee to preserve the truth of being because there was no place or room for it in school, home, or community. The overstructured milieu omitted the being of youth, calling for a sacrifice the youth were not going to make: they preferred to sacrifice their societal status to preserve the truth of being. They could not affirm who they were in their parents' houses or in school and sought and found not "nature" but the landscape wherein their own being could be affirmed, wherein their own being could affirm itself, wherein being could affirm itself in being. This was no mere personal predilection on their part, however, and if it were there would be no historical significance to the youth movement. It was, rather, a call to being: the youth answered a summons that is inherent in human existence, the summons to affirm oneself as precisely who he is. Because human being is self-conscious being, man must affirm who he is. Individual men have to affirm who they are, and the person is who he is in affirming who he is. Before an individual can affirm who he is, however, he must first of all affirm *that* he is, i.e., he must affirm the truth of his own being. This affirmation of the truth of being is made possible by the prior affirmation of belonging to the earth.[12] To be able to affirm belongingness to earth, one must be confirmed in his being by being. He must dwell in a world wherein the world can world itself, wherein being can clear a space for itself in landscape, wherein being can be. He must be in the truth of being.

THE WORLD AS
LANDSCAPE AND GEOGRAPHY

In the Youth Movement, the German youth came to dwell in landscape, to be their landscape. This use of the word *landscape* involves it in a quite literal sense. The word also can be used to designate the "outer pole" of prereflective, nondiscursive consciousness. The world that the child lives in immediate relationship with when he is living directly into the world, before he distances himself from the world through the learning of names of things, is landscape. It is landscape, as distinguishable from the geography that surrounds him after he has learned the names of things that are embodied in "ordinary language." The human world, the world as the correlate of individual consciousness, is both landscape and geography. It is correlative to both the prereflective and reflective planes of consciousness. In terms of consciousness, one has to be prereflectively, nonpositionally conscious of something in order to posit its existence as an object in reflective consciousness. One has to be continuously projecting to the world prereflectively in order to become reflectively conscious of objects and instrumentalities in one's project of being, i.e., in order to be. The landscape as the correlate of immediate awareness or prereflective consciousness is enclosed within a horizon that has to be surpassed to attain the human world, but the surpassing of the horizon of landscape, of nonpositional, nonthetic consciousness of objects, is a continuous nihilating movement of consciousness: the horizon of landscape is perpetually surpassed in the worlding of the world that is the very being of consciousness as such, that is the very being of man.[13] The horizon of landscape is necessary, however, for simply because its surpassing is a continuous nihilation of landscape, landscape continuously re-emerges from its nihilation, unless there is an alienation from the world as there was for the youth of the wandering movement while they were still in school. To affirm that one belongs to the earth means that one has to commit oneself to the limitations of landscape and to its correlate, i.e., to one's own finitude.

Insofar as schooling deals with logically ordered materials, it attempts to establish geography, the common world in which private landscapes become ordered and intersubjectively available. In and of itself, this has nothing to do with the individual person living into his own world and the worlding of his world. Objective knowledge, as Kierkegaard noted, does not exist—pupils do. Insofar as an aim of schooling is to establish a common world, it matters not so much which "logic" is used to order instructional materials or how the common geography is "acquired" in the pedagogical relation. A more primordial concern is its relationship to landscape so that the pupil does not lose himself in geography. The more primordial problem is the necessity of relating the geography of schooling to the landscape of the individual: the problem is one of ontology rather than psychology or epistemology.

There can be little doubt that the acquisition of geography is necessary to the human development of the child, that his world has to be structured with geography. If he is to become available to the common world or that world available to him, he has to achieve that world through having the things of his world become the objects disclosed by ordinary language. In his playing with the house slipper, he becomes aware of its various qualities and uses. This is landscape and the basis of later visualization of its possibilities of being, the basis of what a psychologist might call "divergent thinking" or "divergent responses." His learning its name is geography and the basis of his later "convergent thinking" and "convergent responses." The point is that both are necessary, as is easily evidenced in the learning how to speak in early childhood but also later in the acquiring of the logical structures of the common subjects of the school curriculum. The latter may seem to be an imposition, resulting in an alienation of the pupil from his own world, but it is no more alienating than the preceding learning how to speak with others. It is difficult to know how this ordering of landscape could be avoided. The talk with the parents establishes a geography for him that is as "arbitrary" as the "choice" of the "native" tongue; Merleau-Ponty was right when he said, "We live in the world where speech is an *institution*."[14] The child has to distance himself from the world as a pure landscape in order to free himself from responding immediately to the qualities and values therein in an animalistic way, and this distancing is accomplished through the mediation of words, or geography; but on the other hand the process of acquiring a geography is not without its dangers. The phenomenon the German Youth Movement illustrates is the alienation from the world through the acquisition of a geography ungrounded in landscape. A world of pure geography can be attained, but then the landscape, the whole of man's affective, emotional life, becomes "unconscious." The attainment of a world of pure geography is the separation of reflective consciousness from prereflective consciousness and a total identification of consciousness with reflecting, structured, "symbolical processes" in a way that alienates the person's reflecting consciousness from his prereflective consciousness. From within that alienation, which is the viewpoint of ordinary, naturalistic common-sense realism, the prereflective realm, the landscape, is "unconscious," and indeed so it seems to be: within inauthentic existence one's state-of-being goes mostly unnoticed, one's own moods are attributed to others, one's more superficial emotions and feelings are disharmonious with the deeper state-of-being, and any self-knowledge concerning what is happening to one is quite accidental. Landscape is not "unconscious," however, any more than are the yellow and orange and pink and blue and violet patches of snow that are invisible to perception structured by the concept that snow is white, and that require the artist's help to make them visible when one is alienated from the world and from prereflective consciousness of it in landscape. When landscape, i.e., being, becomes not understood as such, it emerges as "nothing" in ontological anxiety over one's unacknowledged being, manifested in the so-called irrational phenomena, emotions, etc., which then have to be "controlled" by the alienated and unhappy reflective consciousness. To live in a world of pure geography, then, is to lose one's home in landscape and undergo an alienation not merely from the world but from oneself and others. To lose contact with landscape, in short, is to be depersonalized.[15] One attains geography by actively nihilating the horizon of landscape, thereby positing the existence of things as they are known to reflecting consciousness, but to dwell in "pure" geography is to lose prereflective awareness of phenomena to posit as things. It is to live by rote in a memorized world: "Snow is white." One cannot leave landscape entirely and maintain a human geography, that is, without an alienation from the world and one's own possibilities in the world, i.e., from one's self.

Thus the authentically human world lies "between" landscape and geography. Landscape alone is the unorganized immediate, or chaos. Landscape is necessary, however, to be somewhere, to be within a horizon, to be situated. Landscape has horizon and direction, a beyond that beckons. It has lived-values, but to dwell in pure landscape is to be at home everywhere. Geography alone is the world of fact and universal concept. Geography is necessary to possess meanings and to be able to relate anything to anything else, but its "horizon" is "mathematical" and fails to lead one forth because the space and time of geography are separated, i.e., decomposed, because its concepts are universal and "timeless," eternal and lacking a living present.[16] One can spatialize and temporalize into landscape, but not into the decomposed space and time of geography. To "dwell" in pure geography is to be at home nowhere. The German youth, then, were at home nowhere in the schooling to which they were submitted, and could be said to have left "home" in order to find a home. Then when the unity with being was regained as they gradually became their landscape, they were at home everywhere. In their union with the landscape, on the other hand, they lacked their own project of being. The return to the origin of being was, in the final analysis, merely the condition necessary to recover their project of being for themselves, after which they had to return to school and society to be able to have a project of being and to become themselves by bringing their own possibilities of being into being. The letting be of being that occurred in the landscape in the wandering was not yet enclosed within the structure of authentic temporality wherein one achieves a self-constancy through open, anticipatory resolve. The pedagogical significance of the youth movement, then, is its pointing out the necessity of finding a way to allow youth to find a home *within* schooling. This is the significance of their being for educating.

Schooling has to have as its major goal the establishment of a common world, or geography (Chapter 8); but insofar as schooling is the acquisition of logically ordered knowledge, it attempts to put pupils into that which is factual, repeatable, and valid for all pupils regardless of who the particular pupil is, i.e., regardless of his individual landscape. This is entirely proper and necessary, but then the more efficient it is, the more it leads to the development of a world of pure geography and the more the pupil becomes a detached, objective, and depersonalized observer. The more effective it is, the more it leads to nowhere; and the more the pupil dwells nowhere, the more alienated he is from the world and from his possibilities of being in it, i.e., from himself. The acquisition of objective knowledge is actually an attempt to be objective, to be subjectless, without perspective. It happens, however, that this is precisely contrary to the conditions of human existence. No one can be objective; he is and will remain a subjecticity: subjecticity is the truth. Epistemology and ontology ought not get confused—to be a perspective on the world is inescapable. Man exists a perspective. The acquisition of objectively valid knowledge, of that which is general and repeatable, in schooling goes beyond the limits of human finitude in an extravagant and impossible project. It has to be accompanied by some continuous contact with landscape if the pupil is not to be alienated from himself and from the world. Because this continuous contact can be achieved, because one can return from universalizing thought to the particular and become truthful, it is not valid to maintain that schooling as the acquisition of geography and as the intentional "transmission" of geography contributes to the alienation of the pupil in each and every case and in all circumstances. It becomes alienating only when it is not grounded in the pupil's landscape, when it is not grounded in his project of being, in the truth of being.

THE EMERGENCE OF ONTOLOGICAL ANXIETY

The youth who has played sufficiently in childhood established an unconditioned relation to being, is well grounded in the landscape, and faces the increasing intellectualization of secondary schooling in comparative safety. The youth who was not at home in the primary world in childhood faces the increased intellectualization that accompanies the intensification of the induction into geography with considerable danger. In addition, the probability of losing contact with landscape, of being alienated from the world, is proportional to the concentration of the geography acquired, i.e., to the academic proficiency of the pupil. If and when the horizon of landscape is lost, there follows the loss of place in the world and social space, because the systematization of geography allows one to travel hither and yon within its objective space, but it does not have room for spatializing and temporalizing from one's own center to the world around one. When the geographical ordering of schooling predominates within an individual youth's existence, the schooling experience becomes very much like a train ride with the shades pulled down—one is nowhere during the trip to someplace, he knows not where, and of which he remains ignorant when he arrives: he does not know why he is there. It takes landscape to be somewhere in social space, but the reconstruction of the world in general concepts in the objective attitude that ordinarily occurs in schooling makes all centers of reference equivalent, i.e., without perspective. The world's quality of being a world, the worlding of its worldhood, disappears without anyone noticing the loss of the world.[17] Overemphasis upon the acquisition of structured knowledge in school overdistances the "self" from the world, and this loss of world is simultaneously a loss of self as the realization of genuine possibilities of the world in one's project of being. If this loss of self is severe enough the pupil's wanting-to-be-someone-himself is frustrated; he no longer explores the world as part of his project of being. When the youth needs no help in disclosing the world that he is not exploring, there is a general authority-crisis. To cover over the crisis in authority through the use of extrinsic motivation increases the alienation of the pupil from the world, the teacher, and from himself and encourages the truthless flight into the pursuit of external rewards, on the one hand, and into the peer group, through the destruction of the pedagogic relation, on the other.

A complicating factor as the pupil grows older is the changing temporal structure. As his conscious existence continues to deepen, as the temporal structure gradually broadens and orients itself forward in the increasing foresight and force of projection into the "future," the danger of the loss of self that inheres in the coming to dwell more and more in geography is aggravated because schooling becomes a period of waiting. Schooling may become largely a period of waiting due to lack of engagement in concrete possibilities. If the youth's geography is separated from his landscape, if he is not exploring the intellectual-historical world as part of his wanting-to-be-independently but "learning" whatever he is supposed to learn, he remains removed from possibilities of genuine action. This alienation from himself is the more severe the more the pupil can and does project further into the abstract future. Authentic disclosure of world in landscape opens possibilities of action such that the world that is ordinarily disclosed is the future world, not the future that is two or three years hence but that which is two or three seconds or minutes ahead— the world ordinarily disclosed is the world that one is futurizing into. This is the ontological presupposition of action. There can be action, or action has future and is not "behavior," because of the spatializing and temporalizing movement to the world. This continuous transcending of the given in the worlding of the world gives present existence its significance. Present being has significance to the extent that concrete action occurs in a world that allows for one's own futuring. When possibilities are put off into the "future," however, as they are for youth, the future is reified and so is the person whose future it is. They both become abstractions. The postponing of possibilities to be realized later, the holding off at a distance of one's own possibilities, takes them out of landscape and puts them into geography through the thematizing representation.[18] This kind of thematization removes the quality of lived-possibilities from them and destroys them as possibilities of being. They no longer belong to the world as world-facts nor exert their obligatoriness upon the youth within his perspective, but they belong to the youth himself as *his* unobservable "potentialities." The reification of the future and the concomitant reification of youth—both in the eyes of his elders and for himself as he takes the external view toward himself, as he reifies his possibilities in the future—changes his possibilities in the world to his potentialities as if they were separable from the world and his project of being in the world. This makes his being and the "future" a matter of indifference.[19] It will happen later.

When the future becomes existentially indifferent, then the present becomes indifferent, for the present moment no longer opens itself toward those possibilities of the future that are presently lacking realization. When the future become reified, the present no longer opens toward the youth's own possibilities as lacking them. Then commitment to them is intellectualistic rather than existential. It is at best a reflective decision rather than a promise to fulfill them that is made with one's whole being. Once thematized, youth's possibilities become "merely possible" and no longer exist as values or demands of the world that issue to him from landscape. The very "future," when experienced as only possible, causes ontological anxiety to emerge, for this anxiety "is precisely my consciousness of being my future in the mode of not-being."[20] Ontological anxiety, anxiety over having to be one's own possibilities in order to be someone oneself, emerges with the taking of one's possibilities from landscape and putting them into geography through reflection on them—it does not emerge when one is actively engaged in realizing concrete possibilities in the world in prereflective landscape.[21] Because schooling can become a period of waiting, the more so the older the youth because the older the youth the less he needs help to be independently and the more the remainder of schooling seems an unnecessary interposition, youth as a life-phase can be characterized as a period in which ontological anxiety is likely to emerge.

Ontological anxiety is inherent in human being because human being is the kind of being that still has its being to be and it always understands this, but it disappears in authentic action because the realization of the present possibilities is achieving being for the time being. Inauthentic existence is characterized by the emergence of ontological anxiety and despair over the possibility of becoming one's self, even though this anxiety may be manifested ontically precisely as its opposite in a dogmatic certainty over who one is. To the extent that youth is thrown into inauthentic existence by the very existence of schooling, it is a life-phase characterized by the emergence of ontological anxiety. It depends, of course, on various factors, principally upon how fully childhood was lived and therewith upon how rooted in landscape a particular individual is. It secondarily depends upon how much the remainder of schooling actually does interpose itself between a youth and his "future" once his life-possibilities come into view. The "in-between" that separates youth from their possibilities of being, then, can alienate them from themselves and encourage a flight from the present moment into the dream present or dream future whenever the present moment is unappealing, which it automatically is when its geography is divorced from landscape or predominates over landscape. Because the youth has foresight and a pre-philosophical understanding that he has his being to be, and because he is his futural projection, he is kept at a distance from himself, homeless, unless the geography of schooling gears into his headlong rush into the future, unless it is grounded in his project of being by intermeshing with his landscape. Because temporality is existentiality, how the youth is enabled to temporalize is how he is enabled to be. This situation is identical for children and for youth but varies in degree relative to the increased complexity of the temporal structure, the existentiality, of youth. If pedagogic efforts are to be existentially relevant, they have to gear into the pupil's project of being, the ground of educating. The pupil's project of being, however, in each and every case has its own origin and destination. The increasing complexity of the temporal structure of youth means that he is related differently to his origin and his destination than is the child.

Amplifying what this difference signifies will bring out the major point for which the German Youth Movement was illustrative. That each person's project of being goes from his own origin to his own destiny can be understood in a preliminary way in a chronological sense. Irrespective of any possible supernatural origin and destiny, the origin and destiny of each person's human existence is the same—womb and tomb. This can be misunderstood, however, if it is grasped objectively, too quickly. By referring at first to the origin as the womb and destiny as the grave, it is meant that everyone comes from a different womb and goes to a different grave, of course, but it also indicates that these primary events are on the one hand accomplished all alone—no one can be born or die for another—and on the other hand are not "accomplished" at all because one is passive in respect to these most fundamental moments. The actual origin, and not the objective birth, develops in the first few years of life insofar as the child forms his basic relationship to the world, to being, in childhood. In fact, to do so is his essential task. It can be said that the rest of the person's life proceeds from the original relation to being that is formed in childhood, from the origin. On the other end, the actual destiny, death, if it comes after senility, is as irrelevant to one's project of being as his objective birth. The destiny each youth goes forward to is the accomplishments that he alone can achieve in the prime years of his life. In a rough sort of chronological way, then, youth as a life-phase is peculiarly "between" origin and destination as no other life phase is. Childhood is "all origin" from within its own experience of itself, and young adulthood is already approaching one's "destiny," as attested by the pre-philosophical expression that "So-and-so has arrived." If life has direction, it is toward old age, but one does not live in order to retire. It is therefore toward whatever it is that one can accomplish in his being as an adult. Adulthood is "all destiny" from within its own experience of itself. The mature adult struggling with his generation, being authentically there in history, has little time for thoughts of retirement. He already has his reward. Then youth as a life-phase is unique in that the youth is "between" his origin and destiny—by definition, in fact. The increasing complexity of the being of the pupil as he advances from childhood to youth signifies that pedagogic efforts that are to be grounded in the project of being of the pupil have to be increasingly aware of the inescapable fact that the pupil is proceeding from *his* origin to *his* destination regardless of external, alienating influences to the contrary. This is the truth of the being of youth. Because he can be alienated from either in a way the child cannot, the youth can lose all sense of origin and destiny and awareness of the need for help in order to arrive, and there can be a general crisis of authority within this free-floating nonexistence. That the youth's project of being occurs between his origin in the world of childhood play and his destiny in the adult social-historical world, then, is the significance of the being of youth for educating.

7

Educating in Youth and the Being of Truth

The chronological sense in which the way the youth's project of being exists between his own origin and destination is metaphoric, based on the image of human existence as a linear process, a journey from childhood to old age. This may yield some illumination and understanding of the phenomenon of temporality (one exists the journey), similarly to the way the German Youth Movement and the metaphor of landscape illuminates the spatiality of human being by spreading out horizontally the equanimity and joy developed in the recovery of being pursuant upon a return to the origin. The metaphoric nature of the chronological understanding needs to be supplemented, however, by the reminder that all life-phases exist at once. The youth does not come from his origin and proceed to his destiny in a chronological sense—he does that objectively, of course, but subjectively he *is* his origin and he *is* his destiny at each and every moment of his life. Like everyone else, he is equally his past, present, and future possibilities in the ekstatic unity of his present world. In his own experience he is not *between* at all. His present, like any other present, is his whole being. It is self-justifying. It is.

In the ekstatic unity of the authentic present, in authentic presence to the world, wide-awake action proceeds from an origin, the zero on the X and Y coordinates, the center of the circle, because the landscape and geography are united and harmonious. Wide-awake action also proceeds to a destination in the realization of one's own genuine concrete possibilities. To say that youth's temporality (or existentiality) is more complex than the child's and that pedagogic efforts have to gear into his project of being to be existentially relevant is not a duplication of what was said to be necessary to take the being of children into account because the youth's project of being proceeds from his origin to his destination. The establishment of the geography of his world can alienate the youth from his world and from himself because it can deflect his project of being away from his destination, i.e., away from himself. The child becomes alienated from the world that is not safe enough. The youth can become alienated from the world in an alienation from his own origin and destination in objectifying, conceptual thought, even in a safe world. He can lose himself because of the increased intellectuality of schooling in youth even if—and especially when—he is exploring his world eagerly as part of his wanting-to-be-independently, because of the alienating effects of acquiring ungrounded "geography," i.e., free-floating concepts, constructs, and general meanings.

THE RECOVERY OF TRUTH

The possibility of acquiring ungrounded geography, or knowledge about rather than of the world, and the extent of the grounding that is possible depend upon the youth's original relationship to being as it was established in childhood (i.e., on his basic at-homeness in the landscape), in some remedial major return to the origin, as in the German Youth Movement or in major therapy, in intermittent and minor returnings to the origin and concomitant recoverings of being, and in the nature and structure of the geography acquired in schooling. Because of these factors, it cannot be said that ontological anxiety arises for all youth nor that its emergence in youth is either a universal or normative phenomenon because of the overformalization of schooling. It cannot be maintained that youth as a life-phase is a period of *sturm und drang* or that "identity crises" are to be expected in youth, for in the normative cases, i.e., where the previous phase and subphases of life have been lived fully, youth projects strongly into the future: authentically, youth in its adventuresomeness plans to conquer the future.[1] In this projection the exploration of the intellectual-historical world integrates knowledge into the project of being and ontological anxiety is minimal. Neither can it be said that landscape should predominate over geography in some form of voluntarism and exaltation of emotions, moods, and choice above matters of evidence, logic, proof, and intellectuality, for in the normative cases it does not. But the constructs of geography can become free-floating and conceal more than they reveal, and thus can contribute to the alienation of youth from themselves, from their own project of being from their own origin toward their own destination, because they are general, repeatable, and the same for all pupils, and then they contribute to the emergence of ontological anxiety in youth because youth cannot become objective knowledge.

When ontological anxiety does emerge in youth, however, there follows the flight from oneself, from one's being toward his own possibilities, from the rush into the future, into inauthentic existence and the phenomena of truthlessness associated therewith, such as self-deception, having one's being for others, and falling into the peer group. Although the phenomenon of the adolescent peer group can be partly interpreted as youth's attempt to flee responsibility for his own existence, it can be partly understood as being responsive to the alienation from the world caused by the increasing formalization and intellectualization of schooling, for some of the activities of the adolescent peer group can be seen to be attempts to step back into landscape, to return to the origin and *recover* responsibility for one's own being. They often can be understood as small wanderings undertaken to recover one's own being after alienation from it in the geography of schooling. The space of the dance, for example, is landscape, as is the space of adolescent music. The space obtained through drinking alcoholic beverages and using marijuana and L.S.D. and other consciousness-freeing medicines is also "landscape," for precisely what "consciousness" can become freed from is enmeshment in an alienating geography. So, too, do folk songs belong to landscape, like gypsy music—like the gypsy or the wanderers in the German Youth Movement, the authentic folk singer is a nomad, a strolling minstrel without a home but home everywhere.[2]

The activities of adolescence and the adolescent peer group that seem to be attempts to go into landscape in a recovery of being may be part of living the life-phase of youth fully, a balance to the alienating effect of schooling, compensation for an alienation in schooling resultant from the acquisition of geography that is ungrounded in landscape (i.e., ungrounded in the pupil's being), a flight from waiting for themselves, or it may reflect not having lived childhood fully and actually be a prolongation of the missing childhood. That it could be a manifestation of many things prohibits a general polemic against schooling as the acquisition of objective knowledge on behalf of the being of youth in the spirit of the more "militant" of the progressive educational theorists. In general, an increase in landscape activities in youth is probably related to an increased alienation in schooling relative to the increased intellectualization of content and/or lack of room for the pupil's wanting-to-be-someone-himself, although, in particular, landscape activities may be a way to balance the existential diet. Unless the geography of schooling remains rooted in the pupil's landscape, the pupil falls into free-floating, inauthentic existence characterized by uprootedness and sophistical and dogmatic talk, and he attempts to know himself introspectively by impure reflection. When the geography of schooling becomes divorced from the pupil's landscape, the pupil's alienation from the world is a state of truthlessness that permits him to say anything, encourages him to have opinions about everything, and induces him to look within to discover who he is because there is no disclosure of world and no disclosure of possibilities of being in what he hears.[3] There is no truth for him. He, too, is entitled to have opinions on everything regardless of how knowledgeable he is, and because he is removed from realizing concrete possibilities wherein he might find out who he can become by finding out what he can do, he looks within where there is nothing to be learned, for it has passed before he is able to focus properly.

The German Youth Movement exemplifies not only the return from inauthentic, alienated existence to the origin of one's own being and the truth of being, but also the return to being in the truth and the being of truth. The distorted view of "bourgeois life" was exactly the distortion of social life that belongs to one form of inauthentic existence, boredom. The distortion of bourgeois life involved in the boys' view was not irrelevant but precisely the point. Even if it were possible to establish the extent of distortion in the boys' perspectives, the relevant concern would not be to argue with the boys, through engaging in direct and explicit treatment of the issues as *they* saw them, but to probe for the miseducative antecedents of that distortion in order to overcome it educationally. It was not the past that in and of itself alienated the German youth from themselves and from schooling, but the past transmitted as a geography divorced from landscape. Their distorted perspective of the life they abandoned cannot be taken at face value precisely because of their being alienated from the pedagogic relation, the schools, the world, others, and themselves, all equiprimordially, but nevertheless it points toward the educational remedy: to allow for an irregular, periodic return to the origin so that the manifold alienations are not incurred. The return to the origin in the German Youth Movement is a large-scale exemplification of a return to oneself through direct contact with landscape that is essential to the person's retention of his originality and depth, to his being in the truth. If he loses contact with landscape, he becomes superficial and alienated from his genuine humanity.[4] For the deepest and most significant acquisition of knowledge, in other words, some kind of periodic return to landscape or continuous development of geography in and with landscape is necessary.

This, however, is identical with the central intuition of progressive education and the major recommendation that "progressive" educational theorists made to "traditional" schools when they maintained that the logical ordering of subject matter, or the structure of the knowledge of the expert, interfered with the "psychological development" of the pupil. They alleged that the imposition of highly structured knowledge gave rise to the problems of motivation, interest, and discipline as these are associated with "traditional" schooling. Because defenses of "traditional" practice often seemed unimaginative and apologetic for a kind of school-keeping, rather than being established in an adequate conception of human nature, it was also alleged that the imposition of prestructured knowledge gave rise to problems within society because of the kinds of persons developed by traditional schooling: either competitive, striving egoists or passive, anomic conformers, depending upon the degree of success experienced in school. The alternative offered by progressive theorists—and this is what made them *progressive*—was to let the knowledge acquired in school become organized by the pupil within his experience by his own, but guided, endeavors. This progressive organization of subject matter allegedly would not only solve the problems of motivation, interest, and discipline, but would also promote the development of the cooperative, democratic person and the democratic society.

THE "PSYCHOLOGICAL" AND "LOGICAL" ASPECTS OF BEING

Among the many writings on these topics the most comprehensive was Dewey's. His whole effort can be construed as an attempt to find the middle ground between the logical and psychological ordering of knowledge for learning: the method of reflective experience was sufficiently flexible and comprehensive to accommodate the "psychology" of the learner; the reconstruction of meanings within this method was to lead progressively closer to the rationalized, socialized experience that is traditionally called organized knowledge. Because the method was individual, all learnings were intimately related to the pupil's qualitative, immediate experience; because the reconstruction was environmental and social, all learnings allowed the pupil's experience to expand with general meanings, thereby becoming socialized such that the reconstructed mediated experience would result in the moral and social ends of education concomitantly with the cognitive ends. The thrust of Dewey's view was the educative intent of avoiding an alienation of mediated experience from immediate experience (of geography from landscape). The difference between Dewey and other theorists who called attention to the distinction between the "logical" and the "psychological" aspects of experience is that Dewey grounded his distinction metaphysically. The distinction between mediated and immediate experience is "grounded" in experience, or that which is "most real" for Dewey, and the referent for the word *experience* is a nonobservable, semimysterious, atmospheric, processlike, quasi-entity. I cannot see your experience, but to understand Dewey I have to be able to see my own experience as sort of a metaphysical envelope extending out and around my own body. Otherwise I cannot make sense out of many of his sayings, e.g., "The self *achieves* mind in the degree in which knowledge of things is incarnate in the life about him; the self is not a separate mind building up knowledge anew on its own account."[5] I also have to be able to see the distinction between mediated and immediate experience, the "metaphysical" or "ontological" distinction upon which the educational distinction between the "logical" and "psychological" ways of arranging instructional materials rests.

It is probably the difficulty of seeing the distinction between the immediate and mediated in experience that results in misunderstanding the distinction between the "psychological" and "logical" in pedagogy. In the first place, Dewey made the distinction to call attention to the realm of immediate experience, for the point was to bring the two aspects of experience together educationally and not to elevate either over the other. He opposed "traditional" schooling for its neglect of immediate experience; he opposed extremely "progressive" theory for its neglect of mediated experience. Some difficulties in seeing the "metaphysical' distinction that grounds the pedagogic distinction cause difficulty in coming to grips with the pedagogic distinction in an adequate way. In the course of a purely *logical* (albeit somewhat emotive) analysis of the "logical" and the "psychological" in education, James McClellan, for example, traced the roots of Dewey's educational distinction to Peirce's philosophical distinction between coming to have a belief and having adequate grounds for a belief.[6] Had McClellan made an *experiential* analysis, as Dewey did, he would have traced Dewey's educational distinction to the distinction between the immediate and the mediated within experience and then traced *that* philosophic distinction to its probable roots not in Peirce's logic but in Peirce's work on the categories. Peirce's categories of Firstness (Quality), Secondness (Existence), and Thirdness (Mediation), with which he was occupied most of his life, is precisely the source of Dewey's conception of experience. Then to follow the argument, McClellan would have had to go to Peirce's phenomenology (as Peirce did) in order to solve the problems residing in the early formulations of the categories; then he would have had to compare Peirce's phenomenology with the phenomenologies of James and Dewey to further examine the validity of the distinction between the immediate and mediated within this tradition; and then he would have had to abandon the naturalistic, objectivistic mode of thought of pragmatism because he would have seen that it is inadequate for grappling with experience, i.e., with subjecticity. Finally, he would have had to go to post-Husserlian phenomenology to better understand the distinction, and then and only then would he have grappled with the educational distinction between the psychological and the logical ordering of knowledge in schooling. That is to say, Dewey's descriptions of experience are phenomenological, but in a pre-Husserlian, *sans* the phenomenological bracketing, sense; and "argument" over the legitimacy of the basic distinction has to be made at the experiential, i.e., phenomenological, level for the issue to be joined. The previous quotation illustrates: when Dewey said that the self achieves mind to the degree knowledge is incarnate in the things around one, the locus of this incarnated knowledge is the human world, both landscape and geography. Dewey presupposes being open to the world and being-in-the-world, i.e., the intentionality of conscious existence. More important, he presupposes human existence. How forgetful of him.

Although he held that experience was transactional in his attempt to overcome the subject/object, or man/world, dualism, i.e., in his attempt to overcome the alienation of man from the world, Dewey nevertheless, probably in his haste to focus upon its cognitive aspects, presupposed that experience exists. As Thomas Aquinas long ago pointed out that Aristotle's matter and form hypothesis omitted the being of things, so too is it suggested that Dewey omitted the being of experience. The hypostatization of being by Aquinas, however, essentially omitted the temporality of being, or the temporalizing that is being, which is to omit being after all. The suggestion that Dewey omitted human being does not mean that it is necessary to drift toward some form of neo-Aristotelianism. Dewey's suggestion that Aristotle's matter/form hypothesis presupposes the experience of things is well taken. But what is the being of experienced entities? On the point at hand, i.e., on the distinction between immediate and mediated experience, what difference would it make to say that immediate experience exists? That the being of mediated experience is at issue? That the being of truth is at issue? If the being of man is the disclosedness of the world, then the ontological presupposition of immediate experience is nonthematic, prereflective consciousness (of) things, that is, landscape; and the ontological presupposition of mediated experience is thematic, reflective consciousness (of) things, that is, geography. Immediate experience depends upon nonthematic disclosure of world, or landscape; mediated experience depends upon thematized disclosure, or geography. The difference this ontological foundation makes (by a pragmatic criterion of meaning, no less) is in the difference that follows for the problematic concerning the psychological and logical ordering of knowledge in schooling within the context of grounding education in the being of the pupil and of grounding the being of the pupil in the worlding of the world through educating.

One advantage in designating the qualitative world of immediate experience *landscape* and the structured world of mediated experience *geography* is that these designations look out at the world *with* the experiencing being rather than *at* him. They describe his world rather than objectifying him and contributing thereby to the alienation between people. They enable one to *see* the "psychological" and the "logical" and to see them as simultaneous, concurrent elements of the presupposition of human experience. For instance, the sun revolves about the earth in landscape (it really rises and sets!), but the earth revolves about the sun in geography (objectively, the earth rotates daily). Since human experience has to include both of these for adequacy (woe to the astrophysicist who cannot see the sun rise!), the use of the landscape/geography distinction allows for a way to combine the "psychological" and "logical" ways of ordering knowledge that is available neither to pragmatism nor to logical analysis.

This can be seen through the case study. From a Deweyan point of view, it might be said that the wanderers were seeking immediacy, or immediate experiencing, but this does not seem to help much unless it is accompanied by a reason for such a hunger (i.e., "felt need"); and this is not available in pragmatism, for pragmatism *assumes* impulsive activity without stating explicity that it is one's being and that one acts in order to be. It might be said that the wandering was pure capriciousness, from a Deweyan point of view, and precisely the kind of effect predictable of the authoritarianism of the way of life that drove the boys to escape, but this does not help much either unless it is accompanied by a reason for precisely this kind of manifestation of capriciousness, which is not available in pragmatism. To say that the youth left school and home to answer the silent call of being, for which there was no room in school, in a return to landscape, in a return to the origin of their own being in order to be able to affirm their own belongingness to earth and to be in the truth of their own existence, yields some understanding of their motivation in terms that they themselves might have found acceptable. This avoids psychologizing or sociologizing their conscious motives away— it takes their being into account. They had to experience their freedom in some manner in order to be, in order to affirm their own being, and deprived of the freedoms of conquest and choice and moral freedom, they had to resort to the freedom of caprice and rebellion in order to be someone themselves. When it is said that for the deepest and most significant acquisition of logically organized knowledge there has to be some kind of periodic, irregular return to the origin or continuous development of geography in and with landscape, Dewey's point concerning the significance of the method of reflective experience is made, but the designations allow one to see how the grounding of educating in immediate experiencing, in landscape, can occur in a "traditional" schooling pattern that not only encompasses the truth of being but also allows for the being of truth. The problem of the "psychological" and the "logical" at the teaching–learning level is usually stated as the conflict of problem-solving versus the structure of the disciplines at the level of curriculum design; the concepts of landscape and geography indicate how to have it both ways by putting the problematic on a level underlying that of alternative epistemologies.

THE PEDAGOGIC PARADOX

When logically organized subject matter is emphasized at the expense of the pupil's existentiality, all pedagogic effort becomes tailored to transmit a body of highly structured knowledge. The curriculum can be ascertained beforehand, and the teacher facilitates the pupil's learning of the basic concepts, etc., of a body of knowledge so that he can think within the conceptual scheme, or geography, of a structured discipline. The progressive educator complained that this ignored the pupil's present interest; the present point is that it ignores his project of being which manifests itself in the exploration of the world or region thereof that the pupil is "interested" in, i.e., pulled into by the values to be realized therein. To think solely within the structure of a discipline is to dwell solely in the existentially deficient theoretical mode of the geography that belongs within the bracketing of the province of meaning of that discipline. The conflict has been between interest and discipline; the present point puts the conflict at its most fundamental level. Under conceptions stressing the structure of the disciplines, the entire scope of schooling tends toward being limited to achieve the objective of the transmission of bodies of organized subject matter. This creates a pedagogical space or province of meaning that is diametrically opposed to the existential pedagogic relation describable as the teacher helping the pupil into the pupil's own possibilities, as the teacher helping the pupil to be someone himself oriented toward his own destination from his own origin. The entire schooling process becomes teleological in effect, separated from the pupil's project of being, from his teleology, by all the distance its geography is separated from his landscape. The schooling process becomes wholly geography when everything becomes a means so that the pupil reaches a developmental stage in order to go on to the next developmental stage so that he can go on to the next developmental stage, and so on, even if the pupil was not going that way. This, however, is when schooling is at its best, yet it is a very one-sided process that comes dangerously close to pedagogizing all of reality: everything is seen from within its place in the developmental process and in the structure of knowledge. Things become seen for their pedagogical value and lose their other values and their place in landscape.[7] When they lose their place in landscape, however, the pupil becomes alienated from the world and can no longer receive disclosures because he no longer explores his world, unless he is allowed some periodic return to landscape, to being. It is not necessarily his "interest" that must be exploited or captivated, as in progressive or traditional views, respectively—the mood of primary optimism has to be restored to terminate boredom. This restores the pupil's wanting-to-be-someone-himself if the primary relation to being that was formed in childhood, if the fundamental orientation to landscape, remains in the background. Then an alienation from the world is not necessarily prevented merely by structuring the curriculum and schooling on the pupil's explorations, i.e., "psychologically." After all, he goes to school to explore whatever is done there if he is living his present life-phase fully. The attempt to structure schooling on his explorations of the world at the very time that that exploring of the world includes his trying to find out what there is to do in school is like two people trying to get through the same door saying, "After you," "No, after you," *ad infinitum.*

The significance of the examination of the Youth Movement and the uncovering of the ontological presuppositions of Dewey's distinction between immediate and mediated experience is, rather, **the pedagogic paradox**. Schooling is bound to goals and objectives associated with the acquisition of organized knowledge. These define its sphere, and the better schools get, and the better individual teachers get, the more efficient it becomes: objectives become behaviorally and observationally defined and materials of instruction become highly selected to achieve the objectives with greatest dispatch. This is as it should be if the pupil is to become situated in the common world, but it is schooling, not educating. It achieves the teacher's objectives, not the pupil's. It is overcommitted to the significance of schooling for the being of the pupil and undercommitted to the significance of the being of the pupil for educating. The full significance of all of schooling and pedagogic endeavor then becomes realizable outside of and external to the pedagogical undertaking as that occurs within schooling because it is realizable only in individuals and in their projects of being, i.e., in their return to the origin and projection to their destination.[8] If schooling does not account for the truth of being, it will not promote the being of truth.

The pedagogic paradox is that the better schooling is, the less likely it is to have room for the pupil's being toward his own destination from his own origin, i.e., the less likely it is to be worth while. This may seem like verbal play (if schooling gets better it gets worse) because of the different senses in which it is being evaluated, now in terms of the efficiency of the organization of the system, now in terms of individual development.

What establishes the truth of the paradox is that both schooling and educating are necessary for the being of the other, yet they are oppositional to each other. As the pupil grows older and schooling becomes increasingly intellectual and logically organized, the success of pedagogical endeavor becomes less and less probable if the pupil becomes more and more oriented to his destination regardless of what occurs in school (or if he becomes more and more alienated from himself by supposing that his project of being coincides with the teleology of the school). Schooling has more and more to do with organized knowledge the older the pupil is, but its major import has to do with the pupil's orientation to the world in his project of being. The irony is that he is separated from the latter by the former even though the former is supposed to have something to do with the latter. The paradox is "insoluble."

The problematic concerns the relation of the pupil to what is known, the place of knowing in human existence, and the relation of knowledge to truth. In the return to the origin in landscape in the German Youth Movement there was a knowing that was obtained when the wanderers attained a personal relationship to everything that involved their whole being in relation to the whole being of the flower, the storm, the stream, etc. The knowing of this open communion was an intuitive revelation of being wherein things disclosed themselves in their essence.[9] Since there was a disclosure, it has to be designated a *knowing*; since it was a non-thematic, prereflective disclosure in landscape, it has to be designated as an *intuitive* knowing. This kind of knowing simply cannot be reduced to "sense perception" because "sense perception" is merely an abstraction of theoretical psychology. Nor can it be gainsaid. It has always been the ideal of knowledge—it represents indubitable truth. On the other hand, conceptual knowledge, geography, or structured perception is necessary, especially from the point of view that attempts to take the being of youth into account, for knowing who one is and understanding oneself requires knowing what to do, how to do it, what one can do, what can be done, and what cannot be done for every future situation to be encountered. These are necessary to the knowing of who one can become, i.e., of who one is in light of the fact that he is his future, and they require all the conceptual knowledge that there is, plus some more that is and will remain unavailable. The general and repeatable, what is valid for all, is necessary, but equally necessary is the return to the origin from out of the general in order to be in the truth and for there to be truth.

To retain both elements of the paradox, schooling has to go on continuously, but then, as the Wandering Movement shows, the person has to be able to be free of the goal-boundedness of schooling in order to experience things in his own being in their own being, and this he has to do to be in the truth.[10] He can know what is true without it, i.e., know propositions counted as true, because that is what comprises geography, but he is alienated from the world when he counts truth as a property of propositions *about* the world. To locate truth as a property of propositions is a secondary and deficient mode of truth that depends upon the previous disclosure that enables the subsequent "correspondence" to obtain after the proposition is reified. It depends upon a previous being in the truth.[11] To be in the truth requires the kind of disclosedness and the personal relation to things of the wanderers in landscape; it requires a return to the origin of one's own being and the recovery of being and truth.

Scope for origin-ality, then, is of the greatest *pedagogic* significance. Letting the pupil be original, creative, in what he does lets him unite the geography of schooling with the landscape of his own terrain and lets him develop his landscape with the values of the geography of schooling. That he does whatever he is supposed to do to accomplish schooling objectives develops his geography; that he does it in his own way allows him not merely to unite the geography with his landscape but to accomplish the prior step of acquiring subject matter not as a school subject but as geography, as a real, intellectual world rather than as a set of symbols, half understood, half memorized. The child explores the physical world, i.e., landscape; the youth should be exploring the intellectual, historical world if his childhood has been lived fully and if he is to reach the end of educating by becoming situated in the social-historical world. The problem of the "psychological" and "logical" ordering of knowledge becomes a problem only for youth and the increasing intellectualization of his being. It is neither a psychological problem, a logical problem, nor a problem of theory of knowing: it is an educational problem and an existential problem for the youth himself. Pedagogically, schooling is structured according to the structure of the disciplines as a continuous process, but the youth has to do things his own way to make sense out of them from his own perspective to keep from becoming alienated from his world. He needs to be originary in order to be in the truth.

Room for the youth's doing things his own way requires breaks—breaks from the continuous process of schooling, breaks from what he has learned, breaks from mechanical routines. The truth of the pupil's being requires room for the expansion of the possibilities of things that are not included in the one-sided schooling process, with its focus always forward upon the objectives, never backward upon the ground of being.[12] The expansion of these possibilities, of the pupil's own possibilities, is his being-someone-himself, which overcomes the depersonalization caused by the learning of the objective knowledge in the "disciplines," for it is the act of reuniting geography and landscape, of putting the geography in its place in his being, and of putting his being in the place of geography.

The pupil needs breaks right in the continuous schooling process to allow for this return to the origin and recovery of being and to be in the truth. The principle of the holiday and vacation has to be instituted in the classroom because schooling, like all of life, tends to get the pupil in a rut, in an inauthentic mode of existing, wherein he keeps going wherever the rut goes because of the difficulty of getting out of the rut once in it: the teacher has to let the pupil "out of the harness" for the occasional return to the origin that alone can make the schooling process worthwhile.[13] The occasional, unplanned return to the origin, scope for the pupil's originality, and a general conception of discontinuous educating within the continuous schooling process, then, are the means for grounding educating in the being of youth. The significance of the being of youth for educating is retention of the pedagogic paradox. The significance of educating for the being of youth is retention of the pedagogic paradox.

Existential paradoxes make people uneasy. It is much easier to choose one side of a paradox in a general falsification of experience and existence than it is to retain the tension consequent upon acknowledging the partial truths of polar values. Human existence is to be found "between" landscape and geography, however, because one attains geography by the leap from landscape that one has to continuously rejump. Human existence has its being in the leaping. There is no honest solution to the pedagogic paradox. Geography *exists* schooling; breaking from it *exists* educating. Schooling supplies the place to leap to; educating, the ground from which the leaping occurs. To choose between schooling and educating is to lose both because to choose between geography and landscape is to lose both—to be at home anywhere in landscape is to be homeless; to be at home nowhere in geography is to be homeless. Although man is homeless in his very being, his home is precisely coming to be at home in the very homelessness of the leaping between landscape and geography. Maintenance of the pedagogic paradox allows educating within schooling to be this homecoming.

Insofar as youth as a life-phase has to be lived fully in order for the crisis of practical experience to be resolved adequately, retention of the paradox enables avoidance of the hedonic and fanatical failures of the reassessment of adolescent ideals. The former is the choice of landscape; the latter, of geography. The retention of both of them in dialectical interplay is the teleological suspension of the ethical that enables mature adulthood to be lived fully, authentically. Insofar as the teacher is a person who has reassessed her adolescent ideals adequately in the crisis of practical experience, she already embodies the larger paradox of which the pedagogic paradox is a part. Overemphasis upon the psychological aspects of learning in a progressive bias is apt to be a reflection of the hedonic failure to reassess adolescent ideals adequately; overemphasis upon the logical aspects of the structure of knowledge in schooling in a conservative or traditional bias is apt to be a reflection of the fanatic failure to reassess adolescent ideals adequately.

The problem of structure within the knowledge to be learned in schools is part of the problem not of the structure of knowledge nor of psychology of learning, but of structure in human being—the problem of structure in existing and in coexisting. The paradox between the "psychological" and the "logical," between landscape and geography, is the paradox between the unique and the universal, the individual and the social, the private and the public, the conservative and the liberal. Retention of the pedagogic paradox in schooling, then, supplies precisely the educational force that is needed to counteract the trends in modern life that promote mass, anonymous existence wherein the depersonalization of forces producing inauthentic existence manifested in a compulsive conformity prevent the emergence of the individual from anonymity and thereby prevent the emergence of genuine community, i.e., that prevent the authentically human and interhuman. The force to balance societal trends toward inauthentically human existence found in retention of the pedagogic paradox is the matter of the intellectual uniqueness that is developed when the pupil does things his own way. Promoting intellectual uniqueness exists the pedagogic paradox: that it is intellectual is schooling, geography, the "logical"; that it is unique is educating, landscape, the "psychological." Promoting intellectual uniqueness in schooling is all that is necessary to promote living the life-phase of youth fully on the level of the individual pupil and to promote authentically human existence at the societal level in response to the social crisis.[14]

Intellectual uniqueness, the union of one's own landscape with everyone's geography, the matter of fitting the geography of schooling into one's project of being from his own origin toward his own destination without losing oneself in geography but also without distorting the geography by one's landscape, cannot be a separate aim or objective added on to the schooling process, but should be the unexpected consequence of maintaining the tension of the pedagogic paradox in the classroom, of allowing room for the expansion of the pupil's own possibilities of being in the midst of instruction in organized knowledge. The pupil unites the geography of schooling with his own landscape at any rate, but distorting it to fit his "frame of reference," i.e., his existing world, in a manner contributing to his alienation from himself, others, and from the world. The problem is to encourage it in respect to the truth of being and the being of truth. When what are often called independence of mind, incorruptibility of thought, capacity for critical thinking, intellectual integrity, perhaps even moral integrity, are seen not as cognitive nor intellectual but as existential "virtues," everything changes. What makes them possible is the pupil's being-in-the-truth, which depends upon his wanting-to-be-some-one-himself. Responsiveness to evidence is as dependent upon one's at-homeness in landscape as it is upon familiarity with geography. To be able to tell the truth and to pursue the truth, one must first of all be true.

To be true is dependent upon one's listening to the silent call of being and willing one's own "nothingness," on choosing to be in the truth and in the truth of being. These require room for the pupil's origina-tiveness to maintain his wanting-to-be-someone-himself so that he can hear and obey the mute voice of being. For him to be obedient, however, re-quires room for disobedience. Whereas the child requires room for dis-obedience mostly in respect to his conduct in order for him to be able to come to genuine obedience, with the increased intellectuality of school-ing in youth, with the gradual shift from the child's exploration of the physical world to the youth's exploration of the intellectual-historical world, the room for disobedience becomes intellectualized. Room for in-tellectual disobedience is the necessary condition for the development of intellectual uniqueness, the resolution of the pedagogic paradox, and the grounding of educating in the being of youth. It allows room for the authentic acquisition of knowledge, i.e., authentic learning, at the same time that it allows for obedience to being. Intellectual disobedience, how-ever, is ordinarily called heresy. So be it. Then there has to be room for heresy in order to make authentic intellectual obedience possible. Other-wise there are the mirrors and echoes that manifest repression of the pupil's being and all the related phenomena appertaining thereto. Room for heresy, however, enables the organized knowledge of schooling to have something to do with the pupil's search for the truth of his own being, for the truth of being, because it enables the pupil to have some-thing to do with the organized knowledge of schooling and still be some-one himself. Room for heresy also enables the youth to have something to do with the organized knowledge of schooling in his search for truth because it enables this knowledge to have something to do with him and still be truth. Where there is room for heresy there is room for the worlding of the world in which being clears a space for itself and establishes the truth of being and the being of truth.

8

Schooling Policy and Ideology

The questioning of the nature and aim of education led through the question of the structure of curriculum to the paradox of educating within schooling. Questioning this paradox obviously leads in two directions. Concrete pedagogics—How ought the teaching-learning situation be conducted to promote educating?—will be investigated subsequent to the consideration of policy, How ought instruction be organized within schooling to promote educating within the teaching-learning situaton?

Schooling policy is not customarily formulated by taking guidance from and giving heed to the requirements of the teaching-learning situation. On the contrary, its focus generally is to give direction to teaching and learning activities in order to achieve societal goals. By definition, it is concerned with how schooling should be conducted, how schooling in general should promote the good society. If it is decided that schooling as an institution should be subservient to other societal institutions, then it is assumed that the "good society" is already here and policy decisions basically support the extension of the present status of society into the future, giving the school a conserving function. If it is decided that schooling should be one of the dominant institutions, then policy decisions will be made to bring the good society into being, giving the school a reconstructing function. There are many ways, some of them conflicting, in which the schools can be conserving, and many ways, some of them also conflicting, in which the schools can be reconstructing, depending upon what is being conserved or reconstructed (and how and why); but nevertheless, "educational" policy decisions of any kind affect the future quality of society to the extent that they affect the organization of instruction and pedagogy and to the extent that these latter affect pupils. If a policy decision affects the way schooling occurs (and presumably this is its reason for being), and if the way schooling occurs affects the pupil's being (and presumably this is *its* reason for being), then "educational" policy affects the kind of society that will exist after the pupils graduate to the extent that their presence in society is part of society and affects society in its very being, for better or for worse. The major horizon within which decisions of educational policy occur, consciously or otherwise, is the operative social philosophy. An explicit and consistent social philosophy may be lacking, yet the value judgments that are operative in a policy decision are a rudimentary, inchoate social philosophy, a version of the good society. This would be discovered if the decision makers were asked several consecutive "why's," although in a representative democracy it may be the anonymous taxpayer's social philosophy, alleged or real, articulate or dumb, democratic or fascistic, that is ultimately operative.

The major trend in educational philosophy in this century toward using the resources of social philosophy to articulate, clarify, and resolve educational problems at the policy level has been somewhat eclipsed with the development of counter-trends at the societal level toward an increasing distrust of vaguely expressed political and social ideals, developing in the nineteen fifties and sixties and symbolized best, perhaps, by Daniel Bell's title *The End of Ideology*, and toward an increasing awareness of the extreme difficulty of relating educational problems to societal problems with any degree of logical or evidential warrant. But is this distrust of political and social philosophy and its reduction to ideology merely another ideology? Those who oppose social and political philosophy for the best reasons have argued against a "proclaiming" and "prophetic" philosophy because it merely results in an ideology, which they think may have been legitimate in prescientific days before the development of the social sciences but which now hardly passes muster as serious, scholarly pastime. But is this distrust of political and social philosophy, this distrust of ideology, merely another ideological proclamation? What accounts for the hesitancy to employ a self-conscious social philosophy in the formulation of school policy? Is this hesitancy the result of supporting alternative educational policy that rests upon unacknowledged or suppressed premises, i.e., upon an ideology?

THE PUBLICNESS AND FACTICITY
OF SCHOOLING

The possibility of the presence of underlying value premises in the determination of educational policy, i.e., of an implicit social philosophy that operates ideologically because of its unacknowledged presence, can be simply illustrated. From *facts* no policy recommendations follow without additional value judgments derived from a social philosophy: from facts such as another nation's technological accomplishments or an increased proportion of people attending or wanting to attend college there follow *no* schooling recommendations at all without additional premises. It is not immediately clear why nations should compete with each other technologically, nor is it at all clear what the best college education is, nor, consequently, what kind of a program would be the best preparation for college. People who possess intuitively clear connections between these things merely have some ready frame of reference which can be recited by rote more quickly than probing into the problems confronted, and this frame of reference is an implicit social philosophy. There has been a rather widespread opinion that there was nothing philosophical about the apparent superiority of the space technology of the Soviet Union with the orbiting of Sputnik I in 1957 and subsequent policy making in respect to the public schools in the United States; but it is characteristic of people in the grip of an ideology to fail to recognize their own value commitments as such, or, recognizing them, to fail to recognize their questionableness. It is precisely this characteristic, however, that makes their values questionable: the fundamental philosophical event of the twentieth century may have been Sputnik I, for never before had the problems of men, of how to live together, been thrown into such sharp focus. That a basketball-size piece of metal floating overhead could have caused the widespread consternation, flurried activity, and apparent loss of perspective that dominated the criticisms of the schools and colleges of education and that prompted many of the "innovations" in schooling in the decade of the sixties is no little reason for astonishment. What Sputnik I demonstrated beyond the power of words was not the terrors of the Cold War nor the economic and political decline of the United States, but the necessary and inescapable unity of human life on the planet.

Because this inescapable unity went remarkably unnoticed, it also established that the fundamental educational and societal problem is the alienation of people from each other. The implications of Sputnik I consequently fall into the noncognitive dimensions of the schooling process, insofar as the "better" society will have less alienation between men, particularly on the planetary level. The consequences of Sputnik I for schooling policy fall into the moral dimensions of schooling, and there has been very little response thus far to the crisis in education stemming from events on the international scene. Because the problems are noncognitive, one does not know how to understand what has happened. No matter what foreign or international policy the nations may adopt to suit the exigencies of international relations, from that policy nothing is entailed for schooling policy. This is true in any case because there is no logic that can bridge the gap. It is particularly valid, however, if the *educational* development of people is to be oriented to balance or to ameliorate the existing state of affairs. If the general problem is how to live together, in other words, it can be approached in different sectors of experience (or provinces of meaning) in different ways that may, in fact, be logically incompatible with each other. The way foreign policy ought to be decided in respect to the attempt to live together at the international level may differ as much from the way "educational" policy ought to be decided at the schooling level as the ways invented between men to enable them to live together while working in a factory differ from the ways appropriate for a man and a woman. In neither case is the latter supposed to be developed from the former, nor is the latter conducted as if it existed primarily to promote the former.

The confusion of schooling policy and international policy resulted from a lack of understanding of the autonomy of the schooling process. To achieve a sense of this autonomy, it is necessary to have the phenomenon of schooling in view. The phenomenon of schooling consists of elementary school, junior and senior high schools, community junior colleges, municipal colleges, and tax-supported universities in Alabama and Alberta, Harlem and Highland Park, Toronto and Tanganyika, Peking and Buenos Aires, Moscow and Montana, and so on and so on. Policy is decided upon to organize instruction in particular schools and groups of schools, of course, but schooling as a phenomenon exists only as public schooling that is free, universal, and compulsory—schooling exists as a phenomenon independent of its incarnation in particular circumstances because it originated so that everyone might have access to education, and this original image of publicness and universalism that existed before the schools did is part of the phenomenon of schooling. Schooling can exist only as public, and public schooling can exist only as free, compulsory, and universal. The basic criterion that educational policy has to satisfy in order to be relevant to schools that are public is that it is equally applicable to all public schools wherever they may be, even where they have not yet been brought into being. Otherwise it lacks scope, comprehensiveness, and adequacy. A policy not meeting this criterion lacks applicability to public schools because its application changes them into something else, into something that serves isolated interests, rather than considering adequately the moral dimension of schooling and respecting the possibilities of children and youth in the various places not taken into account, especially if those places are under- or overprivileged. The criterion of applicability to all public schools in order to be relevant to schooling by bringing it into being is not a proclamation of a vague, humanitarian sentiment, because it is precisely opposed to the humanitarianism associated with the "white man's burden" or "Yankee imperialism." It is not ideological because it is descriptive. It indicates the *only* means available to avoid an ideological protection of a private interest and to assist in the derivation from the phenomenon of public schooling that which might prevent parochialism, provincialism, ethnocentricism, and cultural relativism. Public is public, arbitrary boundaries to the tax bases of school financing notwithstanding.

From the viewpoint of what exists public schooling, it appears that the preliminary step to reduce the alienation of people from each other is the establishment of a common schooling system and a common curriculum on a worldwide basis. This is somewhat tautological because the common school came into being precisely to overcome various aspects of the alienation between men, but its illuminating point is that the question does not so much concern the response the schools should make to the apparent crisis precipitated by the onset of space age, but rather the response that should be made through schooling when one realizes that schooling in its very being is already a response to the alienation between men. It suggests that part of the "remedy" is merely to enhance the schoolingness of schooling, i.e., to increase its publicness, universality, and commonness, through the employment of the criterion of publicness in the formulation of schooling policy: a common curriculum exists the schoolingness of schooling. Analogously, any policy that could not be instituted universally contributes to the alienation of men because it arrogates to some children that which is thereby denied to other children. The criterion is almost but not quite a version of the Kantian categorical imperative to act so that all one's actions are capable of being legislated universally to assure that they are dictated by reason rather than by limited desires and to insure that one did the right thing. It is not an imperative, an ought, at all. It indicates how one can recognize policy that shows privateness, partiality, or narcissism, that fails to recognize the responsibility involved in the publicness of schooling and what schooling signifies. It is not an ought because it has not yet been said that policy should guide schooling so that it functions to alleviate contemporary problems: it is merely descriptive of the essence of the phenomenon of public schooling and indicative of what the outline of a response to Sputnik I would be were it to be taken seriously. The landing of men on the moon in 1969 did not so much indicate that it was taken seriously as it signified the same crisis. It is passing strange that very few people raised the question concerning the response that schooling should make to the curriculum crisis manifested by Apollo 11. Prior to the existence of common schooling, i.e., prior to the establishment of a common curriculum on a worldwide basis, mere attendance at school forces the child to live immorally in an unjust world. He must and ought to attend, yet his actions are not universalizable because it lets and encourages him to arrogate to himself possibilities that are not accorded to other children. Prior to the existence of universal schooling on a planetary scale the child is indeed forced to be over- or underprivileged, and the former appears to be the less moral of the two because it forces the child to live in a world that tolerates the latter. Prior to a common curriculum, the child is forced to grow up immorally, alienated from others, and guilty.

Insofar as this is so, public schooling is inherently mass schooling. It is not the schooling of the masses as if they existed somewhat differently from you and I, but schooling is the generalized and leveled-down feature of educating in the pedagogic relationship that can be considered on the general policy level. Only the everyday characteristics of mass education are amenable to policy making and reflection on schooling. That schooling is compulsory and universal makes it inherently mass schooling, for it occurs in the realm of anonymity. Not in respect to the pedagogic relation but in respect to schooling are teachers and children anonymous. Anyone who undertakes to be prepared can teach. Anyone can go to school. Schooling occurs as a form of average, everyday human existence, particularly when it pretends not to be by encouraging "individuality" to compensate for its embarrassment over itself. Self-conscious attempts to achieve "individuality," in school as elsewhere, are express recognition that one is not individualized. It requires a previous comparison of oneself with others. In the assumption or "recognition" that people are different is to be found the basic alienation, for before they can be said to be alike or to be different they have to be compared on some isolated impersonal "dimension" or "property." To see that John is taller than William, for a not always so trivial example, is to be alienated from either, for John is as tall as he is, which is just right for him, and William is as tall as he is, which is also exactly right for him. In spite of the tremendous volume of research into individual differences, *that people are either the same or different is not understandable.* Each person is simply himself, nameable only by his proper name. Individuation is a modification of the temporal structure of human being. It is a modification of the way in which one projects futuringly into his own possibilities and achieves a "self-constancy" through the completion of concrete tasks—attempts to be individualized or to individualize another have to occur through the way in which concrete tasks are accomplished. Then whatever is done in schooling cannot contribute to individuation directly because of the way in which the universal and the particular are combined in the pedagogic paradox: schooling and policy deal with one half of the paradox, the other half belongs to the concrete pedagogic tasks and to the particular person. Policy cannot promote the development of individual existence because it cannot by its very nature deal with the particular case—it is precisely policy that deals with schooling in general. Pedagogic decisions that deal with particular instances are guided by the details of the individual situation that are necessarily omitted from policy consideration and formulation. Public schooling, therefore, is mass schooling perforce.

Not only does schooling constitute itself within the realm of anonymity, it is the "instrument of society," i.e., of anonymous everydayness. Schooling is the attempt to perpetuate "society" in its averageness. Phenomenologically, "cultural transmission" is the development of the ordinary, common world. Schooling *is* average, everydayness—the everydayness that belongs to schooling is its facticity, its that-it-is, such that to try to avoid the averageness of schooling is to try to avoid the existence of the public school. The word *schooling* refers to the same thing as do the words *mass education*. All departures from the mass aspects of schooling are departures from how public schooling constitutes itself—they have to "fail" when instituted because they establish the new form of average existence in schooling by being instituted.

An examination of one such departure will serve to show how policy might be decided were it deemed desirable to accept the facticity of the publicness of schooling. One item will suffice as representative of a way to relate educational problems to societal problems, to indicate the kinds of policy decisions respecting educational problems that might be made to promote the educational development within schooling of the kinds of persons who might be able to resolve or live with the societal problems of the post-Sputnik world. "Ability grouping" may be paradigmatic of the "innovations" that have been widely advertised as remedies to cure whatever was alleged to ail public schooling.

LOGICAL ANALYSIS

The decision to group the people in school according to "ability" (and other factors in order to yield "homogeneous" classes) can be made upon "empirical" or political grounds; either to increase the acquisition of knowledge, as allegedly indicated by "empirical" studies, or to suit the majority, the most powerful interest groups, or the "power structure" of a given community.

"Empiricial studies" can be discounted because the necessary information is not forthcoming. An adequate study of the effects of various instructional groupings would require the kind of controlled experiment that is not possible within the context of schooling. It would require perfectly matched instructional groups, perfectly matched teachers, continuous and perfectly matched instructional methods, and, given all of these, an equivalence of "empirical facts" and values. Without the first three of these, no research study can result in the kind of generalization that can be used as the basis for a policy decision. Given the first three, the absence of the last would still militate against using the valid generalization as the decisive factor in a policy decision. The first three, however, involve variables that cannot be sufficiently controlled to yield the requisite warranted generalization.

To match instructional groups includes matching individual for individual and classroom interaction for classroom interaction. Two people who are perfectly matched on all the objectively attainable data, including Rorschach and T.A.T. findings (to indicate how complex the matter is), may not be matched at all on the subjective data, for they would have differing projects of being, i.e., different origins and destinations and differing temporal structures. In empirical language, they would still have differing experiential backgrounds and differing motivations. They also have differing home lives and different people across the aisle from them during experimentation. To be matched on all the "objectively" attainable "data" is not to be matched at all, except in the never-never land of mathematics: "matched" people are still different people. To rest content with statistically matched groups or random sampling is to be very arbitrary on two accounts: it is to remain within a very gross, abstract preconception of what is being investigated in the research, and very remote from the phenomenon inquired into. It also postulates a metaphysical thesis when the "findings" are taken out of context and used for something other than the direction and redirection of further research. When "empirical findings" are taken to represent the real, a nonempirical system of natural law is postulated in the traditional rationalistic, realistic metaphysical manner, for it is implicitly asserted that the findings extracted from their context represent valid generalizations that are operative in and govern human events that occur elsewhere than the actual experiment. This is what was formerly postulated by the designation *natural law*. To rest content with statistically matched groups in relying upon "empirical findings" in making a policy decision to group homogeneously or heterogeneously in effect asserts that one is according to natural law, the other not. The "findings" have to be presumed as embodying general laws of human conduct that exist in the world as soon as existential, experiential decisions of policy are based upon them. The scientific researcher himself does not have to assume his findings are generalizable or that they correspond to anything apart from his own context and method of inquiry. He will not assume this if he is cognizant of the limitations, i.e., of the nature, of his inquiry. He cannot make it without leaving the area of his specialization and competency and entering into the area of philosophy.

To match teachers involves matching teaching within the controlled experiment, and an adequate study would necessitate teaching all groups the same way—same teaching style, same personality, same method, same classroom atmosphere and mood (i.e., the same prevailing state-of-being), same competency in subject matter, and so on, so that all pupils in all classes within both heterogeneous and homogeneous groupings and within both experimental and control groups, including both "fast" and "slow" groups within "homogeneous" grouping, are in fact taught the same way. After perfectly matched populations are obtained, in other words, everything else has to be rigidly controlled to isolate the variable of grouping to assure its ontological independence and the validity of the experiment. This means they would have to be taught in the same way in the most minute of detail, including the teacher's tone of voice (her state-of-being), to insure the stability of the variable and to make a common achievement test possible. If they were taught differently, or if any of a multitude of variables were not held constant, a common achievement test would not be possible and there would be absolutely no way of knowing what occurred in the experiment. There is no way of knowing whether all the variables are identified and controlled, furthermore, so that there could be no way of knowing what occurs in such an experiment. Because there could be no way of knowing that only the variable being examined, the grouping itself, was what happened, there really can be no inquiry into the benefits of various instructional groupings.

In order for there to be perfectly matched instructional groupings not merely at the beginning but throughout the experiment, continuous study habits throughout the experiment would have to be assumed. This is just one of the many variables that would have to be controlled, but it is perhaps the most crucial and least amenable to control. It would have to be assumed that all the people in all the groupings worked equally efficiently from day to day, always at the same rate according to their "capacities." This would be a very atypical teaching situation. To assume that day-to-day differences were statistically negligible or unresponsive to the groupings is rather bold, convenient, and question-begging; yet this must be assumed in any application of findings. To ignore the issue is to remain on a very gross level of experience.

Supposing that these difficulties were surmounted by some fantastically complex research design and assuming that the relevant information respecting the merits of "homogeneous" and "heterogeneous" groupings were obtained, it requires an additional value judgment to leap from the empirical "is" to the practical "ought." In this kind of thinking, Aristotelian logic is still illuminating: the major premise of a practical syllogism is missing. With simply the information from an adequate study, there are two sentences:

A. Students, by and large, learn most when X-grouped.
C. Schools ought to have X-grouping.

If schooling policy could be established directly from the findings of empirical research, these two sentences are the form that the thinking process would take. The policy statement is labelled "C," however, to indicate the absence of B, that schools ought to be organized to promote the greatest amount of learning. Actually, A ought to be labelled "B," for the research finding is the *minor* premise and the value judgment is the *major* premise, so that the correct syllogism should read:

A. Schools ought to be organized to promote the greatest amount of learning.
B. Students learn most when X-grouped.
C. Schools ought to have X-groupings.

That the prior judgment is necessary to apply findings of empirical research has been stated in Chapter One; what is noteworthy at the present is that to accept the major premise as definitive for policy-making, one must reject other normative judgments such as "Children ought to be happy in school," and "Schools ought to embody egalitarian democracy." Disagreement over groupings turns out to be not a matter of the application of the findings of research but of alternative philosophies of education. Not only is the major premise necessary to derive the normative conclusion or policy statement from the "empirical facts," it is not sufficient. Many other considerations are necessary as well. That schools are a place for any kind of learning is still an open question, despite the proclamations of some ideologies to the contrary. What "learning" is, what constitutes learning, is still an open question, despite the proclamations of ideologies to the contrary, because what it is depends upon what knowledge is. The question of knowledge is still a wide-open question, despite the proclamations of some ideologies to the contrary, because, believe it or not, current argument for "revelation" and "intuition" make as much sense and have as much appeal and exert as strong an influence among first-rate philosophers on the world scene as do various forms of positivism. This suggests that *experimentation* in instructional groupings could not be carried out unless a *decision* were made *concerning the nature of knowledge* so that teaching might occur within the experiment, which would probably mean, incidentally, that any findings were limited to groupings wherein teaching was confined to that kind of knowledge. It also suggests that even if it were accepted that the implication of Sputnik I were the maximal diffusion of knowledge through schooling, there are still other considerations that prevent the linear thinking of the syllogism from being valid. Which kinds of grouping promote which kinds of learning and the diffusion of which kind of knowledge? Which kind of students learn more? How much of which kinds of learning are learned by whom over the entire span of schooling and have the greatest long-run transfer value? Is "sufficiently more" of some kinds of learnings by some kinds of people enough to warrant priority over other kinds of learnings and other considerations? Because "maximal diffusion" of knowledge is two words, the maximal diffusion is not necessarily the maximal acquisition of knowledge, even if it were clear as to what knowledge is. It is not clear which the schools should promote even if "ability grouping" were proven to excel at one rather than the other. This in turn means that from neither the world situation in the years subsequent to Sputnik I nor from the increasing enrollments in college and university does it follow that the maximal acquisition of knowledge by a minority of pupils should have been preferred to the maximal diffusion of knowledge as it was in the increasingly widespread adoption of "ability grouping" in various forms since Sputnik, except for some ideologies.

ONTOLOGICAL ANALYSIS

The value dimension of this or any other item of policy, in other words, is the decisive factor and the decisive issue. It is what makes a decision possible. It is decisive particularly when it may sound as though it is facts that are referred to, for it is precisely then that the value issues dominate in a decisive way. It is then that they dominate thinking analogously to the way that the submerged part of the iceberg determines which way the current will float the visible portion. To accept the moral point of view for the development of policy in order to organize schooling to respond to the social crisis means to pay notice to the *fact* that "ability grouping" contributes to the alienation of men from each other and from themselves because it institutionalizes differences and qualities that are unrealizable in personal experience. This alienates the pupil from himself and others because it objectifies him and others within his experience. Within one's own experience, one cannot feel or see or experience in any way one's own "level of intelligence" and one cannot perceive "levels of intelligence" in others. This is why standardized tests of "intelligence" were developed. "Ability groupings," however, develop an illusory perception of levels of intelligence in others and in himself within the pupil's awareness through an alienating structuring of his consciousness of himself and other people through the structures of schooling. People who think they can experience levels of intelligence in themselves or in others are living their decision to approach living situations in a stereotyped and preconceived manner. Their awareness, and with that their interpersonal being, is obstructed and the flux of human existence objectified in such a way that a living encounter with other people is not facilitated but prohibited. The being of levels of intelligence and intellectual achievement lies out there in the world in a more (or less) finely articulated, more (or less) coherently interrelated contexture of meanings that become possibilities of action through projecting into them: differences between apparently "slow" and "bright" pupils are differences in the structures, fluidities, depths, and possibilities of their worlds, in the referential totality that is out there in front of them, but the institutionalization of "ability grouping" suggests to them through their experience of the structure of schooling that the differences reside over here inside the skin as properties that one already has. This considers human being with categories appropriate to non-human entities, places societal expectations upon pupils with respect to what they are but not with respect to who they are, structures the world of pupils to make authentic coexistence improbable, and institutionalizes the desires of dominant societal groups who collectively constitute an oppressing class. Explication of these four points will indicate how policy is inadequately formulated when it is decided upon political grounds.

When various "ability groupings" are institutionalized, they define a predominant structure of schooling and thereby suggest through the "institutional press" that the decisive aspect of human being in respect to schooling is "intelligence" or "intellectual capacity" or "academic achievement." Because the horizons of the child are opened in the space they establish, they suggest to him that the most important aspect of human being in school and in general in societal life and in the cosmos is the same as that by which he is grouped in school. The child is learning all of these at once regardless of the attempts of others to isolate the school from its social and cosmological context, because these attempts do not isolate but define a different relation to the outside world. Within the child's experience "ability grouping" seems to structure not merely the school but the society and the universe as well, because the school is his first contact with the broader world. He assigns far greater societal and cosmological significance to it than perhaps merits. It is not that "intelligence," etc., are unimportant to schooling but that they are reified in schooling under "ability grouping," and that pupils are concomitantly reified. "Intelligence," "intellectual capacity," "academic achievement," or whatever do not exist as static entities but in process. They exist in action as qualities of action. The atmosphere of the school where there is "ability grouping" not only reifies them but reifies them as the most significant "attribute" of concern to the school (and hence to society and the universe): what seems to the child to matter most in the world is "how smart you are." More important than the value hierarchy—hence ideology—that is obviously thereby involved is the fact that the major criterion for making room for the child or youth within schooling is an unrealizable quality. He cannot make room for himself in the same space that room is made for him without undergoing an alienation from the world, because he cannot spatialize from his own origin into the geography of an unrealizable. Because it is an unrealizable, he cannot be conscious of this "thing" by which he and his friends are grouped, nor can he go to the world making room for himself in it by what he can be conscious of. He cannot be someone himself and the tension of the pedagogic paradox cannot be maintained when schooling is structured by "ability grouping."

Although no one else can become conscious of the reified "thing" by which "ability grouping" is instituted either, the practice nevertheless implies that "ability" is something one already has. It becomes a metaphysical, unknowable *Ding an sich* that allegedly determines the pupil's futuring: it overstructures and delimits his own futuring from his own origin to his own destination. Whereas the traditional conception of the superiority of "character" to "intellect" probably underestimated the place of "intelligence," in respect to the achievement that was called "character," it does seem correct to estimate the significance of schooling in terms of long-range achievement: if the "honors student" does not contribute significantly five or ten or twenty or thirty years after the completion of schooling and if the "B" or "C" student does, then the significance of the latter's *schooling* achievement is greater than the former's, report cards notwithstanding. It may be correct to predict greater achievement from the former, but nevertheless this "prediction" is only probable and schooling achievements are in some respects irrelevant to who one is, particularly when human being as a totality is considered. They may in fact be irrelevant to future achievement (i.e., low correlation). Predicting future achievement, moreover, is largely irrelevant to the accomplishment of the tasks of schooling. Then advocating schooling policy on the basis of a future promise overestimates the significance of schooling to authentic achievement, committing the schoolman's fallacy of overestimating the importance of schooling. It overlooks the possibilities of the present for the sake of a nonexistent future, which is characteristic of the doctrinaire failure to reassess one's own adolescent ideals correctly after the crisis of practical experience. To neglect present possibilities for a future that does not exist is existing inauthentically—it is failing to be authentically there in the situation, letting its possibilities disclose themselves and realizing what is possible. This is the danger endemic to schooling policy-making.

What is required, if one wishes to place policy-making on a solid "empirical" ground, are tremendously comprehensive and extensive longitudinal studies that are more precise and controlled than Terman's or the Eight Year Study. It might be interesting to discover, for example, precisely what becomes of National Merit Scholarship winners to see if the expense, disruption of school life in almost every school in the country merely to administer the examinations, and the distortion of the curriculum entailed in attempts to prepare for the examination, are actually worth while in terms of the societal contributions of "winners." What kinds of contributions would be expected from them in order to make the examinations worth the time? What percentage of "winners" would make wholesale administration of the examinations worth while? What kind of criteria could be used to evaluate these contributions? Perhaps the money involved merely to administer the tests would be as well spent if it were donated to any college selected at random. How would one know?

In general, that is, there has been little awareness of long-run effects of recent "innovations," including "ability grouping" as a paradigmatic case, and little attempt to examine thoroughly those things that are made to sound "good" with the use of rhetoric and Madison Avenue promotional techniques.

The absence of longitudinal studies of such "innovations" is the lack of significant estimates of their value. One can only wonder why they are considered desirable, particularly in the face of their widespread acceptance, for part of the phenomenon of being a "good student" has been a "capacity" to learn more from any schooling experience than "average" pupils, and part of the phenomenon of "giftedness" has been doing whatever is assigned and finding more to do on one's own: *academic talent* has always been used to designate those people who have stood in less need of help of schools and teachers. *Less.* Conceptions of "good students" or of "academic talent" that do not focus upon the pupil's active exploration of the world and his "self-motivation" as revealed in action are based on a belief in "magic": "ability" or "talent" or "giftedness" is an entity that resides within the person that he already has, separable from what he does, and his actions are explained by naming the "cause" that was constructed in order to explain the action. The mode of reasoning is from effect to cause, naming the inferred but unknowable cause, then invoking the name not merely to "explain" the effect but *to produce it.* The paradigm for this mode of reasoning is magic. It is also reminiscent of faculty psychology: "ability" or "academic talent" or "intellectual excellence" can be improved through the special exercises of the faculties that are facilitated by "homogeneous" groupings. "Ability grouping" is either supposed to accelerate the acquisition of "knowledge" or develop "abilities" (i.e., faculties). Because there is nothing restraining any "talented" or "gifted" pupil in any "heterogeneously" grouped class, however, except his own lack of imagination and responsibility for his own existence, and because both magic and faculty psychology are as outmoded as they are indefensible, one can only wonder why "homogeneous" groupings are deemed desirable, in the absence of signs as to their worth.

If there are any children or youth who do not need "innovations" on their behalf, they are the "good students," the "academically talented," by definition of what these designations mean. All they can possibly signify is doing well in school. "Innovations" in schooling to help those who do well in school not only smack of favoritism, they actually are redundant. One can only wonder how and why redundant items of policy are taken to be a response to a major societal crisis. One can only wonder at the motivations of people who advocate redundant innovations with great missionary zeal.

It is not appropriate to question motivations of people when philosophizing or when formulating policy, nor is it appropriate to question the sincerity of people teaching "fast" classes. Such questioning would be *argumentum ad hominem* instead of confrontation of the issue, which is not so immoral as it is a diversion of attention and an alienation from the problem, and the appropriate and valid reply would be another *ad hominem*. Consideration of policy, however, has to suppose a context wherein the decision is open to decision, i.e., a specific school or system that is contemplating institutionalizing "ability grouping." This supposing can be purely imaginative, for imagining what might be suffices to free thought from the bonds of previous decisions. In imagination one can and must question motivations, for motivations, ulterior and otherwise, are as relevant to the outcome of deliberative proceedings as evidence and logical argument are unless everyone involved is free enough to let the situation be what it is. One can question motivations particularly if they are the value judgments that are more decisive than logic and evidence. If so, then the reasons "talented" or "gifted" pupils would want "ability grouping" can be questioned. To attempt to achieve their whole being at one stroke? To avoid both immediate and future trial by concrete action? To avoid the anguish of not being able to be conscious of one's own "talent"? To achieve merit once and for all, as if it were not the kind of thing that had to be won anew in each situation? To avoid the risk of schooling with the average?

Why would parents want it for their own children? To insure a head start in later-life competition? To put their children's being out of question?

Why would teachers want it?

In spite of the slant of these questions, the item takes on new dimensions approached from the viewpoint of *why* rather than *whether*. The most relevant questioning concerns the pupil's desires for "ability grouping" and the way these are affected through his existing in a world where they are permitted. Some of the desires might be related to an unwillingness to accept the responsibility of relying on merit, on action alone, without the aid of special privilege, which is an alienation from oneself because it is a failure to live up to the condition of human existence of being responsible for one's actions—to ontological anxiety over who one can be when it is motivated by accepting societal "values" such as vocational success in a narrowly prescribed direction, before having the experience that would enable their acceptance to be a responsible choice of concrete alternatives and when, therefore, it has to constitute an alienation from his wanting-to-be-someone-himself—to an alienation from others insofar as it arrogates to oneself possibilities of being (in later societal success) that are concomitantly and actively denied to other children and youth—and to an alienation from himself when it is the prestige or success or power as such that is desired, inasmuch as these require the complicity of society to subsist as well as requiring the admiration and compliance of the "unsuccessful" in order for them to be constituted as "prestige" or "success" or "power," which is an alienation from oneself because it delivers one's own being into the hands of others in one's being for them rather than for one's self. Where "ability grouping" is already instituted, the person ought to realize the possibilities of the situation in which he finds himself, but nevertheless these alienations occur because of the categorization of pupils on the nonhuman categories used to structure schooling.

This categorization places societal expectations on children and youth not in respect to who they are but in respect to *what* they are: it omits their being and alienates them from their being from their origin toward their own destination, particularly when "ability grouping" is part of a broader attempt to develop "human resources," to discover, motivate, and develop "talent" for ends that are thrust upon "gifted" pupils, regardless of who they are. In the "search for talent" the suggestion is made that the "talented" child or youth has no right to solve the problem of existence for himself (with authentically pedagogic assistance) and that he is to be converted to wanting to excel in school so that he can participate in whatever patterns of "success" happen to be societally dominant even if it is contrary to his whole being to do so, as if the "talented" youth has no right to dirt farm, paint, write poetry or novels, wash dishes, park cars, or to do any of a great number of things to which schooling is not necessarily a help, and to which "ability grouping" is less obviously a help, but which might nevertheless contain the individual's own possibilities of being. On the other hand, the adoption of "ability grouping" as part of a large project to seduce youth into the "establishment," into the successful routes of the economic system and the "industrial-military complex," can have the reverse effect of what is intended when youth arrive upon university campuses and no longer remember why they are there, because the reasons they formerly thought they had for wanting to go to the university were never their own and have faded from view in the retrieval of the youth's own being from being-for-others that is made possible by the extrication of himself from the mores of family and neighborhood.

Advocating the discovery and motivation of "talented" children, in other words, is arrogant, deficient solicitude, for it presupposes that "gifted" children and youth can be helped by schooling without waiting until the help is asked for, until it is required as part of the child's or youth's exploration of the world. A great variety of questions concerning the motivation of "gifted" people, of which very little is known, thrust themselves forward.

What if the greatest possible motivation for the greatest possible contribution to society on the part of the "gifted" stemmed from or was related to neglect, frustration, and indifference on the part of schooling? Or what if it resulted from imaginative wanderings during dull classes unimaginatively taught? Or from impatience with mediocre teaching or rebellion against the "duly constituted" social order? Or from compassion developed through insight into the problems of quite ordinary classmates? What if premature recognition, or simply recognition, ruins "talent" or its "motivation"? What if a long period of solitary, unrecognized gestation is necessary to any solid creative accomplishment, and what if schooling has to be precisely such a period of unrecognized and unexpressed gestation? How would a "talented" person be recognized so that the "investment" had its proper "returns"? What if Sartre was at least partly right when, after his existential psychoanalysis of Genet, he said, "Genius is not a gift but the way out that one invents in desperate cases"? Might it not make as much sense to institutionalize the conditions conducive to the happening of desperate cases as to institutionalize the conditions tending to prevent them, particularly with post-affluent youth who have no need to achieve according to the canons of the Protestant Ethic, but who seem often to hunger for personal tragedy in order to make their existence seem more real to them? Who would be willing to try that experiment?

These questions, slanted as they are to shatter some glib and superficial idols, are not the kind of questions that can be "empirically" investigated: if something is once tried, it is not possible to tell what might have happened had it not been tried or had something else been tried, except with different people. Unlike the medical profession, moreover, the teaching profession never sees its own failures: teaching and schooling failures are all mixed up with pupil's failures (and the reverse) during school years. Apparent school successes may manifest themselves as "failures" ten or twenty years later in another town in another state or country, or there may be later "failures" that never manifest themselves as such at all. If "potential talent" is ruined by schooling, either by channeling through accelerated classes, by failure to be channeled through accelerated classes with other students of more discernible talent, or in a myriad of other possible ways, it never shows because it cannot show. What might have been never shows. The apparently "positive" results of "ability grouping" might sometimes appear to be ascertained, but only to a degree, because for all one can know results might have been better. The negative results simply do not show. Unfortunately, schooling can always blame the pupils for its own failures.

"Ability grouping" structures the life not merely of the school but of the world of the pupil, in and out of school, during school and after. Because human temporality is not a linear progression as if one's life were a magnetic tape that rolled through a recorder, a remembrance of school in later years brings the "social structure" of the school, of the past, into the present world. A remembrance of the past can be closer and more relevant to the present situation than incidents of the same day. Later remembrance of childhood and youthful friends in the categories of the "ability groups" of schooling prohibits authentically human interpersonal relations because of the earlier inauthentically human relations. "Ability grouping" is being there in school inauthentically with others because the grouping is based upon ontic grounds: it has no foundation in human being, i.e., is not based upon ontological differences between people. The "differences" are "real" within a province of meaning that enables their disclosure as real, but they have no being apart from the bracketing of a particular province of meaning and its method of inquiry. Groupings upon ontical properties prevent the formation and development of a common world and the concomitant underlying understanding that "we are in the same situation" that is necessary for genuine coexistence.

IDEOLOGICAL ANALYSIS

If Sputnik I demonstrated that there is only one world, and if the schooling development of the world of pupils should be oriented to promote the kinds of persons capable of overcoming societal difficulties, then "ability grouping" runs counter to what the main schooling intent should be: the development of a worldwide common curriculum so that all children and youth can come to dwell in a common world. As children are forced to grow up immorally prior to the institutionalization of common schooling that is genuinely public and universal, so too is the implication on a more specific problem *within* a school the institutionalization of the other conditions promotive of a common world, and so are children forced to grow up inauthentically where instruction is organized in a way wherein schooling is not genuinely public and universal. That children can come to "accept" and "adjust" to "ability grouping" if it is introduced early enough is not the mitigating but the damning factor. It is precisely where tragedy lies, because this is nothing other than becoming adapted to a world that is too safe for the explorations of some pupils, and hence men, and not safe enough for the explorations of other pupils, and hence men; and the inauthentic modes of coexistence "learned" at the schooling level will be projected on a larger scale at the societal, planetary, and cosmological levels to the point where the Almighty himself, no less, is on "our" side.

To be either too much or not enough at home in the world because of a "realistic" acceptance of "ability grouping" in school when it is begun early enough, on the one hand, insures that the crisis of practical experience will not be survived and young adulthood entered through an adequate assessment of adolescent ideals, and, on the other hand, manifests itself in ways of existing characterized by arrogance and shame or "master" and "slave" mentalities, both characteristic of inauthentic coexistence, both constituted by having one's being for others.

In his criticism of "American culturalism," i.e., of the prevalence in the United States to accept the *theory* of sociology and cultural anthropology as definitive truth, Sartre suggested that its mechanistic approach treated societal roles as essentially things of the past. The way "roles" and "role expectations" were held to be *causes* of "behavior" removed from them the temporality of a living perspective, but freedom is restored if "society" is considered as being presented to each person as a perspective of the future. Rather than "role expectations," then, what appears within a person's horizons are his possibilities in "society." The societal possibilities visible to him are his possibilities.[1] His statement seems to be of particular value transformed into the educational development of the perspectives of children and youth through schooling: To understand a society it is necessary to study the structures of the future that are presented to children and youth in schooling. How are the structures of the future, the societal possibilities, presented to children and youth in schools that are structured by "ability grouping"? How are they presented to children and youth within their temporalizing?

As each person is his future by being his future possibilities, he is at the same time his societal possibilities, for who he can become is not contained within himself but is rather who he can be in realizing possibilities in the world in and among other people, i.e., in "society." As each person is "defined" by his societal possibilities (or societal destination), so too is he defined negatively by the societal possibilities that are generally available but not available to himself in particular: he is defined negatively by each societal possibility that is impossible for him. For the underprivileged, each societal enrichment is one more impoverishment when it is seen to be a possibility that is impossible.[2] Then each schooling possibility that is added for only some of the children or youth becomes another impossible for others, becomes another impoverishment, because it increases the number of routes forward that are not attainable. It increases the number of doors marked "No Admittance," thereby negatively defining the schooling "have nots." Whether people in "slow" or "average" groups are college-bound or college material or not, "ability grouping" cuts off their future by institutionally defining it negatively. That it is done institutionally appears to the pupil as being done legally because schooling regulations have the force of law upon his being. The institutionalization of "ability grouping" is necessarily premature because it murders hope, thereby essentially murdering children and youth insofar as it destroys their possibilities of being.[3] Separate facilities, even in the same building, are once again inherently unequal.

"Homogeneous" groupings provide segregated schooling that is necessarily unequal; the ontic properties upon which it can be based are as irrelevant to schooling as the ontic properties of skin color or hair texture if schooling has to do with opening up future possibilities of being to children and youth, which it does if it is public and universal and which it must do if it is compulsory. It is very difficult to understand it as doing anything else. If this be so, then the institutional elevation or denigration of some people on ontic differences is inherently immoral because it alienates other pupils from their future possibilities, i.e., from themselves, insofar as it murders hope, as well as alienating them from each other in their major institutional deliverance to the broader society. This conclusion respecting the item of policy that is being used for illustrative purposes, that "ability grouping" militates against the authentic coexistence in society that is demanded by the post-Sputnik crisis, is phrased in the terms of the 1954 Brown Case respecting school desegregation intentionally and prophetically: sooner or later "ability grouping" will be declared unconstitutional because it is a policy that is in opposition to the being of the public school as public.

In light of the preceding, there is no explanation for the existence of "ability grouping" in any school or system other than to reinforce the dominant societal groups by "filtering off" or "co-opting" the "talent" from possibly dissenting groups for their own preservation as dominant groups through the selection process institutionalized within schooling (except for unawareness of the ramifications). This constitutes oppression of those not so selected, of those not deemed "acceptable": the parallel with the racial segregation issue indicates that just as there was oppression of an excluded group in the "separate but equal" principle, so too is there a similar oppression of the group that does not do well in school under "ability grouping," although it may be less visible because it is not a black and white matter. To define other people negatively by defining their impossibles for them under the guise of disclosing their genuine possibilities is oppression. Any other term would be descriptively inadequate, and where there is oppression there is the arrogance/shame or master/slave mentalities characteristic of inauthentic coexistence.

A few factual considerations help. The trend since Sputnik I has been a return to traditionalism: renewed emphasis upon college preparation and the equation of that with education, acceleration, enrichment, "ability grouping," the return to "standards" and "hard" subjects in the suburban curriculums, as well as "team" teaching, programmed and computer-assisted instruction, and educational television. These "innovations" tend to equate "educating" with the transmission of factual, informational knowledge and "education" with the mental acquisition of this kind of material, and all belong together as part of a Thermodorean reaction to progressive education in an "authoritarian backlash." Against this, students themselves lash back in favor of forms of progressive education with the cry of "Relevance!" The recipients of these "advances," of these "conservative innovations," however, had not reached the labor market by the time of Apollo 11. It is now clear that it was no shortage of trained personnel and hence no fault of the schools that Sputnik I was Soviet rather than American. There will continue to be major difficulties abroad in the world that are *not* caused by any shortage of trained scientists and technologists, and there is far less assurance that solutions to major problems of the planet are to be found simply through having greater supplies of trained personnel available. The truth can be stated more strongly: Apollo 11 succeeded through the efforts of people who acquired their public schooling before any of the "conservative innovations" began to have widespread effect. They would have had to have graduated from high school before the institutionalization of the "new" curriculums in order to get through college with a bachelor's degree to participate in the Apollo program at all. It is correct to infer, then, that the excellence of the public schools before the scapegoating criticisms of the post-Sputnik era occurred is now established beyond a doubt by the success of the Apollo missions and that the efficacy of the subsequent "innovations" remains wholly to be seen. In fact, the post-Sputnik controversy in education can now be seen to have been a tremendous *faux pas*, the tragic result of which may have been the loss of most of what was achieved in the improvement of schooling throughout this century. The schooling response to Sputnik I and what it was assumed to signify, in other words, has been out of proportion because it has been a response not to the societal crisis but to the demands of some, and only some, organized interest groups who collectively constitute a dominant or oppressing class in respect to schooling because their impact has in fact dominated and has in fact tended to negatively define children and youth in forgetfulness of their being. Because their impact has exploited the rest of the public insofar as it amounted to the utilization of public facilities for private interests, wherever there is "ability grouping," e.g., there too is oppression in the strictest Marxian sense—of the "proletariat" by the "bourgeoisie."

This use of "Marxian" *constructs* to come to grips with schooling policy in respect to reducing alienation requires further elucidation to avoid misunderstanding, particularly in view of the parallel with Marx's ethical concern for the alienation of the worker in modern industrial society. It is simply too generous to let the Marxists have Marx (it is already well known that Marx prided himself on not being a Marxist), for Marx invented, after all, neither the Industrial Revolution nor modern technology nor the way technology is used in modern society. It is no subscription to Marx's sociology, social philosophy, or metaphysic to say that sometimes his sociology of knowledge seems to be a valid explanation of events. Perhaps so in the case of "ability grouping." The previous critique, which owes more to Mannheim's sociology of knowledge and its technique of unmasking an ideology in an exhibition of Utopian thinking (in Mannheim's sense) than it owes to Marx, merely applies the criterion of the publicness of schooling to distinguish the policy alternative that requires an ideological justification from the adequate "Utopian" alternative. Policy is viewed from the vantage point of trying to resolve societal problems before the revolution occurs. If one begins with the phenomenon of worldwide, compulsory, free schooling and reflects upon the organization that permits of the educational development within schooling of the kinds of persons capable of resolving contemporary problems, one finds it is "heterogeneous" grouping. Other items of policy could be examined in an analogous manner if it were decided that the basic educational and schooling issue raised by Sputnik I were in fact that of how to live together and that this problematic ought to guide policy decisions. All that need be done to escape ideological justification would be to keep the phenomenon of the publicness of schooling in mind.

This may be easier to imagine in the United States after the successful moon landing, for many people envisioned a unified world in the flush of victory after Apollo 11 and may have something of the necessary broadened vision. The difficulty with *that* unity, however, is its imposition upon the globe by one side of the great dichotomy at the expense of the other in the superficial blindness customarily associated with "Yankee imperialism." To have recognized the unity of the world in the Soviet successes of the first unmanned and first manned orbital flights would not have been narcissistic self-aggrandizement, for to have recognized the stature of that achievement would have been to recognize that "they" are somebody, too, and that "they" collectively as a nation want-to-be-some-one-themselves. Perhaps a full understanding of the publicness of schooling, however, would require its prior institutionalization in a common curriculum because of the difficulty of transcending ideological justifications and because of the difficulty of transcending one's own alienation as a child. It may not be possible to transcend a Marxian sociology of knowledge until there is a common curriculum and a common world. This is what Marx would have said. That it requires revolution to achieve a common world is open to disproof through the adoption of schooling policy that is not designed to exploit other people's children, i.e., through taking the significance of their being into account in policy decisions.

9

Educating
and the
Power of Being

Because the "conservative innovations" in schooling in the post-Sputnik decade were largely manifestations of the forgetfulness of being—because they were largely manifestations of the blind, technological mentality that calculates what it wants and then manipulates objects and people as if they were objects in order to obtain what it wants, instead of participating in the world to let the situation constitute itself as such and exert its demand in order to do what the situation demands and to rise to the occasion— because they were manifestations of the irrational pursuit of nonterminating, inauthentic passionate projects that exist the will to will in the oblivion of being—the imaginary "confrontation" with established societal power structures ended the consideration of schooling policy.

Within established societal power structures the relations between people are reducible to dominance/submission patterns, to commanding/ obeying relations, by definition of what "power structures" are. Where there is not at bottom a commanding/obeying relation there is no element of a power structure. Within societal power structures, however, man's power over man is consolidated and objectified, and it can be investigated as a thing theoretically and artificially separated from the people involved. As such, the interrelations are inauthentically human, but they are the means whereby aggregates of people become organized and capable of collective (but not corporate) decision and action. If the latter are as necessary as they seem to be, then there can be little quarrel with the political institutionalization of man's power over man and the resulting commanding/obeying relations within some kind of organized power structure. Insofar as the one treats the other as his object within commanding/ obeying, these relations are reducible to the coercive use of power, i.e., to force.[1] Force is violent power. Because educating requires room for disobedience to be grounded in the being of the pupil and for there to be genuine obedience, there is no room for the violence of societal power structures in the form of some kind of commanding/obeying within the pedagogic relation. The pedagogic relation brackets out any form of commanding/obeying in order to come into being. It may be necessary for the existence, for the very being of society to have an established power structure, with its inherently violent power in all the variety of commanding/obeying relations that obtain, because the corrective use of force may be necessary to curb men's passions, men's passions being what they are, but the kind of relations between men thereby established can extend only to schooling and general policy, whose being may in fact be inextricably involved with societal power structures. It can extend only to one half of the pedagogic paradox or the paradox itself is eliminated, which eliminates as well schooling in any significant sense. If it extends to the other half, to educating within the pedagogic relation, it destroys the relation by prohibiting the transformation of political power into the power of being. Political power is used to establish schools in order to make the corrective use of force that is sometimes necessary in adult society no longer necessary. It becomes unnecessary when the rising generation has been educated to citizenship in the broad sense. To educate to citizenship is the reason political power establishes schools. This transformation of violent power into the nonviolent power that belongs to the authority that can educate to freedom, this transformation of political power into the power of being, cannot come about if the forms of power that may be appropriate to the societal realm find their way into the pedagogic relation.

THE DEFICIENT
PEDAGOGIC RELATION

When various forms of commanding/obeying or coercive force enter the pedagogic relation, they transform the teacher/pupil relation into a dominance/submission relation in which it is never clear as to who is dominating whom, or why. On the surface, the teacher dominates the pupil through orders, approval and disapproval, loud talking, sheer physical size, commanding presence, and so on, but underneath all this the pupil submits unwillingly, when he chooses, and under the conditions he chooses. He will keep on whispering to his friend, for example, until the teacher raises her voice to the level at which he will stop. He thereby determines the conduct of the teacher, to a considêrable extent dominating her by deciding what conduct will be required in order to obtain his "submission."

When various forms of commanding/obeying enter the pedagogic relation, they transform it into a relation within which both parties have their being for the other in the unstable transcending-transcendence/transcended-transcendence reciprocating conflict of having their being for the other. Because human existence is open to the world, transcending to the world, because human existence is this transcendence that lies underneath the intentionality of being conscious of entities within the world, the human reality of another person cannot be made into an object by and for "my" consciousness. In my transcendence to the world I can, however, attempt to transcend another person's transcendence to the world by becoming conscious of him in the same manner in which I become conscious of nonhuman objects: I can attempt to transcend the other's transcendence, to be a transcending-transcendence in respect to another person.[2] Since he is not an object, however, this project to make him an object of my consciousness fails and I cannot dominate the other in an enduring way, for he can always attempt to transcend my transcendence, which, when I accept his evaluation of myself, changes my transcendence to the world into a transcended-transcendence. This attempt to become the object for another's project of conscious being, however, also fails because I am not an object and still have my being to be: it is in bad faith that I can attempt to be the object of another's consciousness because I have to freely sustain this project of "being an object," and the project is fated to failure.

When commanding/obeying enters the pedagogic relation, then, the teacher assumes as the mode of existing toward the pupils that of being a transcending-transcendence, which throws the pupil into being a transcended-transcendence insofar as the teacher's project is successful. As a transcended-transcendence, however, he is no longer transcending to the world that he should be exploring to necessitate the pedagogic relation. Insofar as the teacher's project is unsuccessful, i.e., insofar as the pupil refuses to be an object of her treatment by refusing to assume the project of being a transcended-transcendence, he is thrown into the project of being a transcending-transcendence toward the teacher because the failure to execute a command can be no indifferent matter. Thus the intrusion of any form of commanding/obeying into the pedagogic relation, i.e., the general constitution of the teacher/pupil relation that relies upon the teacher's dominance, puts the pedagogic relation into the conflict of being for others—teachers and pupils pursue the goals that develop in the efforts to transcend each other or in the efforts to become the object for the other's consciousness. There is no "moralistic" objection to be made: it is merely that consciousness cannot be conscious of things in the world while it is involved in the conflict of having its being for others in either the transcending-transcendence or the transcended-transcendence pole. The objection is not that one can never tell who is dominating whom, although each project shifts to the other as it fails to resolve the conflict and who dominates whom is never completely clear, although individuals might choose as their fundamental project to be either the master or the slave—the objection is that the consciousness that is entrapped in having its being for others in dominance/submission patterns is alienated from others, from itself, and from the world, all three alienations occurring equiprimordially. Within these alienations there is little room for the authenticity of the teacher's speech, for the pupil's explorations of the world, for his wanting-to-be-someone himself, and for educating as the matter of helping the pupil to be independently: there is little room for schooling to be grounded in the pupil's project of being, to be educative.

THE ALIENATION
OF COMMANDING/OBEYING

Whatever form commanding/obeying takes in teaching, its very use indicates the prior existence of these alienations. Commanding/obeying is to be found within the practices of taking attendance; giving surprise quizzes to "keep them on their toes"; in the use of reward and punishment (or "positive and negative reinforcement"); the administering of examinations, when these become a threatening or mandatory rather than a challenging experience; the use of "peer group" pressure to promote desired conformity of conduct or belief; the use of propaganda, rhetoric, oratory, and eloquence to gain conformity of belief; and scoldings, beratings, sarcasm, and so on, including explicit verbal commands. Whatever its form, its very use indicates that within the teacher's point of view the people who are there in class having their being as pupils are already alienated from the work of the classroom, from the person who is having her being as a teacher, or from the school itself. Insofar as the use of some form of commanding is justifiable within the educational philosophy of the teacher, i.e., insofar as a particular instance occurs wherein the use of some form of commanding is justified (albeit erroneously) by the operative educational philosophy, its very use indicates that the pupil involved finds himself there only through some externally compelling, coercive, and inauthentic reason. Further moves on the part of the teacher involving coercive force of any kind, however subtle and subdued and however justified by some ideology of power, increase the alienation of the pupil.

The use of commanding within the pedagogical relation aggravates that which it intends to cure because it appears to give symptomatic relief but it increases the cause of the malaise. Increasing the pressure of a dominance-submission relation increases the alienation of the "inferior." Ontologically, the reciprocating the polar conflict becomes the more involuted and inescapable the more the transcending-transcendence attempts to transcend the other, for the more he does this, the more the other has to struggle to be someone himself and the more alienating is the final capitulation to becoming a transcended-transcendence or the final overt rebellion. The use of commanding tactics on the part of the teacher to cope with manifestations of alienation from the pedagogic relation increases the extent and depth of the pupil's having his being for others, which increases his alienation from the world, which makes him more inauthentically there in the classroom, i.e., more alienated from himself and from the work of the classroom and from the teacher. The use of any form of commanding does not clarify why he is there and enable his consciousness of his situation to be more lucid and responsible, but rather increases his mystification and alienation from wanting-to-be-someone-himself as it promotes the illusion that the reasons of other people are his own—as he, through inauthentic obedience, obeyingly submits to the commanding and allows himself to become the teacher's object, he loses sight of his own destination and begins to accept the reasons of other people for his conduct as if they were his own; and he is not helped in establishing his own reasons for being there based upon the authentic possibilities of the classroom.

As it happens, however, the person who is having his being as a pupil, in each and every case, even in compulsory schooling, is in class precisely because he wants to be there, precisely because of his own perfectly gratuitous choice to be there. Exactly like everyone else, he is where he wants to be, all things considered. His problems then center in living up to his condition as a student fully, of living in harmony with previous choices and their consequences, of being there in full lucidity of his condition as a student as a consequence of an existential choice to be there, of being there with his whole being. Because he is lacking awareness of the consequences of a previous choice to be there or lacks the courage to be, no form of commanding can help him, because no form clarifies his situation for him, but rather increases his situationlessness in its pushing him away from the world into having his being for others in its displacing with the project of the teacher his own spatializing and temporalizing from his own origin to the world.

That the student's alienation from the pedagogic relation is related to his not living up to his condition as a student has to be carefully understood. On the one hand, his "condition as a student" is the result of his own previous choice to be there, although the consequences of the alternatives may appear to him to be so overwhelming as to remove the actual choice, but this can happen only when some other choices make the alternatives overwhelming. Parental, vocational, or societal pressures may make it seem no choice at all to attend school, but these can be overwhelming only on the basis of a previous choice to obey the parents or to live in a certain way. On the other hand, so too is the person who is having her being as a teacher there of her own free and gratuitous choice, all things considered. Either the pupil or the teacher could have committed suicide last Saturday but they did not; because they did not they are in class *together* of their own free choices to be there, all things considered. It is part of the pedagogic task on the part of the person who is there as a teacher to be clear as to why she is there, part of which is to help the pupil become clear why *he* is there. The teacher, too, however, may be there for inauthentic reasons, for reasons stemming from having her being for others rather than for herself, rather than simply to be as a teacher. No use of the coercive force of some form of commanding, of so-called power, will assist her in her own clarification of why she is there, but will further alienate her from herself and her authentic possibilities as a teacher, i.e., from the authentic possibilities of teaching, because it will further alienate her from the pupil's own possibilities of being. The attempt to displace the pupil's possibilities of being with her own alienates the pupil from himself, and, here as elsewhere, the more the alienation of the other is demanded, the more one alienates himself. If the pupil is his future, if he has his being in his possibilities of being, and if these possibilities of being extend outward to the world and forward to the future only insofar as he can spatialize and temporalize from his own origin; and if he has his own being to be, i.e., if he has to bring his own possibilities into existence by projecting into them in order to be; and if he has to accept responsibility for this projecting into these possibilities in order to be independently, in order to maintain his transcendence to the world in his project of being—then all attempts to coerce him into the pedagogic relation essentially estrange him from his own possibilities of being, from his project of being, from himself and from others, including the teacher. At the same time, they alienate the teacher from the pupil because within them the pupil can no longer be seen in his projecting toward his future— in his being. Because the freedom of the pupil is not recognized within the use of any form of what is ordinarily called power, the pupil as a human being is not recognized: What is the significance of the being of children and youth? Because the teacher can no longer see the pupil as who he essentially is, as himself, within any form of commanding, the intrusion of this mode of power into the teacher–pupil relation is precisely an avoidance and destruction of the authentically human pedagogic relation as an encounter between two people, one of whom is charged with helping the other liberate himself for his own possibilities of being. It is precisely opposed to what can bring the pupil back into a pedagogic relation with the teacher because it encourages him to submit to domination when he should be striving to be independently, for the necessary presupposition of educating is the pupil's wanting-to-be-someone-himself. His wanting-to-be-someone-himself, it must be recalled, is the condition necessary for the exploration of the world, which is the necessary condition for needing help, for the constitutive attribution of pedagogic authority, and for the attainment of the end of educating in the independently functioning adult.

The intrusion of various forms of commanding/obeying into the pedagogic relation, in other words, at its best is an attempt to relieve the manifestations of the pupil's alienation from the teacher, and could be allowed only by people who are inauthentically there as teachers, who are alienated from the pupil in their alienation from their own being as teachers. No use of this so-called power, however, can relieve the teacher's anxiety over the fact that the "symptoms" of the pupil's alienation from the pedagogic relation put her own being as a teacher in question in its being, over the fact that the pupil's refusal of her offered help is a venture in his very being that challenges the teacher in her very being as a teacher. These refusals place the teacher's power of being as a teacher on trial. The power of being, however, depends upon the amount of nonbeing that can be tolerated and accommodated.[3] The use of any form of commanding, what is ordinarily called power, i.e., power in the sociological or political sense, is a manifestation of the lack of the power of being. It is a sign of weakness, of the absence of the power of being, for its presence betrays the incapacity to accommodate the threat of nonbeing that the pupil's venturings away from the teacher bring to her. Its use cannot restore the pedagogic relation in which the one helps the other to become a person in his own right, because it encourages the pupil to hide behind appearances in his seeming to be whatever or whoever will pacify this arrogant use of violent power. It has the effect of making it difficult for the pupil to be able to accommodate the threat of nonbeing, and he resorts to a self-concealment that is not so cowardly as it is lacking courage.

In seeming to be other than who he is in order to pacify "power," the pupil's consciousness becomes structured within having his being for others in a surface mode of transcended-transcendence, but this repression of his own being is undergirded by a project of transcending-transcendence: the student uses the teacher as an object in his own grade-getting. More important, however, his actions lose the quality of action and become gestures that no longer disclose his world: his speech becomes free-floating even when it is the correct words, for he says the words that suffice to pacify the "power" and that constitute the phenomenon of being for others, and he says them regardless of whether or not he understands them in a grounded way, whether or not they disclose anything to him. In this gesturing his words manifest a geography not rooted in landscape, as they become a means to achieve his own preconceived ends that are kept concealed, perhaps even from himself. They disclose neither who he is, his situation, his world, nor what he has learned; neither to the teacher nor to himself. He has no authentic learnings because his words become his own retaliatory use of force against the teacher, however concealed, subdued, and academic this force may be. This use of force, however, is an essential powerlessness, for it is generated not by the power of being but by the threat of nonbeing, analogously to the way the teacher's use of commanding is generated.

More significant, the gesturing that is used to pacify power does not allow for the emergence of the power of being that arises between people when they are able to create a space for their appearance by disclosing who they really are.[4] Without this disclosure, there is no disclosure of world, no worlding of the world. When any form of commanding/obeying enters the pedagogic relation, then, the power of being cannot arise within it. It cannot arise because the teacher does not rely upon the power of being to establish a genuinely pedagogic relation in which the worlding of the world can occur.

THE EDUCATING ENCOUNTER

Within the pupil's conscious experience, authentic learnings do not happen to him but to his world. As he explores the world, dark areas become lightened as the possibilities therein become dis-closed. The opening up of possibilities occurs in the child's explorations of things as toys and in his concomitant learning of "language," for as he learns the names of things, he learns what they are because this naming unconceals the thing named, causing it to shine forth as the thing named. It causes it to come into being for the child. What is learned are the possibilities of the thing, or, rather, some of the possibilities of its being, and this learning occurs on the face of the thing in the child's world, not primarily inside of him as if he were not a transcendence. With authentic learnings, the child's world becomes increasingly brighter, richer, more complex, and more fully articulated and interrelated, as his world becomes a referential totality as more and more possibilities are disclosed. As his exploration of the world gradually shifts from exploration of the physical world to the exploration of the intellectual-historical world as he moves into youth, the disclosure of things becomes more and more mediated by geography, to be sure, but nevertheless authentic learnings occur to his world as his world worlds itself, i.e., as the regions therein become opened and articulated in discourse and speech and as the latter bring the possibilities of being in those regions into being for him. When educating is grounded in the pupil's being, the possibilities disclosed belong both to the pupil and to his world simultaneously: he exists his world and his world exists him.

At the same time, however, the possibilities that are disclosed in educating belong to the teacher and to her world, for she also exists her world. Within the authentically human pedagogic encounter that is adequately founded on both the teacher's and pupil's transcendence to the world, i.e., within educating, when the teacher is speaking authentically and the coexistence that constitutes pedagogic authority is established, teacher and pupil both project into the possibilities disclosed in the aforementioned co-disclosure of possibilities of being. In this projecting into them, the possibilities are brought into the teacher's being and into the pupil's simultaneously. Since their being remains in the world, however, this bringing them into their being simply brings them into being in a primordial worlding of the world. The co-disclosure of possibilities of being that occurs in educating brings the possibilities of the world into being by clearing a place for their appearance. The co-disclosure lets the possibilities of being be, thereby allowing the world to world itself. This means that in educating, being clears a space for itself. If educating action allows being to clear a space for itself by disclosing possibilities of being, this signifies that educating allows being to be. But who or what could let being be except the power of being? What lets the power of being emerge within the pedagogic encounter?

Educating action brings the possibilities of the world into being through mutual participation in their disclosure. By projecting into them, in being conscious of them, teacher and pupil become those possibilities. Educating action thus brings the possibilities of later action into being, into awareness, for the pupil at the same time that they are brought back into the teacher's being in her renewed awareness of them, which remembrance occurs with her projection into them in authentic disclosure. Educating action can occur, however, only when the pupil understands, at least implicitly, that he requires help in the disclosure of the possibilities of the world, for only then can he project into the disclosure with his whole being and actually bring it into being for himself, and only then is he able to coexist with the teacher in the possibilities opened up. On the other hand, educating action can occur only when the teacher understands that it is required of her to help the pupil explore the world, for only then is she able to project into the disclosure with her whole being and to coexist with the pupil therein. This coexistence, that is, occurs only when both the teacher and the pupil are authentically there in the classroom, i.e., only when they are aware of their gratuitous choices to be there within the teacher–pupil relation, and are living up to the conditions of those choices by being authentically as a teacher and being authentically as a pupil. This occurs only when the person teaching understands that her being as a teacher is in question in its being, for the pupil can always turn away from her. On the other hand, it occurs only when the pupil understands that *his* being is in question in its being, for otherwise he would not be there as a student. It can happen, in other words, when the participants do not succumb to the "role" of being a teacher or being a student as if they were not their own futurizings that are in question in their being. This is none other than when they are living in accordance with the conditions of human existence in general, however; for it belongs to human being to be in question in its being. Because of temporality, because of tomorrow, one never knows who he is and who he can become in the situations in which he will find himself: his being is in question in its being. This means that the coexistence of co-disclosure occurs when the people who are having their being as teachers and pupils simply are who they are.

To avoid reifying the person who has his being as a student or the "subject matter" or the "language" through which educating occurs, and to avoid an analytic reduction of the phenomenon to something else, the only way to describe the coexistence that occurs in educating in the pedagogic encounter is to designate it as the co-disclosure of possibilities of being. The "language" of the classroom that serves as a "medium" of the interhuman is not a self-subsisting entity, and cannot be considered as such without omitting the being of the speaker and the listeners. The "language," so to speak, places both the speaker and the hearers into the situation "referred to" by the words spoken in the locus of their "referents," i.e., in the possibilities of being in the world, when there is a genuine co-disclosure: "It is only language that affords the very possibility of standing in the openness of the existent. Only where there is language is there world."[5] The nonreductive and nonobjectifying way of saying that both teacher and pupil have the same "referents" for the teacher's "words," which must obtain for there to be authentic learning, is to say that they coexist in projecting into possibilities in the world that are speakingly disclosed, or that educating is the co-disclosure of possibilities of being. This co-disclosure of existential possibilities grounds educating in the world, and thus in being.

When the teacher speaks authentically with the pupil, the world is created anew each moment. Its horizons are under constant co-creation by both teacher and pupil: the world worlds itself. In inauthentic speech the talk goes into mid-air, not quite understood, as a dead "language" that is an intrusion of the past into the present that covers over the present, and is not revelatory of the world because it becomes thickened and substantialized, to be learned as a "symbol system" separated from the referential totality to which it belongs, to be memorized because it conceals more than it unconceals. Without being, it lacks truth. When the teacher speaks inauthentically, every word ordered ahead of time, the pupil remains aloof, a spectator of what the teacher is saying; but authentically pedagogic speech, like any genuine speaking, transcends the present by plunging into the future that is so close that it hardly seems to require the plunge, but does if one is to futurize into it and bring it into being. The spoken "sentence" is a sally into the future, requiring not a little courage, because it is a futurizing leap into what does not yet exist, into a nothingness that contains the possibilities of being that can be brought into being by completing the sentence in their way and that guide the development of the sentence even from their locus in nonbeing, and in this transcending of the present in futuring, authentically pedagogic speech makes the present moment luminous through lighting it with the possibilities disclosed presently. When the present moment becomes luminously present, when teacher and pupil coexist in the possibilities therein co-disclosed, when possibilities of being are brought into being in the pedagogic clearing of the space for their appearance, then the teacher has authoritativeness because the disclosures are accepted as disclosures because they are revealed as such. In the truth of being, truth has being. Then there is no need for the use of violent power because the pedagogic encounter within which the power of being arises has established itself.

The power of being, authentically human and nonviolent power, forms itself within the pedagogic relation in the luminous present as the teacher reveals possibilities of being,[6] i.e., as possibilities of being prompt their revelation by addressing the teacher, much as alternative ways of completing the half-spoken sentence present themselves to be chosen and spoken, i.e., to be brought into being by being spoken. The power of being does not come from the teacher but from the possibilities of being that address her and demand their realization by her.[7] Her power, the power that apparently is generated by her and that permits her to be together with the pupil, that permits the teacher and pupil to be authentically there together, does not come from the teacher's own being as if this were cut off from the world but comes from the world and the possibilities disclosed, from the possibilities of being that are disclosing themselves to her as she says the words that reveal them to the pupil.[8] The power of being comes from the possibilities of being that lie dormant in the teacher's world, from the possibilities as they are disclosed in her "words" as openings into the world or region thereof that the pupil was searching for. Her power comes from the opening into being that is simultaneously an opening out of being into the disclosing speaking to each other that constitutes the shining presencing of the pedagogic encounter.

Viewed anthropocentrically, the co-disclosures are openings that are generated from the teacher extending to the world; they are openings into being. Viewed non-anthropocentrically to include the initiation of the disclosures by the possibilities of the world, they are the worlding of the world. Viewed ontologically to include the initiation by being, they are the opening out of being into the pedagogic relation. This opening out of being is the work of being clearing a place for its own appearance; it is the being of being. The being of being depends upon the power of being to be.

The power of being forms itself within the pedagogic encounter, then, insofar as it is genuine possibilities of being that are disclosed: insofar as the teacher lets being be. A nonviolent and authentically human power emerges to govern the pedagogic relation when there are genuine disclosures: When the teacher is in the truth of being, she is a guardian of being, and when she establishes the being of truth by means of the word, she establishes being. She can be a guardian of being only insofar as she lets being be her guardian and refuses to surrender her being to the anonymous power objectified in the schooling role of the teacher; i.e., when she has the courage to be, is able to disclose herself, and is someone herself. When being is her guardian, the power of being emerges within the pedagogic encounter, for being is the power of being.[9] This power, this being, enables the pupil to be someone himself. Increasing the possibilities of his being through educative disclosures increases his power of being; increasing his power of being enables him to let things and other people be through participation in their being. The more the pupil is able to let things be what they are and to let others be who they are, the more he is able to be someone himself and to be prepared to cope with societal difficulties (Chapter 3). The reliance upon the power of being by the teacher develops the pupil's power of being, which is the educative way of promoting authentic individual existence and authentic coexistence, of promoting the educative development of the kind of persons capable of alleviating current societal difficulties.

EDUCATING AND SCHOOLING

Reliance upon the power of being is the necessary presupposition of the pedagogic encounter, which is why forms of commanding are foreign to pedagogy. As the kinds of authority that are to be found in the community are not the models for the genuinely pedagogic authority, so too are the forms of power to be found within established societal power structures inappropriate models for the kind of power involved in founding educating and promoted by education. Whereas the philosophical attempt to take societal power into account in the consideration of the policy appropriate for schooling led to the final opposition to policy that contributes to the alienation of men and aggravates the societal crisis—which opposition could be categorized, no doubt, as a "liberal" protest—the attempt to take personal power into account in the educative process is neutral with respect to the dichotomy between liberal and conservative social and political philosophies.

This can be seen through a minor digression to ,a recent attempt to come to grips with education and power. The formulator of a widely known fourfold classification of educational theories according to their orientation in social and political philosophy (according to whether they were at bottom the concomitants of ultraconservative, conservative, liberal, or radical social philosophies), Theodore Brameld, recast his classification in terms of power in *Education as Power.* He presented four views of the relation of education and power: essentialism is the adoption by the schools of a program that is geared to supporting the nation's power struggles with other nations, particularly by preparing the academic elite for positions in the established power structure within the nation to assist that power structure in its external conflicts; his own reconstructionism is the adoption of the goal of building a unified world governed by the majority of the people of the whole planet; perennialism stresses the development of the power of reason and is traceable back to the Greeks and to Plato's "Knowledge is virtue"; and progressivism emphasizes the development of the power of intelligence through the solving of experienced problems.[10] It should first of all be noticed that the previous chapter is very compatible with Brameld's own reconstructionism: it employs the Utopian thinking (in Mannheim's sense) that Brameld also employs, i.e., it "unmasks" the ideology of social-political-economic interests through the counterbalance of a broader and more inclusive perspective, although it is not optimistic about achieving any Utopian goal, because the distance from here to there is unimaginably vast and the route not understandable. Because of this agreement with Brameld's orientation, it is not ideological to say that Brameld overlooked two basic distinctions, thereby oversimplifying his otherwise important attempt to confront the phenomena of power. He did not distinguish between schooling and educating, on the one hand, and between violent and nonviolent power, on the other. Employing these distinctions to reclassify the theories of his classification yields the following results. Essentialism and reconstructionism are the conservative and liberal positions concerning the power of schooling, concerning violent power. (In Brameld's classification they are philosophies of schooling.) Perennialism and progressivism are the conservative and liberal positions concerning the power of educating, concerning nonviolent power. (In Brameld's classification they are philosophies of educating.) Brameld's concern with developing the power of schools as a dominant societal institution implicated him in a conception of the essence of power not unlike that of essentialism, albeit on the opposing side of the societal problems involved, for it partakes of the violence of societal power struggles and would use forms of commanding/obeying within the teaching/learning relation that forget the significance of the being of children and youth, particularly in the mythologizing of the Utopian goal through the use of drama, symbol, and ritual that mystifies the pupil rather than liberating him for his own possibilities.[11]

The powers of reason and intelligence, on the other hand, are non-violent powers that should be developed in educating, according to the views, and there is no direct concern with schooling except that the advocates of the views wish to suggest most strongly that schooling ought to be educating. The difference between them is that of the two, the power of reason is more theoretical and contemplative because the individual is predominantly concerned with his own adjustment to society and the universe, whereas of the two the power of intelligence is more concerned with adopting the environment to one's own desires and values and with solving societal problems or with changing institutions so that social problems can be solved. The difference is between theoretical and practical reason (or between theoretical and practical intelligence), but both are intellectual and focus primarily upon the personal development of the student, upon educating, rather than upon the schools. Instead of engaging in phenomenological inquiry to determine whether reflective consciousness is more like classical conceptions of reason or more like pragmatic intelligence, suffice it to say that either or both are probably genuine possibilities of being that could be developed through educating (providing that both landscape and geography were retained). What matters for the present is that the existence of either or both depends upon, i.e., existentially presupposes, the nonviolent power of being. The nonviolent power of being is the necessary but not sufficient condition of the being of theoretical understanding and/or practical intelligence. A simple illustration will suffice. A violent person can neither reason nor act intelligently—he habitually substitutes commanding for reasoning and intelligent thinking because he remains within the conflict of being for others; the violent person lets neither things nor others be. He cannot think adequately (by either paradigm of the essence of thinking) when his prereflective consciousness projects his moods upon the landscape and then within this inauthenticity dominates the reflecting consciousness. Reason and intelligence, insofar as they have being, are ontic manifestations of the ontological power to be. The educational development of the power of being is therefore neutral to a preference for reason or intelligence, unless it is subsequently disclosed that one rather than the other is ontologically grounded in a more authentic province of meaning. Then insofar as the power of reason is individual and therefore conservative and the power of intelligence is social and therefore liberal, the neutrality of the power of being toward the conservative/liberal controversy is established: it is fully compatible with both authentic conservatism and authentic liberalism.

The ontological criterion for evaluating the adequacy of policy of the preceding chapter is also neutral to various social philosophies, because the latter are ontic matters. Because policy itself is a very ontic affair, the policy resulting from utilization of the criterion (ability grouping is eliminated because it is founded upon ontic, not ontological, differences) would support some societal groups rather than others and thus in effect be very non-neutral. It is true that perennialism says that education is everywhere the same, that essentialism advocates general education for all, and that both progressivism and reconstructionism advocate common schooling, i.e., it is true that the policy resulting from the application of the ontological criterion is compatible with all four educational theories and hence with all four places on the sociopolitical continuum. The ontological criterion in a very refined sense is neutral to the various social philosophies. Nevertheless Brameld is right when he indicates that the selection and training of the technological élites has in fact been advocated by those who wish to orient the schools behind established power structures such as the "military-industrial complex." The effect of the application of the ontological criterion of adequacy to policy in the present societal context would be to make the schools reconstructionistic: they would in effect take the societal lead in trying to reduce the alienation between men and of men from themselves. But this orientation is not due to the bias of the criterion so much as it is to the societal context and the social crisis and it concerns schooling as a whole; analogously, it may very well be that the development of the power of being in educating would in effect be not neutral toward various political philosophies.

If the effect of relying upon the nonviolent power of being to promote the pupil's power of being in educating is not neutral toward differing social and political value orientations, its effect would not be neutral to societal interest groups and established power. The fault and blame lies with the bias, arrogance, and lack of ontological grounding of these various partialities, however, insofar as they err in wishing to perpetuate the power structure as such through continuation of forms of commanding/obeying rather than wishing to educate for citizenship. The ontological fact remains that authentic individual existence (to advocate which would be conservative) and authentic coexistence (to advocate which would be liberal) are peculiarly combined within the pedagogic encounter that responds to the call of being. This encounter exists the pedagogic paradox: the genuine coexisting in the co-disclosings is the means whereby the individual pupil becomes someone himself. The genuine coexisting is the source of the teacher's authority and power and is the way whereby educating is simultaneously grounded in the being of the pupil and the being of the world. Equally paradoxically, in the co-disclosing the teacher lets the pupil be, but in this participation in the pupil's being the pupil becomes other than who he now is as the possibilities of being revealed to him become grounded in his being. As his being becomes grounded in the possibilities of the world he becomes less and less the "self" he already is and more and more the future "self" that he equiprimordially has yet to be. That this is not alienating depends upon the pupil's lack of coincidence with himself, upon the ontological fact that his being is having his being to be, upon his being what he is not and not being what he is. But this is to elucidate a paradox with more paradoxes. That it is not alienating (and also not Hegelianizing) depends upon a remarkably unnoticed feature of the peculiar combination of schooling and educating that exists the pedagogic paradox. Schooling is in its very being a continuous "process": it occurs within the public time regulated by clocks and calendars. The pedagogic encounter, i.e., educating, is in its very being a discontinuous "process." Schooling is continuous; educating is discontinuous. Within continuously occurring schooling and continuous and ongoing instructional patterns here and there, now with this pupil and then with that, occurs a genuine pedagogic encounter. Proximally and for the most part, the teacher-pupil relation has its being within schooling, within the inauthentic existing of the continuous, average, everydayness, but here and there authentic historicizing historicizes itself, genuine being emerges, and it is worth while.

To promote the development of the power of being through educating, then, it is necessary to clear the way for the establishment of the pedagogic encounter: it is necessary to lay the groundwork so that being can clear a space for itself within the teacher-pupil relation. The basis of this groundwork is the recognition that authentic individual existence and authentic coexistence, being-oneself and being-with-others, are equiprimordial. From the viewpoint of educating within the pedagogic paradox, they are co-primordial. For the teacher to recognize this co-primordiality of authentic individual being and authentic co-being with her whole being while she is in the teacher-pupil relation exists the pedagogic paradox. This recognition is the significance of the reliance upon the power of being to let the truth of being establish the being of truth.

10

The Call to Being

The significance of the being of children and youth for educating and the significance of educating for their being confront the teacher with the problem of relying upon the power of being to clear the way for the pedagogic encounter. The encounter establishes itself as the teacher-pupil relation becomes a place where being makes its appearance. The problematic for the teacher concerns ways to let being emerge within the relationship: how to let the being of the teacher, the being of the pupil, and the being of the world shine forth. These three elements of the encounter—pupil, world, teacher—indicate the three aspects of the founding of the authentic pedagogic relation: leading the pupil back to himself in a return to the origin of his being to restore his wanting-to-be-someone-himself so that he can be authentically there as a student; leading the pupil to an encounter with "subject matter" as disclosing regions of being as part of his explorations of the world that he might become more at home in the world; and leading the pupil to an encounter with the teacher herself as a person who is able to supply the help in disclosing the world that the pupil requires in his explorations of the world in the regions thereof constituted by so-called subject matter. These three aspects are not separate processes that occur chronologically in sequence that are only afterwards interrelated. They correspond to the three participants in the encounter—pupil, world, teacher—whose being has to emerge simultaneously to establish the being of the encounter.

In any encounter there has to be someone there to encounter. The pupil (or teacher) who has let himself fall into having his being for others, who has chosen the alternative of being a transcended-transcendence or a transcending-transcendence in relation to others, the pupil who has fallen into the anonymous role of being a pupil cannot enter into an encounter with the person teaching. He may, and probably will, be more capable of a surface sociability and cleverness, more capable of saying the nothings of formality and ceremonial talk, than the person who does not fall into the role of being a pupil, but this talk does not clear a space for his appearance because there is no one there to disclose unless he wants to be independently. Surrender to the anonymous power objectified in schooling as an institution by succumbing to the role of being a student (or teacher) causes the pupil (or teacher) to lose himself in exteriority: the center of consciousness moves out to the periphery, causing his being to be off-centered because an image of himself (a "self-concept") enters consciousness and divides attention. He then acts according to the image he would like to maintain, closing himself off from the situation and the possibilities of being concealed in it. No longer capable of a lucid awareness of the possibilities of the situation, the pupil then is not clear about his choice to be there because the projection to the world has been narcissistically deflected back into itself, guided by the image of being a pupil rather than by the possibilities, i.e., the values, of the situation, for these are perceived distortedly as through cracked sunglasses in terms of the inauthentic "self" that does not exist, that does not concretize its reality by realizing concrete and therefore authentic possibilities. Because he is inauthentically there, alienated from the world he should be exploring, he becomes guided by role expectations rather than by situational demands. To adopt the role of being a student, which is a project that is ontologically impossible for he can only be *as* a student by doing the things appropriate to studenting (i.e., by studying), causes him to pretend to be a student, to gesture. In this gesturing he pretends to pay attention, rather than really engaging himself in the matter on which the teacher speaks; he pretends to write papers, rather than putting down what there is to say, and so on, because nothing touches the pupil in the core of his being and so that core cannot leap forth into the work that belongs to him. In this nameless, meaningless gesturing everything done in school becomes academic in the pejorative sense and schooling becomes an elaborate game: abide by the rules, do what you are forced to do, fill in the blanks, and earn the diploma (or degree), even if nothing happens along the way, because "they" say it is important. Whatever is learned, no matter how highly intellectualized, remains free-floating, specious talk because of the pupil's alienation from the world and from himself as his futural project of being in the world. To lay the ground for the possibility of the pedagogic encounter and meaningful learning, the teacher has to lead the pupil back to himself so that he can recover his being and find the world safe enough to explore without having to pretend to be other than who he is.

As the pupil recovers responsibility for being who he is, he no longer equates the achievement of his own being with the fulfillment of the goals of schooling, he is enabled to be dissatisfied with any being he may have achieved, and he realizes he still has his being to be, still outstanding in the realization of further possibilities of being. Responding to the call of being throws him into the world exploringly and allows him to be authentically there *as* a student as he becomes aware that he requires help in his explorations. People who have their being as teachers are able to help the pupil's explorations not merely through co-disclosure of possibilities of being but also by eliminating blunderings into the inauthentic possibilities that the teacher and her teachers and their teachers have had to explore and eliminate as being inauthentic,[1] but their perspectives are available only to those pupils who ascribe authoritativeness to what she says, only to those pupils who want to be independently but who explore so intensively they become aware that they are not yet independently functioning adults and require help.

The first element—the pupil—is the most important to the work of educating, of course, and the restoration of the pupil to the truth of his being possesses pedagogic priority, for the pupil's wanting-to-be-someone-himself is the fundamental means of educating. If the pupil is alienated from the pedagogic relation, it is because he is first of all alienated from the world and his own authentic possibilities of being in it. Despite appearances to the contrary, he no longer wants to be independently, to be someone himself, to take up for himself his having to be, to assume responsibility for his own existence. He lacks the power of being. His power of being, the power to be in the truth of being, can be restored through the establishment of the safety of his world, but more than this is needed to pull the pupil into a relation with the teacher. Folklore wisdom suggests that a commanding firmness can create the requisite safety, for example, but the fault with all forms of commanding/obeying is that they further convince the pupil of his own powerlessness rather than establishing the condition that makes an encounter possible. Leading the pupil to the pedagogic encounter requires methods that reestablish not only the safety of his world but also his power of being, that enable him to have the courage to be someone himself in participation. Forms of commanding/obeying customarily used to "motivate" the pupil maintain schooling as the continuous process with its somniferous effect, but what is required to promote the occurrence of the encounter is precisely the opposite. The need is for a means whereby the pupil can be wakened from the semi-conscious state of inauthentic existence to the wide-awakeness of authentic existence. Schooling as an ongoing continuous process is a necessary presupposition administratively, but the continuity of the course of education and life is neither a necessary nor a tenable presupposition of educating. If the pedagogic paradox signifies that here and there within the continuous process of schooling this and that pupil now and then enters into the genuinely pedagogic relation with the teacher, then to prepare the way for the encounter and educating within the encounter the teacher has to employ means to assist in the wakening of the pupil. This passage from inauthentic to authentic existence, this passage from powerlessness to being, from not-being-obligated to being-obligated, from being-in-the-world to being-in-the-truth, is a true awakening.[2] The educative awakening is a conversion, more or less temporary, more or less permanent, of the pupil from a truthless state to one of the truth of being, and consequently to the being of truth. Among the means whereby the educative awakening can be promoted are the admonition, the provocation, the challenge, the summons, the request, the invitation, the beckoning, and the appeal. Of these, the admonition is paradigmatic.[3]

THE ADMONITION

The admonition has its inauthentic and authentic modes, depending upon whether it occurs within inauthentic or authentic solicitude. The inauthentic admonition can be designated *admonishment* or *exhortation*. These, primarily because of their futility, have no place in pedagogy. Ordinary pedagogic common sense recognizes their futility and characteristically, moralistically, and correctly opposes the use of moralistic admonishing and exhorting. They too readily serve as vehicles of projected blame, disguise poor teaching, signify a lack of patience in waiting for the pupil's growth, and actually hinder that growth by promoting the alienation of the pupil through the consequent rebellion, resistance, or pretended submission and repression of his own being. Utilized within continuous schooling to allegedly assist in the transmission of skills and knowledge in step-by-step instructional patterns, admonishment indicates an inadequate curriculum, lack of pedagogic planning, and/or the teacher's own inadequacy.[4] It manifests the teacher's lack of genuinely human solicitude, because its attempt to dominate the pupil occurs within the transcending-transcendence resolution of the conflict of being-for-others rather than within a qualified respect for the being of the pupil that wants to help him liberate himself for his own possibilities.[5]

The authentic admonition, on the other hand, is neither a manifestation of the teacher's vexation nor a technique to maintain the continuous process of schooling, because its intention is to lead the other person into the encounter and educating.[6] The structure of the genuine admonition can be most readily seen through contrast with more familiar devices. The use of reward and punishment (or praise and blame in the broad sense, to include all forms of "positive" and "negative" reinforcement) attempts to maintain schooling as a continuous process. First of all, it can "work" only on the validity of the presupposition that pupils do in general prefer praise and reward to blame and punishment. This assumption is obviously gratuitous in spite of its apparently truistic qualities. To be sure, "research" seems to indicate that "positive reinforcement" works better than "negative reinforcement," but it "works better" at maintaining schooling as a continuous process. That it works at all in promoting educating has not been shown, nor can it be shown. It is "beyond the testable" by definition: education does not occur extrinsically motivated. The extrinsic motivation of positive and negative reinforcement refers to things that have already been done, and in this major reference to the past they indicate to the pupil that he has already achieved being, or a small amount of being, as if he had to be told this and as if this were not accomplished in the performance of the task itself. They are unrelated if not oppositional to the pupil's accepting responsibility for his being, for his having his being to be. The admonition, on the other hand, is explicitly forward looking; it may be closer to blame than to praise because it does contain a slight rebuke, but this is only the result of its temporary focus upon the blameworthy past precisely in order to transcend the past through reorienting the pupil toward his own future. It is thus based upon the temporal structure of human being and this is its significance as a means of awakening the pupil.[7]

Reward and punishment, to the contrary, alienate the pupil from himself as his futural projection to his own destination from his own origin by diverting that projection into alien channels: they manipulate him to become whoever it is that other people want him to become. The donkey-carrot analogy is appropriate if understood nonemotively: if the donkey's eyes are on the carrot he cannot see where he is going and is apt to fall into the ditch the minute the reins are slackened, or if he gallops to avoid the whip he does not care where he is going and could run into the ditch for all he cares. The donkey, furthermore, stops when the carrot is gone or when the whipping stops because he was not going anywhere on his own. The use of reward and punishment, in other words, creates a splitting of the pupil's consciousness, i.e., a fragmentation of his being, whereas the educative process is precisely identical with achieving an increasing clarity over where in the world one is, where one is going, and the possibilities of where one might be going. When continuous instruction is supported by reward and punishment, the educative increasing lucidity of the possibilities of the world is prohibited because conduct and disclosure of world is deflected into the social fantasy system, which is thereby enlarged and intensified, contributing not a little to the alienation of people from themselves and from others that is found in present society.

The pervading meaninglessness of modern life that some commentators upon the societal scene seem to find is directly consequent upon the deflection of the pupil from his project of being into the situationlessness of the social fantasy system by the use of reward and punishment in pedagogy. It is consequent upon the elimination of the educative process in this, the most enlightened of all ages. The alleged meaninglessness is sometimes attributed to the catastrophic events of the century, but there have always been calamities. Once there has been a catastrophe, or once the conditions change so that a new kind of catastrophe is possible, it becomes part of the human situation, part of the limitations of the situations in which one has to find himself by finding what is possible within those situations. The possibility of the human race to commit racial suicide through nuclear holocaust may be a readily available excuse for one's own lack of the courage to be when ontological anxiety emerges, but this threat can be individually experienced authentically only as the threat of one's own death "at any moment." The immanence of death, however, has always been part of the human situation. It is difficult to see how the present peril makes life any more contingent than it has always been. Any meaninglessness attributable to the peril of nuclear holocaust, therefore, merely manifests a prior lack of lucidity over the possibilities of the situation, one of which is always one's own death. This threat, then, rather than contributing to the sense of powerlessness, can and should be the occasion for an authenticating conversion from the somnolence with which inauthentic everydayness is drugged, from the semi-consciousness of the social fantasy system wherein death is something that happens to other people. The events of the century, in and of themselves, are neither catastrophic nor noncatastrophic. They can only seem so to those people who found their own significance in the compulsive security of an impossible reward system and an impossible future; they can remove the significance of human existence, of future existence, for the people living into that future only if they are alienated from the world in pursuit of extravagant and inauthentic goals in an extreme lack of clarity over the difficulties of human existence at any time, only for people who expect too much from the world. This, of course, results from the lack of education for which schooling, training, and instruction have been generally substituted. This in turn is attributable to the pervasive use of reward and punishment, praise and blame, at the various levels of schooling, because this use constitutes a definitive program of alienation. It is a persistent encouragement of the pupil not only to let others decide for him what is important and what is unimportant but also to believe them. This in its turn is attributable to the general forgetfulness of being.

The educational task, however, is to take the being of the pupil into account by enabling him to say for himself what is important, to speak in his own voice, to determine for himself who he is, and to accept responsibility for his being and for his being there with others. That many people might say that the same things are important, or that adults already know what is important, does not nullify the fact that everyone has to be able to say this for himself and that education is the matter of finding out what to say in this regard. To find out for himself who he is able to be requires the room for disobedience that is prohibited by the form of commanding/obeying that occurs through reward and punishment, praise and blame. The admonition, on the other hand, always allows room for the pupil's disobedience.

In the admonition the teacher calls the pupil's attention to what was left undone and re-creates the possibility of completing it. This offers the pupil the opportunity to transcend his past and change the meaning of it for his present being and encourages him in his futural projection. Reward and punishment, on the other hand, call his attention to what was already done when he should be awakening to the next task already. The momentary calling attention to what was already done slips a nothingness between the pupil and his futuring, causes him to take the view of others toward himself, and deflects his transcendence from the world in this objectification. The admonition, however, pulls the pupil out of himself toward the future because it is not unlike an enhanced reminder. The ordinary reminder is calm, theoretical, and emotionally neutral. The admonition is more significant existentially because it is both a reminder and an incitation to action with the specific characteristic of summoning the pupil to his being there as a pupil. It summons him in his very being as a pupil by calling his attention to a neglect task belonging to schooling and by creating anew the opportunity to complete it. Reminding pertains to what was forgotten, whereas admonition pertains to what was neglected, with or without forgetting. That the admonition is directed to a neglected task rather than to a forgotten one enhances its reminding effect: it has to be directed to a task that has been neglected from the pupil's point of view, i.e., to which he bore some commitment to do but neglected. Without some degree of commitment, the task was ignored, forgotten, or simply not done; but the admonition is directed to a negligence, and this is what enables the pupil to transcend the past and catch up to himself that is important to the temporal structure of the admonition. It challenges the pupil to do what he was supposed to have done but has not done.[8]

Although it is directed to a particular neglected task, the admonition turns the pupil in his being toward his own possibilities by bringing him to recognize his being obligated to complete those things to which he has pledged himself. The specific sense of being obligated aroused by the obligatory situation implicates the state-of-being of being-obligated. The admonition returns him to himself when "successful." It enables him to have power over his own being in the existential recognition of being-obligated, and the power of being enables the being-obligated to turn him to the neglected task or lesson to complete it. Because the admonition is not an admonishment for not having done the neglected task, and because it is not an exhortation to complete it, because it is merely the reminder that receives its enhancement from the prior commitment of the pupil to doing what was neglected, the teacher ignores noticing whether or not the neglected task is subsequently completed. This allows room for "disobedience." In the authentic admonition she ignores the actual completion because she recognizes that that is none of her concern. The concern is to waken the pupil to responsibility for his own being, not to complete a task that is inconsequential to the pupil.

The teacher cannot become concerned with the actual completion of the neglected task without turning the admonition into something else, without falsifying it into a means for continuous schooling or corrupting it into an element of a "learning theory" as reward and punishment are. The point of the admonition is to waken the pupil to being-obligated after he has become alienated from himself; it concerns how and when and what can be done to waken the pupil to the existential imperative of having his being to be, of how to establish the power of being so that he can be in the truth of being; of how to help him liberate himself for his own possibilities without intrusiveness and without false dramatization. Whenever in the teacher's judgment there is a pupil who has neglected to do something that he knows he should have done, the admonition is in order, for then it can call him to himself and allow him to be in the truth of his own norms.[9] Because he might not authenticate his existence upon this occasion, and because the teacher capable of delivering a genuine admonition recognizes that her judgment can err, the completion of the task is ignored, room for disobedience remains, and the being of the pupil is recognized. If the intent were to get the lesson done, the apparent admonition would be ungenuine; it would be a reminder, a suggestion, a threat, or a command. The intent of the admonition, however, is to confront the pupil with the strongest moral authority that exists, with the demand of a moral authority that can require of him what he previously pledged: his self as his futural project of being. Because the admonition is used where there was a prior commitment to a task, it confronts the pupil with a call from his own wanting-to-have-a-conscience, and this call from his own futural possibilities is a morally requiring demand from his own authentic "self" that he has yet to be. The surface appearance of the admonition (its explicit content) is to get the pupil to redeem his pledge by accomplishing the task, but its real intent is to enable him to respond to the call to being as it may be disclosed through the objective demands of his situation. The particular lesson, task, or pledge is of no pedagogical significance; not so the response to the call of being. Not so the return of the power of being to be.

The admonition is able to call the pupil to be authentically there in the situation and to realize its and his possibilities because it is grounded in his being. Its foundation is ontological guilt: that guilt which is inherent in human being.[10] Ontological guilt is the primordial guilt resulting from having limitations but not having these limitations within one's power. The ontic forms of guilt—the psychological and the moral—are possible only on the basis of this more primordial guilt: reward and punishment, praise and blame, depend, when they are effective, upon the promptings of the superficially experienced guilt derived from being for others. They fail to tap the deepest source of guilt in a failure to reach the pupil in his very being. Their failure to reach to the heart of the pupil's being can result in his leaving the school, as in the German Youth Movement, because they can result in the pupil feeling ontically (morally and psychologically) innocent when he is accumulating ontological guilt for not being someone himself. They also result in his feeling ontically guilty when he is merely responding to the call of being, i.e., when ontologically innocent.

The foundation of ontological guilt lies in the fact that individual human existence is its own origin, its own basis, but this basis is given rather than chosen. All choices proceed from it, but the origin itself is a brute given. The ontic experience of this sheer givenness is the "existential moment" when one consciously understands something similar to "I am I and nobody else, and I did not ask to be born but here I am with no justification for being." It is the experience of the contingency of one's own existence. Ontologically, the basis from which all projection, all existing, all transcendence, occurs is not chosen. In existing from it, one exists the basis. Because the origin of all action is not chosen and is a pure nothingness that one has to be, human being is constantly lagging behind its possibilities. This existential lag constitutes ontological guilt.[11] The experience of psychological or moral guilt is founded (except when it is free-floating) upon the more primordial having-things-to-do-that-one-should-do and not-having-done-that-which-one-should-have-done, which are unitary structurations of human existence. Because human being is constantly running behind its own possibilities, it is constantly lapsing into the state of inauthentic existence, into not-being-obligated. The admonition is the means whereby the pupil recovers from this guilt, and as he recovers his being, the not-being-obligated shifts into a being-obligated, the pupil takes up his project of being in futuring from his origin, and the task is completed.

Because human existence is constantly running behind its possibilities, the child and youth keep neglecting things that they acknowledge they should do and have to be given an admonition again and again and again. They require the awakening of the admonition coming from outside because they keep lapsing into the immanence of inauthentic existence wherein they no longer want to be someone themselves. This phenomenon is not peculiar to the life-phases in which educating occurs, but it is peculiar to those life-phases that educating should occur. Because no one is able to develop to his possibilities by himself, the person who has his being as a pupil requires the admonition in order to catch up to himself by making up for his neglect.[12] The repeated awakenings of the admonition, prompted with indefatigible patience, help the pupil to become himself.

THE APPEAL

Although the pupil requires the admonition, again and again, to counteract the falling into the null basis that he is, to counteract the falling into everyday averageness, the admonition can by no means be considered to be a moralistic nagging. This can be seen through contrast with the appeal and the explicit command. The appeal also belongs within the pedagogic area, but it does not contain the slight rebuke for unrealized passed possibilities of the admonition: it is completely concerned with the future. Whereas the admonition can be considered as an enhanced reminder, the appeal resembles an enhanced request. The request is for something specific, however, whereas the pedagogic appeal is directed generally to whom the pupil can become, i.e., "All you have to do is take it one day at a time." To constitute itself as an appeal, it appeals to the pupil's "better self" in the face of some discouragement or overwhelming setback. When the pupil's wanting-to-be-someone-himself has been frustrated, the appeal is in order, for it can summon him out of superficial existence into his own possibilities.[13] Because the appeal is essentially to the pupil to want to be someone himself, it is a call to conscience. When he hears the call, it comes from his own future self. It is the call of being. The authentic response to the appeal, then, is not made to the teacher but again to a moral demand that comes from the authority existing within the pupil, to his own "conscience," i.e., to himself as his own future possibilities as they impinge backward upon his present being.[14] Authentic responses to both the admonition and appeal, then, occur outside of the conflict of being for others and thus fall within the conditions necessary for the establishment of the pedagogic encounter.

An appeal can and should be made by teachers in appropriate circumstances, but it does not belong within the pedagogic area proper because the pupil should not be exposed to the kind of existential frustration to which the appeal is appropriate and because the presupposition of the appeal is that the other person is completely free, but complete liberation belongs to being-adult and occurs only in the adequate reassessment of youthful values after the crisis of practical experience. As long as the pupil requires pedagogic help, he does not exist completely independently, is not completely free, yet the appeal as such is a relation between two completely liberated persons. In this sense it is opposed to the command, for the command presupposes that the other person is completely unfree. As such, it is foreign to the pedagogic area except for small children who "obey" without question, as a matter of course, because their conscious existence has not yet deepened to make the freedom of choice possible. The command is no longer pedagogic once the child's world has developed sufficiently to enable the transformation of the freedoms of caprice and conquest into the freedom of choice: by the time schooling begins the child can decide things for himself and then momentary obedience to commands is opposed to the main pedagogic intent of helping the pupil to become someone himself by helping him to become responsible for his own existence. As praise and blame are opposites, the command and the appeal are opposites. The command treats the other as completely unfree and is pedagogic for very small preschool children; the appeal treats the other as completely free and is "pedagogic" for post-school adults. The admonition lies midway between the command and appeal, both chronologically and existentially. It is definitive of the area of schooling and educating. Lying midway between the command and the appeal, the admonition is partly each. It differs from the command in its application to something the pupil knows he should have done and in its allowing "disobedience" as an open possibility. Commands force a response for or against, but the criterion of the authenticity of the solicitude within which the admonition occurs is lack of concern for completion of the negligence in letting the pupil choose to do it or not. In admonition his freedom is always recognized; not so in the command.[15] The admonition differs from the command in that it is partly an appeal. It differs from the appeal in its relativity to some particular negligence, e.g., "Haven't you done your book report yet?" Although it is partly an appeal, it is nevertheless spoken with the calm assurance that belongs to the command rather than with the humble hesitancy of the request, although it also contains the pleading openness of an appeal: "Haven't you done the book report yet?"

Again, from the perspective of the pupil the admonition is heard almost as strongly as a command because values that he has already chosen are implicated. It is also heard almost as gently as an appeal for the same reason. Because his wanting-to-be-someone-himself is also implicated, he becomes readied for the pedagogic encounter. If the particular negligence was at least partly due to a need for pedagogic assistance for which the pupil was unable to ask (he does not know how to get started on the book report), the availability of the teacher is manifested through the admonition. The words, "Haven't you done the book report yet?" spoken in the tone of voice that constitutes the admonition, contain in an unobtrusive way the unspoken question, "Do you want my help?" The perceived availability coincides with the emerging awareness of the need for help resulting from the more vigorous projection to the world consequent upon the restoral of the pupil's wanting-to-be-someone-himself. Thus the pedagogic encounter is prepared for. When the admonition is heard as an admonition, when the pupil takes up the neglected task because the values in the task address him and pull him into it, and when he then looks to the teacher for help in exploring the part of the world constituted by the task, the maximal focusing and heightening of conscious attention occurs.[16] Correlatively, the world is allowed to world itself and truth comes to being. Under these conditions the pupil encounters the task and the teacher; he learns with his whole being.

THE INTELLECTUAL ENCOUNTER

This awakening to authentic existence involves more than a superficial even if captivating interest.[17] A very intense and enthusiastic interest may in fact be a sign of the inauthentic existence that diverts its attention from its own being in despair over its own being, that never dwells anywhere but constantly flits from fad to fad. It may be a way of filling the existential vacuum that arises when one is in despair and unable to be someone himself. It may be compensation for the emptiness that develops when one is not able to be independently, that is, it may be a distraction to fill the time, and since "time" is one's life, such pastime may be "symptomatic" of the insignificance of one's own existence. That the encounter that may be aroused by the admonition involves one's whole being, on the contrary, indicates that what is encountered is met and grappled with on its own terms. It is experienced in its recalcitrant otherness as a completely other than oneself with which there is something to do, which places claims upon one's own being. What is encountered is experienced as an intellectual reality that places one's own prejudices, opinions, and beliefs in question, that places one's own present being in question, for compared to the intellectual reality encountered, one's own views count for nothing and the respect for the new possibilities disclosed compels an intellectual and existential struggle with them.[18] It is this struggle with one's whole being that creates the modification of one's whole being that effects a permanent change in one's being, i.e., that grounds education in the being of the pupil. This struggle is the historicizing, or worlding, of the world as it comes into being.

The variety of things that can be encountered is as numerous as the facets of the intellectual-historical world: intellectual and moral ideas (which are experienced as truths when encountered and subjectively appropriated), notable and great people of the past and present, works of art (such as poems and novels), authors, previous and present times and cultures (such as the Greek world), and so on.[19] The pupil in his being as a pupil is supposed to be exploring the intellectual-historical world in order to be able to exist authentically, i.e., to be independently as an adult struggling in and with his present generation and making his own mark in the social-historical world. The task of the teacher in general is to guide the encounter of the rising generation with the intellectual-historical world,[20] which is accomplished in particular by preparing the way for the encounter of particular students with particular intellectual ideas, etc. Insofar as the child has lived his childhood in a safe world and explored that world fully, he goes to school expectantly. He has heard some rumors about school from older children, but insofar as he has lived the preschool life-phase fully by adequate exploration of the physical world about him, he enters the school as part of his exploration of the world: he wants to explore whatever is done there, to do whatever is expected of him. He trusts his parents and will trust his teachers and whatever undertakings they plan, at least for the first week of the first year. As this attitude of expectation is maintained through an adequate grounding of education, the explorations develop into explorations of the regions of the intellectual-historical world constituted by subject matter. The pupil will commit himself to do those things that are relevant to his explorations. He will commit himself to the various tasks that arise as the teacher attempts to fulfill her responsibility to develop the pupil's world. Her task can be considered as arranging, rearranging, and rearranging again the materials of instruction in order to promote the educative encounter. This occurs within the daily routine of schooling, but it would involve a pedagogic subjectivism in the pejorative sense to confuse the continuous process that constitutes the *attempt* to get the pupil to have an educative encounter with the encounter itself. It is true that a reliance upon the encounter and discontinuous educating involves different learnings for different pupils, but there is no pedagogic subjectivism (in the pejorative sense) involved: alternative ways to ground knowledge in the individual's existence are not available. The continuous process of schooling deals with the common world and geography; the discontinuous encounter grounds this in landscape.

The ordinary, garden variety of schooling wherein the continuous process is assumed to be the normal course of education occurs within the theoretical bracketing of "objective knowledge," but this objective mood is a deficient state-of-being.[21] It is a bracketing that prohibits full wide-awakeness. Since all understanding occurs enveloped in some mood or state-of-being, the advocacy of the continuous process of schooling and disinterested learning creates a dominant mood of dullness. However appropriate this dull, disinterested mood may be for the theoretical understanding of the scientific researcher, the consequence for schooling is that the kind of learning occurring within it is as deficient as the encompassing mode of being. What is learned is learned superficially and is quickly forgotten. To want to promote this kind of continuous learning when one can predict it will be soon forgotten is pedagogic subjectivism in the pejorative sense.[22] It is pedagogically irresponsible because it neglects the being of the pupil. This subjectivism is avoided through maintaining the pedagogic paradox by continuously preparing the way for the discontinuous, unplanned encounter that grounds knowledge in individual being.

THE PROVOCATION
AND THE REQUEST

The encounter cannot be planned; it can merely be prepared for. Although the admonition is the principal means to promote it, the materials of instruction can be arranged to provoke, challenge, summon, invite, and beckon the pupil into an encounter with them. The teacher's talk can contain provocations, challenges, summonings, invitations, and beckonings, and insofar as these are based upon features of the world, they encourage the pupil's explorations and awaken him to authentic existence. If the provocation, for example, comes to the pupil not from the teacher but from the materials of instruction, it means that something in those materials differs somewhat from the pupil's present world in such a way to provoke him into resolving the incongruity through further exploration, e.g., going to an encyclopedia or other reference material. For a provocation to be a genuine provocation and promotive of the pedagogic encounter, it has to be received by the pupil as nonthreatening to his wanting-to-be-someone-himself, i.e., in a safe world, but as somewhat disturbing: it creates dissatisfaction with any being already achieved and creates an implicit awareness that he has further possibilities to explore, i.e., that he has his being to be. The challenge allows his wanting-to-be-independently to manifest itself through the experience of the freedom of conquest if he is allowed freedom to refuse and therefore to accept the challenge. The summons is a subtle challenge to his desire to be. Invitations and beckonings are but mild requests wherein the pupil's freedom is so sensitively respected that it is too obvious to point out that they, too, like the admonition, provocation, and challenge, let room for disobedience and thereby adequately take the being of the pupil into consideration. They are more like the request, however, because they are not necessarily world-centered. The admonition, etc., have to be world-centered to be constituted as such and to be a means whereby the inauthentic coexistence of being for others is avoided. The invitation and the beckoning, to the contrary, can also serve to prepare the way for the pedagogic encounter of the pupil with the teacher herself inasmuch as they lead him directly into authentic coexistence with the teacher similarly to the mode of being of the request.

As the admonition is the principal means to promote the encounter with "subject matter," the request is the most important means to promote the encounter of the pupil with the teacher herself. In this respect it is opposite to the command. When the pupil who wants to be independently hears a command, he is placed in a highly ambiguous situation. If he is already alienated from himself he can obey and not suffer further repression of his being, but only because he already lives a mechanistic existence. If he still wants to be someone himself, then in order to be independently he has to disobey, because he cannot experience the freedom of choice or the freedom of conquest through obeying. This leaves freedom of caprice and revolt as the only authentic actions and removes any possibility for genuine coexistence. The pupil remains in the pedagogic relation as an inferior, as a transcended-transcendence, or he leaves the relation to be someone himself. The request, on the other hand, presents the pupil with a situation in which he finds another person in need of *his* help. He is confronted by an obligatory situation, a situation in which a moral demand appears. If he fulfills the request, he is able to transform the freedoms of caprice, revolt, conquest, and choice into the exercise of moral freedom and still be someone himself, because it is his choice.[23] If he refuses, he still has become aware of the teacher as a person who addressed him as a person. In either case he has entered genuine coexistence with the teacher, which prepares the way for a genuinely pedagogic encounter with her. He has not only remained someone himself but has gained additional power of being someone in his own right. The problem is not which is most efficient in the short run. The efficiency of the command is overrated because the teacher does not know if insight occurs when a command is obeyed. Even in the short run, however, the request might be as efficient as the command, for it confronts the pupil with the obligatory situation, and if he trusts and respects the teacher, and if the use of the request is judicious, he will respond affirmatively.[24] If his consciousness is free from ulterior motives, which can be expected if the request itself is free of ulterior motives—which it will be if it is genuine—the affirmative response to the request establishes the reality of the coexistence that can be extended toward the pupil by the teacher. The request addresses the pupil as a person worthy of respect; the affirmative response makes this mutual. This mutuality of respect is genuine coexistence. With this, the pupil becomes open to encounter the teacher herself and to coexist in the co-disclosures of educating.

The various ways that have been indicated as promising for the clearing of the way for the establishment of the pedagogic encounter differ from the violent power to be found in all forms of commanding/obeying in the following ways. They confine themselves to different ways of awakening the pupil, enabling the teacher to encourage the pupil to be someone himself and to depend upon the power of being. They can arise within action without premeditation and its accompanying alienating manipulation, enabling the pupil to share in the teacher's power of being in direct participation. They invoke the nonviolent power of being, enabling authentic coexistence to be established in the classroom. They are future-oriented and thus based upon the structure of human temporality, i.e., upon human being, enabling the pupil to hear the call of being, to take up responsibility for his being, and to gain power over his existence. They help the pupil to emerge from the everydayness of schooling to educating by calling him back to himself, and thus constitute the significance of the being of children and youth for educating.

They are the meaning of the being of children and youth for educating because they acknowledge the hazardous character of educating. To rely upon the power of being and prepare the way for the encounter, the teacher has to allow room for disobedience so that the pupil is free to venture. If he is free to venture, he can explore the world in his project of being and educating can be grounded, but this makes educating hazardous for the teacher. If the being of children and youth is to be taken into account, this hazardous character of educating cannot be avoided as if shipwreck were not inherent in the being of man.[25] If education is to be safe for the pupil, however, it has to be hazardous for the teacher, for if the teacher makes it safe for herself, she does this through making it hazardous for the pupil, which halts his venturings and leaves pedagogy ungrounded in his project of being. This might be designated "education for the teacher's tragedy." Allowing the pupil the freedom to venture means that he is free to reject any and all teachings, to frustrate the pedagogic endeavor entirely.[26] He has this freedom at any rate, as any teacher only too well knows. The teacher has to recognize this possibility in order to be authentically there as a teacher with a full lucidity of the possibilities of the situation, to prepare the way for the encounter, to maintain her own status as a free being, to respect the pupil as a person, to maintain her dignity, the dignity of the pupil, and the dignity of the educating. She has to recognize it to fully accomplish the act of educating.

A restriction of the use of auxiliary devices to those that invoke the power of being (such as the admonition and request), that acknowledge the hazardous character of educating and maintain at its core one free being addressing another free being, not only takes the being of children and youth into account in educating and grounds educating. This confinement to methods that do not go out of the pedagogic relation also fulfills the teacher's responsibility for the development of the child's and youth's world and grounds their being in the world that they might be authentically there in the social-historical world as adults. Unlike the progressive education that also attempted to allow children and youth to live their present life-phase fully, the constant readying of the teacher for the encounter through the rearranging of instructional materials and through the use of the admonition, the provocation, and so on, recognizes that part of what living those phases fully signifies is a gradual situating of the individual in the historical context, so that he might enter into history and historicize in and with his generation. This is "education as preparation" after all, but in a recognition of the fact that it is in this world that one has to be free. It also fulfills the ontological function of the teacher, for it indicates how she can let pupils be through participation in their being, thereby recognizing the significance of educating for their being. It also indicates how teachers can let being be through participation in being, thereby establishing the significance of educating for being.

11

Traditional Aims of Schooling

By asking the question concerning the significance of the being of children and youth for educating in juxtaposition to the question concerning the significance of education for the being of children and youth, the preceding chapters have indicated how to guide the educational development of young people to help them endure, alleviate, and perhaps resolve the difficulties of contemporary mass society.

The difficulties generated by and manifested as the "loss of identity" are responded to through attending to the meaning of the being of children and youth for educating. How this can be done in schooling appears in the articulation of the relation of values to life-phases and in the claim that each life-phase has to be lived fully (i.e., authentically) if the individual is to achieve the responsibility for his existence that belongs to being-adult (Chapter 4); in the description of the genuinely pedagogic authority that depends upon the possibility of disobedience to come into being (Chapter 5); in the formulation of the return to the origin and recovery of his being that encourages the pupil to be someone himself (Chapters 6 and 7); and in the disclosure of the nonviolent power that fosters a return to the origin and establishes the educational encounter in its replacement of customary continuous school learning (Chapters 9 and 10).

The difficulties of contemporary society generated by and manifested as the "loss of community," on the other hand, are responded to through attending to the meaning of educating for the being of children and youth.

How this can be done in schooling appears in the articulation of living each life-phase fully as the essential condition of the adequate reassessment of adolescent ideals and the subsequent realization of the values constitutive of genuine coexistence in adult society (Chapter 4); in the formulation of the ontological foundation of the learning of the native tongue that indicates how the child's learning to speak with others brings him into the common world, as does authentic pedagogic authority and the co-historicizing that occurs within the historicizing of world that constitutes authoritativeness (Chapter 5); in the description of the gradual transformation of the world that the child explores from the world of objects to the intellectual-historical world in order to establish his being in the social-historical world, which transformation occurs through maintaining schooling as a continuous process (Chapters 6 and 7); in the presentation of the criterion for judging whether or not schooling policy is ontologically adequate (Chapter 8); and in the articulation of the alienating effects of various forms of commanding-obeying and the disclosure of alternative means whereby genuine coexistence in co-historicizing might be promoted to overcome the inevitable but temporary flagging of the pupil's exploration of the world (Chapters 9 and 10).

The philosophical resolution of the problem of educating to restore both "identity" and "community" occurred through the disclosure of the pedagogic paradox. This "paradox" is not really paradoxical, because authentic individual existence and authentic coexistence are equiprimordial. The pedagogic "paradox" can appear paradoxical only to someone who assumes a permanent conflict between the individual and society, between education for oneself and schooling for others, between personal development and socialization; and who also elevates one of these to an honored position. Claiming that (individual) existence and coexistence are equiprimordial not only refuses to prefer one over the other but asserts what is claimed to be an ontological fact that was elucidated within the explication of the encounter with respect to the dependency of an individual for the realization of his very own possibilities upon their prior disclosure by others within genuine coexistence. To claim that individual existence and coexistence are equiprimordial, or, rather, co-primordial, is no philosophical synthesis of intellectual ideas about human life, however, for the claim that they are co-primordial presupposes that they are indeed disparate phenomena that are ontologically independent of each other, and that this independence has to be maintained not only in order for them to be co-primordial but as the necessary condition for the being of either. When there is no authentically individual existence there is no authentically coexistence, and vice versa, for in either case everything slips into the anonymous gray of inauthentic everydayness wherein people are neither themselves nor with one another in any meaningful sense. The easiest way to grasp their co-primordiality, however, is through the designation *paradox*, for by all ordinary methods of understanding it is indeed a genuine paradox.

By formulating the problems of education with reference to societal difficulties, the societal function of philosophy of education has been fulfilled. Although it may seem to be too facile to classify and interpret all societal problems as "loss of identity" and "loss of community," this kind of generalizing about a welter of particular phenomena is the only means available to expand the horizons of a given problematic to attempt to achieve and maintain a broad perspective.

By formulating problems of education in terms of being, the ontological function of philosophy of education has been fulfilled and the horizons of the problematics pushed back to disclose them in their utmost depth. Although other forms of inquiry may disclose more specific and detailed aspects of the problems, these ontic investigations have to become integrated within a phenomenological, ontological articulation of the educational problematic at hand before their results can be "applied" to guide the educative process without distorting it and without contributing to the alienation of the pupil (unless they unconsciously presuppose an adequate ontology).

Whether or not specific schools in specific social-historical contexts should develop programs to reduce or increase the alienation of men from themselves and others is an ontic matter that involves ontic choices that can in no way be derived from the preceding ontological analysis. Any preferences in this respect, conversely, have no bearing upon the validity of the preceding examination of educational problems in ontological context. It has not been said, thus far, that it is *better* to struggle in the societal context toward the reduction of the alienation of man than not to. *Objectively* considered, it may be better to hasten the thermonuclear annihilation of this mankind in a vague hope that this will allow a new species to appear in a grand, new beginning. Perhaps this mankind is merely being itself in its haste to commit racial suicide (*cf.* Freud's death instinct), and perhaps it is better to fulfill its very own possibilities in this way. If so, then it would be better to promote the hastening of the end through promoting alienation in schools in particular context. *Objectively* considered, there should be no surprise, shock, or misgiving to say or to hear it said that racial suicide may be better than enduring the agony of the struggle to avert it. The dismay that emerges either indicates the presence of an inveterate human narcissism or indicates that subjectivity is the truth—if the desire to be exists subjecticity, perhaps both. If it seems odd to say that there may be insufficient objective grounds for an ontic preference for the survival of the human race, if it seems strange to point out that human existence is not necessary, this feeling of uncanniness is already the beginning of a silent response to the mute call of being. It is already a response of "I will and we will" to the existential imperative of having one's being to be.

The ontological analysis of the conditions necessary for the being of educating cannot indicate which ontic decisions ought to be made, nor can it indicate any preferences. It can only hope to illuminate the context of education that the pre-existing but prephilosophical and nonconceptual understanding of the call of being might clarify and strengthen itself and respond to the call as it comes through the situations in which this understanding finds itself, in which it perhaps ought to find itself in order to let being be, not in response to what has been said but in response to the call from being. The ontological investigation can only attempt to disclose general features of situations, but particular responses to the call of being are situated in the socil-historical context responding to situational demands by being authentically there in those situations. What demands these situations will extend depends upon the situation and the power of being to be, i.e., upon the power to be authentically there in the situation. Whether or not being will respond depends, however, upon how thorough the technologizing of the world has been. It is not a matter of small oases of being, scattered here and there, wherein the encroachments of the technological mentality have not yet contributed to the alienation from the world, that might function as the "saving remnant" or the catalytic agent to avert the mobilization of the planet. It is more a matter of the domination and destruction of the planet by calculative, manipulative thinking motivated by the blind will to power having already sufficiently run its course that mankind may be ready for a resurrection of being. It is not a matter of evading technological nihilism but of going through the zone of nihilism that exists the forgetfulness of being in order that there may be a listening for the call to being. In schooling, consequently, it may be mostly a matter of plunging into the zone of the nihilism that forgets the being of children and youth completely in order to fulfill the meaning of this nihilism and to create the conditions, as in the German *gymnasium* preceding the German Youth Movement, that will permit children and youth to respond to the call of being and ask the question, in a more primordial and authentic way than can be done in philosophizing about education, What is the meaning of being?

Of these ontic matters the ontological inquiry must remain silent. This can seem strange only because of the "cognitive nearness" of ontology to ethics. The situation resembles that of applied physics: the physicist can describe the conditions necessary to get a man on the moon, but he cannot qua physicist say either that a man should be put there or that it is good to put him there. Such ontic decisions and preferences cannot be made within the province of meaning within which physics has its being.

Be this as it may, ontology is not ethics, and the kind of generalizing necessary to fulfill the societal and ontological functions of philosophy of education leaves something to be desired.

TRADITIONAL AIMS
IN CONTEMPORARY CONTEXT

The traditional aims of schooling can serve as a source of the desirable. The ontological analysis can be transformed to philosophical anthropology to match the level of concreteness of these aims. Character, vocation, and citizenship have been the aims of schooling from the Renaissance to this century, from the Puritans to Dewey. In this century the major trends have been to replace the aim of the development of character with some form of what can be designated, for want of a better name, *psychological ideals* (personality integration, emotional maturity, etc.) and to replace the aim of promoting citizenship with some form of implementation of democratic ideals within schooling. With the post-Sputnik crisis, however, a good deal of this orientation became lost and only vocational preparation remained. Character and citizenship were too old-fashioned to be revived, and psychological and democratic ideals were too soft for the hard realities of college entrance examinations and the Cold War.

The transformation of character and citizenship to psychological and democratic ideals had the merit of modernizing talk about education by abolishing emotive moralization, but something was lost in the process. The traditional aims of schooling were comprehensive in scope. Vocational preparation served the major hours of wakefulness as an adult, citizenship training prepared people for their societal contact with people beyond the circle of friends by attempting to structure their conduct in accordance with laws, and character training prepared them for areas of life beyond and "above" what can be demanded through laws, especially a willingness to obey them. This completeness of the intent of the traditional aims of schooling became lost in the transformation of character to psychological ideals because character should have been replaced by psychological ideals plus some moral code. An independent moral code is necessary for personality integration (at least for Freud's theory),[1] and cannot be replaced by psychological terminology *by the pupil*, who still needs moral education in order to be able to adopt a moral point of view. The emphasis of those who advocated education for democracy through some form of practicing democracy in school omitted obedience to laws in an analogous manner. The transformation of character and citizenship to psychological and democratic ideals, in other words, retained the formal aspects of character and citizenship but forgot the material aspects (i.e., the behavioral manifestations) as these would appear when conduct is regulated by moral or legal code. The traditional aims of schooling always presupposed that schooling would result in conformity to the local mores (or so-called conventional morality) and to local laws. Such regulation of an individual's conduct was largely omitted through the emphasis upon psychological and democratic ideals unless it was promoted surreptitiously in the old-fashioned, pedagogically untenable way.

There seems little doubt that the traditional ways of defining the traditional aims of schooling require modernization to be tenable, meaningful, and relevant to contemporary mass society.[2] Neither suburbia nor urbia has any commonly accepted set of values, and the phrase "conformity to the local mores" is literally nonsense where there are no such "mores." It still appears in school-board talk and in professional codes of ethics, however, as supposedly referring to something solid enough to enlist the teacher's support in the educating of the young. With the breakdown of a common set of values at the semi-conscious level of mores that accompanied the breakdown of the nineteenth and early twentieth century community, there also occurred a breakdown in an implicit faith in, and obedience to, laws. A return to the older conception of citizenship would be as anachronistic as a return to the older view of conformity to the "local mores." Because the mores became codified into laws and obedience to laws helped shape the mores, the traditional aims of character and citizenship worked together. The breakdown of the mores qua mores through urbanization and the development of a multigroup society signifies not only a breakdown in the traditional conception of character but also of citizenship. Citizenship training as traditionally conceived is pointless without the support of a widely accepted common set of values at the ontic, verbalized level.

The social crisis, the crisis in the being of man, is manifested in this breakdown of law and mores as effective guides to conduct, and it can do little good to revive that which is elemental in generating the crisis. By no means is it implied that a return to the traditional aims of education can help solve the problem of educating for the resolution of the current "societal" problems if those aims remain traditionally defined. For example, one response to the crisis in human existence is to shout for "law and order." These cries of "law and order" are right in their implication of a need for citizenship as an aim of schooling, wrong in their assessment of the social crisis and in their recommendations to simply repress symptoms of the loss of community, rather than trying to restore an underlying sense of identity and community that might make "good character" and "good citizenship" possible. They are wrong because they remain too much involved in the crisis and respond too immediately in too obvious a way, rather than turning to education and schooling to see what might be done to establish the conditions for the eventual solutions of the problems of deepest concern. They are wrong because they exaggerate the significance of a certain "virtue" or "virtues" and neglect the significance of the wholeness of the person and of human being. Education, however, cannot be identified with the formation of a particular "virtue" or set of "virtues" without committing a fallacious reductionism and failing in its task. The person who is capable of this or that virtue, such as obeying laws, is so because he lives with his whole being and is responsible for his life, i.e., because he exists independently as a social-moral being.[3] Authentic existence is the requisite and constitutive condition for the being of any "virtue" or "ethic." All codes of ethics or forms of citizenship require ontological foundation, because all require the responsibility for one's actions that is available only in wide-awakeness, i.e., in authentic existence. The social scientists are right when they remove responsibility from a person's actions when he is not fully himself and succumbs to the facticity of the human situation, but it is precisely the educational and ethical task to enable the pupil to recover this responsibility and establish the necessary condition for the being of any ethic, any form of "character," and any form of "citizenship."

Any ethics, whether personal ("character") or social ("citizenship"), is an ontic affair and is neither compatible nor incompatible with the preceding ontological grounding of education. Any ethics presupposes the responsibility for one's own actions that is depicted therein as the pupil's projecting into possibilities of the world, i.e., into the demands of the situations in which he finds himself that exert their demand upon him when geography is grounded in landscape, i.e., when he has the power to be someone himself and lets being be, i.e., when he lets the situation disclose itself as a situation without projecting his own everyday concerns into it, i.e., when he lets it disclose its possibilities and they exert their demands upon him. This, however, is precisely the definition of "good character" and "good citizenship": "The morally good man is the man who is seen as being guided by an apprehension of objective demands in the situations which confront him."[4] This leaves undefined the content of those objective demands, i.e., of those demands experienced as coming from the lived-situation, but it nevertheless is the phenomenological explication of what was often meant by "character" as a traditional aim of schooling.

CHARACTER: FORMAL ASPECTS

It is a phenomenological description of the formal aspects of "character" rather than of the material (i.e., specifiable and behavioral) aspects, but the traditional concepts were also based upon the distinction between the formal and material aspects of character. Although often a certain *kind* of character was desired (e.g., the Christian gentleman), which placed emphasis upon the material aspects and the consequences of actions in respect to their rightness and wrongness, this expectation was often very vague because it occurred within an ideology whose values were more presupposed than explicit. What was equally desired was a person who had "character," "backbone," integrity, which placed emphasis upon the motivations or intentions of actions and not upon the consequences in respect to their correctness. The development of a person who "had character" and could withstand the shifting winds of temptation and fortune was the aim of schooling, even when a whole configuration of actions in accordance with some particular moral code was also implied. It is this formal aspect of character that has been replaced by psychological ideals in this century, for what was desired was none other than "emotional stability" or "personality integration." There is more than a verbal similarity between the concepts of personal integrity and personality integration. What was omitted when character as the traditional aim of schooling in the sense of personal integrity was transformed to personality integration was the self-conscious ethical concern of the pupil to achieve personal integrity by achieving a self-constancy through acceptance of personal responsibility for his actions and for his whole way of being. What was omitted was his being. By and large, it was assumed that the introduction of flexibility, the relaxation of standards, the injection of personal regard and warmth into schooling, and a rejection of moralistic concerns from schooling would allow for personality integration and the development of emotional stability, but by overlooking the self-consciousness of the pupil, the possibility of his taking over his project of being, and his accepting responsibility for his existence, the genuine possibility of his becoming a person in his own right was denied him.

The omission of the significance of educating for the being of children and youth followed necessarily from the fallacious equation of educating and "therapy" that necessarily occurs with the introduction of psychological ideals into schooling. Educating is not therapy and does not resemble it in the slightest. It takes up where therapy leaves off. At its best, all that any therapy can possible do within its province of healing is to establish the person's power of being to enable him to be someone himself and exist independently once again. Its task is precisely to free the person from dependence upon the therapist by enabling him to recover responsibility for his being. For the child or youth, therapy involves restoring the frustrated wanting-to-be-someone-oneself by establishing a world safe enough for him to explore so that the process of education can begin. By definition, therapy during the life-phases of schooling can merely attempt to restore the preconditions of educating. For the teacher to engage in some bastardized form of therapy through a misequation of therapy and educating in trying to implement some version of psychological ideals is precisely to avoid educating, to avoid responsibility for her own being as a teacher, to avoid the responsibility of development of the child's or youth's world, and, withal, to avoid even the possibility of achieving the "psychological ideals" that have replaced the educational aim of helping the pupil to become someone himself through achieving responsibility for his existence. It may be that there are times in the classroom when the situation may seem to call for therapy rather than educating, but the appeal, the request, the challenge, etc., are appropriate and do not leave the pedagogic area. Nor do they offer excuses to the pupil for evading his responsibility for having his being to be. Because they encourage him to take up his project of being for himself by helping him to emerge from the inauthentic existence into which he has lapsed, their use is a means to establish a pedagogic relation. Although the appeal, the request, the invitation, etc., do not leave the pedagogic arena, they do, on the other hand, serve as quasi-therapeutic devices that promote "psychological ideals" in their strictly pedagogic way. It can be shown quite easily how the use of means that restore the pupil's power of being such as the admonition, the request, the summons, etc., accomplishes the same thing that was intended by the implementation of psychological ideals in schooling.

A great mystique has developed around the phenomena of "abnormal psychology." There is a distinction between psychiatry and those forms of healing that accomplish their cure through conversation. If the medical is restricted to that which is cured through medicine, i.e., by chemical and surgical means, then illnesses are physiological in nature, and any "neurosis" or "psychosis" is a chemical imbalance or bodily disturbance that manifests itself in a bizarre pattern of behavior that can be classified as "neurotic" or "psychotic" for heuristic purposes only. As a matter of semantics, psychiatry as a branch of medical science is the one and only field that can develop strict, technical, operational, medical definitions of "neurosis" and "psychosis." Its definitions are inviolate to the layman, psychologist, or philosopher, but as a branch of medical science it has to confine its definitions to that which can be cured through applied medical science, i.e., through ways that are at bottom a matter of chemistry and surgery. This, at least, is the way it should be, and everyone else should expunge the medical terms from their technical vocabulary to avoid quackery. Clinical psychologists, psychotherapists, and psychoanalysts, however, claim their curative effectiveness with respect to patterns of conduct that they also wish to classify as "neurosis" and "psychosis." These "cures" are effected by the encounter with the therapist and by talking, rather than by medicine, so that there seems to be something that they designate as "psychoneurotic behavior" and "psychotic behavior" that is not reducible to physiological origin. Whether or not there are these kinds of "neuroses" and "psychoses" should be decided by medical science rather than by clinical psychology, psychotherapy, or psychoanalysis, for it can be decided by the latter only to the extent that they are part of medical science.

If it be granted, however, that there are "talking cures" or "experiential cures" effected by the various forms of therapy or analysis, then what they "cure" are forms of conscious experiencing or ways of existing —inauthentic, ungenuine forms and ways. The nonmedical, nonbodily "neurosis" or "psychosis" is only a variation of human experiencing.[5] Once the "magic" and "mystery" are dispelled from "mental illness," it can be readily seen that any form of nonmedical therapy merely helps the "patient" come to grips with the problems of his existence in a more authentic way. As the general practice of ascribing the powers of witchcraft and demonology to "insane" people that prevailed in the Middle Ages changed to one of confining them in chains in the eighteenth century of enlightenment, and as this attitude toward confinement gradually became replaced by the recognition that "deranged" people were merely "mentally ill" and that "insanity" was a "disease" that could be cured, throughout the latter half of the nineteenth and first half of the twentieth centuries, so, too, is the next step of enlightenment the recognition that so-called mental illness is either a matter for medical treatment, when it is physiological in origin, or a matter of conscious experiencing and self-conscious existing that is somehow deficient in some manner. Once non-physiological "neurosis" and "psychosis" are recognized as variant forms of human existing, all the magic and mystery disappear and *any* form of therapy becomes a matter of helping the patient to acquire responsibility for his existence. The acceptance of this responsibility is the "cure" regardless of the "demonology" under which the "therapist" labors.

As a view of the totality of human existence from birth to death in all its forms, existential phenomenology includes the nonmedical phenomena of "neurosis" and "psychosis" within its conception of inauthentic existence. When one lapses into the immanence of inauthentic average everydayness, there is a failure of this transcendence to the world and projection into being. His existence is then no longer individualized, he is not someone himself, and the general anonymity of the "mass man" who could be anybody takes over, as it were. This loss of freedom and responsibility is what is found in the nonmedical phenomena of "neurosis" and "psychosis." On the one hand, when a person is unable or unwilling to be someone himself, when he lacks courage to be independently because of his existence in groups that are intolerant toward deviancy from group norms, and when he then becomes dependent upon the opinions of others for his self-understanding and for the affirmation of his being in the use of the group identity to resolve his own problem of identity in bad faith, his life "may well be that of the neurotic."[6] Falling into everyday existence in a falling away from oneself through a "compulsive conformity" results in the situation "in which the unauthentic existence is in truth what may be regarded as a 'neurosis without symptoms.' Not infrequently, however, the inauthentic existence develops into a neurosis with fully manifest symptoms."[7]

On the other hand, when a person is unable or unwilling to be someone himself, when he lacks courage to be independently because his existence is submerged in immanence and he is unable to intend a world, unable to spatialize and futurize from his own origin in the realization of possibilities, this inability to go into the future eagerly through acceptance of responsibility for being is of great significance to the psychopathology of the "neurosis" simply because the "neurotic" is captured by the past and keeps throwing the past into the future, dreading it, rather than throwing himself forward in letting the future be.[8] The ontological foundation of the nonmedical "neurosis," that is, lies within the possibilities of inauthentic existence, in the possibility of becoming entrapped in immanence, alienated from the world, from one's future project of being in it, and from having one's being to be.

Inauthentic existence is midway between dreaming and being wide-awake: it is a state of awakeness in which the world happens to one, but of which one is conscious of it happening, in dread. Only because the person can lose the power over his own existence can he become inauthentic; only because this self-estrangement can become dominant can he become "neurotic." To fall into the immanence of inauthentic existence and to be more or less stuck there, unable to project freely into the future, is to be dominated by one's thrownness into existence. If at any given moment, individual existence is a null basis from which projection has to occur (if one has his being to be), this sheer state of being, this pure facticity over which one has no choice, is one's thrownness. Even if human existence is gratuitous, without excuse, it is given to the individual that he has to be. He is thrown into existence. The falling away from oneself as one's futural project into immanence and being dominated by thrownness, the escape from responsibility for having to be through submission to this thrownness, is manifested ontically in claims that one has already achieved being and knows who he is, as if his being were not still in question, i.e., it results in the ontic denial of the basic conditions of human finitude. It results in bad faith, corresponding to the lived-denial of the temporal structure of human existence as the ekstatic unity of the three moments of past, present, and future. To fall into everydayness is to omit one moment, the future. If the present is made present by projecting futurally from the past, the strength of the projection can easily weaken and allow the past to dominate. Each day becomes the same dull space through which one lets himself be dragged because he does not futurize into the day but lets it happen. The past and present taken without the future, however, is the sheer "that one is." The existential structure, however, is a unity of that-it-is (or the past) and that-it-has-to-be (or future). Both the null basis from which projection occurs and the projection from the null basis are equally real; authentic existence exists the reality of the two moments. Inauthentic existence, however, conceives of its being as if it were a nonhuman object without the moment of having its being to be, and in this lapsing turns into a nobody precisely because it imagines itself as a someone who already exists. By not futuring to achieve being, one becomes merely the null basis from which projection might occur, and this null basis is precisely that, a sheer nothingness. To fall into inauthentic existence is precisely an attempt to be this nothingness, i.e., the formless nonentity of the anonymous mass man, but it is manifested ontically in loud claims that announce that one already exists totally as the person he is in an outrageous denial of the limitation of having one's being to be from the null basis or particular origin that he is. Regardless of what they allege to be doing, the various forms of therapy merely assist the person to gain power over his existence through achieving some kind of commitment to these limits of human existence, for only by a basic commitment to thrownness and projection, to facticity and freedom, to that one is and has his being to be, is he enabled to become "unneurotic."[9]

The various ways of therapy merely help the "patient" to reestablish the power of being. This is their only task. The means whereby the teacher can call the pupil into the pedagogic relation have the identical purpose, but they are not "therapeutic" in any significant sense: they simply will not work with a pupil who is so alienated that he requires therapy. Because the pedagogic means do help to restore the pupil's wanting-to-be-someone-himself and are based upon human temporality, however, they are the pedagogic analogues to therapeutic practices and thus suffice to fulfill "psychological ideals" as these have come to replace character as an aim of schooling. Their focus upon the pupil's responsibility for his own existence, moreover, includes that which was lost when it was thought that "psychological ideals" could replace character as an aim of schooling.

They can do this precisely because the lived-responsibility they evoke is the futural projection from the null basis that is self-consciously understood as such. The traditional aim of promoting character development basically sought a person who was responsible, but one *becomes* responsible only by *being* responsible. Because even the small child can be responsible for small things (going to the bathroom, eating his meals, putting his toys away, etc.), the range of his responsibility extends coextensively with his being. The whole of education is becoming more and more responsible until one is totally responsible at the end of education. This lived-responsibility for one's having his being to be is omitted in any version of the application of psychological ideals to schooling, because those ideals become couched in the objectifying conceptualization of personality theory that reifies the pupil and omits his being as it stretches out toward the world futuringly in front of him (Chapter 1). This psychology is often designated "ego-psychology," and the problem is precisely the status of the "ego." Within the phenomenological reduction, there is no ego, no self. The "ego" can appear as the center of all acts, as a pure nothingness (Sartre), as O in the X, Y coordinates; but this remains a null basis, a pure origin, that cannot be reified into a metaphysical, unknowable *Ding an sich* without ascribing more reality to something that is not accessible to consciousness than is attributed to that which has this evidential ground, i.e., without alienation from oneself. The "ego" can appear as the unity of the transcendental field of consciousness, as the totality of one's lived-world as this is constituted by one's perspective upon the objective world, but that this differs from the "objective world" that allegedly exists independently of one's consciousness of it is not understandable, for consciousness always tries to grasp the objective world with no remainder, but remains within a perspective no matter what. The transcendental field is a referential totality, but it is never a totality that is finished totalizing itself. It is a totality that is continuously accomplished in the historicizing of one's being and cannot be reified into an ego; it remains a totalizing nothingness. The "ego" can appear as an object for consciousness in the transcendental field, but only when consciousness becomes alienated from itself and tries to become conscious of itself in the phenomenon of being a transcended-transcendence. Then, however, one is alienated from the world and cannot become fully conscious of possibilities in the world during the time that a self-concept inhabits consciousness as an object of awareness. This "ego" cannot be reified because others' evaluations of oneself are always changing, and the split in consciousness that develops when part of it becomes an object for the other part depends upon the instability and temporality of the latter part that is conscious of it for its being. The "ego" that can appear in the transcendent field as an object of consciousness depends upon the nothingness of the sustaining consciousness in order to be.[10]

Within the province of meaning of a naturalistic psychology, on the other hand, the "ego" or "self" can be postulated and defined whichever way the theorist gains most explanatory power, logical rigor, symmetry and simplicity of theory construction, unification of data, and so on. In no case, however, can he claim that his constructs, to which the "ego" or "self" is central, are both explanatory and descriptive. There is no "ego" or "self" accessible to purified reflection or present in wide-awake action; the "ego," the "self," the "person," remains a construct, a metaphysical fiction, or a real, live, particular individual who still has his being to be. The "self" is the null basis and projection from it in a project of being.

An attempt to replace character as an aim of education with psychological ideals, then, particularly through identifying pedagogy with therapy and pedagogic theory by personality theory, omits the being of children and youth by replacing it with a static "self" that is not self-consciously responsible for its own existence and that is therefore incapable of being educated. This reductionism deals with a pupil who is not capable of achieving a self-constancy through the realization of possibilities in an expanding world into which he is futurizing in order to be, because it forgets the basic pedagogic task of challenging the pupil into the educational encounter through the content of the materials of instruction. It deals with a "self" that is not consciously capable of integrating itself. The admonition, appeal, request, etc., to the contrary, can challenge the pupil into accepting responsibility for his existence and into responding to lived-values in situations because they take his being into account, to be sure, but more particularly because they take his nonbeing into account.

CHARACTER: MATERIAL ASPECTS

They also serve to take the material aspects of character into account, as did the traditional aim of schooling: the person who deviates from "conventional morality" is likely to have fallen into inauthentic existence. When schooling becomes overstructured and does not take the pupil's being into account, there might be an increase in landscape activities. These activities include the dance, the drinking of alcoholic beverages, the use of drugs, and the pursuit of sexual relations (Chapters 6 and 7). It is true that these appear to establish room for the youth to be someone himself and tend to violate "conventional morality." They are, however, symptomatic of an alienation promoted in schooling. Their reduction accordingly requires modification of schooling to take their being into account to allow them to project across the given in their own project of being, to enable schooling to have meaningfulness. Their reduction involves allowing youth to transform the freedom of caprice and revolt into the freedom of conquest, choice, and moral choice within schooling.

If the landscape phenomena are the result of alienation and if they violate conventional morality, then the attempt to turn schooling into educating by taking the being of youth into consideration means that authentic existence would support conventional morality, that people who authentically existed would live, by and large, in the way conventional morality describes. This means that whoever desires to promote the development of character as in the traditional aim of schooling should find it desirable to ground educating in the being of the pupil (Chapters 4 to 10), so that the aim is achieved.

Because some of the young people pursuing landscape activities protest most strongly against conventional morality, and because they might vocalize their protest in existentialistic vocabulary, however, this point requires considerable amplification. It is true—the articulate members of the beat generation and the articulate hippies adopted certain texts of existentialistic literature as Holy Writ, particularly some writings of Sartre. Because the present inquiry relies considerably upon Sartre's phenomenology, there is no evading a direct confrontation. The question is not who understands Sartre more correctly, but how to ask the question of the meaning of being in the most primordial way, although the claim will be made that Sartre asked the question more authentically than his followers who philosophize at the level of folklore. In *No Exit*, for example, Sartre made the claim that "Hell is other people." No, *he* did not. In the play, three people are caught up in having their being for others according to the transcended-transcendence/transcending-transcendence polar conflict. One of these alienated people says "Hell is other people." This is based upon the phenomenology of inauthentic coexistence of his *Being and Nothingness*, which has been rightly judged by a medical psychiatrist to be a picture of "neuroticism." In *Being and Nothingness* Sartre also said, "Each one is alienated only to the exact extent to which he demands the alienation of the other."[12] Within inauthentic existence, within bad faith and before the ethics of deliverance, the dominance/submission patterns of inauthentic coexistence are the supreme torture, "Hell." In *Nausea* Sartre depicts the experience of one's own contingency wherein the world and one's own existence seem to become absurd. The main figure is between projects. He is directionless because of his own lapsing into facticity and ensnarement in the immanence of inauthentic existence, and ontological nausea emerges. This "nausea" is also discussed in *Being and Nothingness*, where he describes how it overtakes one in abandonment of one's project of being,[13] where one can also read about freedom as being situated in a resisting world and as a constant, engaged, surpassing of the given.[14] To understand *No Exit* and *Nausea*, one also must understand that twentieth-century *avant-garde* belles lettres knows no heroes and no messages. Those readers who looked for guidance on how to live in *No Exit* and *Nausea* found what they wanted, but why should anyone look for messages in literature except to escape responsibility? In *No Exit* and *Nausea* Sartre is exploring the phenomena of inauthentic everydayness; one has to go to *The Flies* to find freedom swooping down upon Orestes in an authentication of human existence, but even this is overdrawn to make the point dramatically to a popular audience. In a review of *The Age of Reason* that appeared in the *Journal of Philosophy and Phenomenological Research*, an M.D., Heinz Lichtenstein, suggested that Sartre took up Heidegger's project of describing inauthentic everyday existence, but where Heidegger failed, to some extent, because of the apparent abstractness of his language, Sartre attempted to give concrete embodiment to the phenomena involved by writing literature depicting people caught up in the triviality of inauthentic existence.[15] Lichtenstein will be quoted at some length, because what he says about some of the characters in Sartre's trilogy seems relevant to understanding the people who apparently attempt to justify their own despair over the possibility of becoming someone themselves in contemporary society with existentialistic jargon, who use existentialism as an ideology, perhaps not to become but to escape themselves. Lichtenstein sketched the plot line of *The Age of Reason*, then said it was:

> A trivial story indeed, but its triviality has a strangely disturbing character because it brings to life a very compelling character of everybody's existence: the all-pervasive banality of human existence to which man is tempted to yield willingly enough at any lived moment of his day. It is Heidegger's "falling away from life itself," his *"Man ist"* that lurks behind the pervasiveness of this triviality. Here are people whose life never becomes as real as they want it to be. Knowing of this character of unreality, they are frantically trying to free themselves from it by using sex, alcohol, drugs, and the thrills of morbid impulses to experience moments of ecstacy that should make them feel more real. The result, however, are pseudoecstasies from which they emerge more unreal, more lonely, more frustrated, and more guilt-conscious than ever. Could it be possible that this group of psychopaths reveals anything at all that makes visible a basic structure of human existence—not just a peculiar and pathological form of existence? It cannot be denied that Sartre's characters are types familiar to every psychiatrist. It is not even difficult to classify them according to the clinical entities of modern psychiatry. There are psychoneurotic personalities, ambivalent, craving to love and unable to form a genuine relationship to anybody. We can easily recognize the addicts, the impulse-ridden psychopath, the pervert—Sartre's awareness of the symptomatology of psychiatric cases is quite keen indeed. But why this preoccupation with morbid characters? Is morbidity a general structure of human existence?
>
> The psychiatrist does not hesitate to answer the question in the affirmative. To be able to become "morbid"—to be psychoneurotic, addicted, perverted, and, indeed, insane is not just an "accident" that happens to some human freaks or "degenerates." It is a basic potentiality of human existence itself. . . . The psychiatrist . . . has observed that disintegration deprives a person not only of the experience of reality (to use Heidegger's term: his being-in-the-world), but makes him subject to the compelling power of impulses that take control of his action against the decisions of his reasoning mind. The stages of disintegration are the

stages of being compelled to do what one has not chosen to do. According to the area of existence that has come under the domination of compulsion—instead of freedom to choose—the psychiatrist classifies the phenomena of disintegration of human existence. Some forms are nearly universal, he calls them psychoneuroses. Others represent the complete "loss of reality," he labels them psychoses. Whatever technical names he uses, he is describing an existential structure of human reality. . . .

It seems fair to conclude that the realm of the psychiatrist is not very far from the existential phenomena Sartre is trying to make visible. What the psychiatrist studies with different aims in mind must appear as a basic ontological structure of man's existence to the existential philosopher. . . . It belongs to the existentiality of man to be able to lose his "freedom to choose," his "freedom to engage himself". . . . All of this is perhaps nothing new at all. . . . Sartre, man of the twentieth century, rediscovers man's existential propensity to fall victim to the "demonic powers" in the phenomena of the psychiatric realm. . . . He depicts [some] modern young people of our days, in the most urbane of all cities, struggling helplessly against the "morbid"—which is the demonic—in themselves. . . . Indeed, these young people are "cases for the psychiatrist." But what else does that mean than the existential fact of man's existence in the face of the danger of disintegration, the danger of losing "his freedom to choose?"[16]

If Lichtenstein is right, then an increase in "landscape activities" among youth, or the attempt to return to landscape in order to be, is, as it has been claimed, an indication that schooling is not grounded in the being of children and youth, for if and when youth are trying to find themselves through the use of alcohol, drugs, sexual freedom, and so on, it signifies that education as the matter of finding oneself in a project of engaged freedom is not occurring. If, on the other hand, education as an existential quest can make schooling more real and lessen the hunger for "excitement" and "thrills" outside of schools, then grounding education in their being fulfills the aim of schooling in respect to character in the sense of "having character," i.e., the continuity of the person, emotional stability, and personal integrity, and, moreover, in the sense of agreement of the person's actions with "conventional morality." The development of the pupil's responsibility for his being fulfills this aim of schooling both formally and materially.

But what can be more trivial and conducive to the boredom wherein all responsibility for being is surrendered than living according to the way conventional morality describes? Has not the preceding description, suggesting that "landscape activities" belong to inauthentic existence, begged rather than answered the question that the young people who participate in them are asking? Is it merely a charge-countercharge argument over what belongs to inauthentic existence and what to authentic existence, or worse, over who is authentic and who not? Is it not precisely the banality of "bourgeois" existence that is the prime example of everyday-ness from which youth have to escape into alcohol, drugs, psychedelia, and sexual freedom in order to live life fully and authentically? Is not the present reading of Sartre, for example, simply enclosed within an impenetrable "bourgeois ideology" that invalidates it? Is not the psychiatrist quoted for authoritative support from medical science merely culture-bound? Did Sartre not warn us sufficiently about the "right-thinking" man?

The first reply is to repeat the claim that human existence is midway between landscape and geography, between prereflective and reflective consciousness, between "feeling" and "reason." Human being is between earth and sky, between the home of the animals and the home of the gods. Landscape activities are a return to immediacy, the home of the ani-mals, wherein there is no direction, no future, no significance, merely the present. This distorts temporality and omits the moment of the future, the having to be. Consciousness expansion may be a salutary return from the home of the gods to earth and a release from being constricted by geography, as the "right-thinking man," the "hide-bound conventional moralist," may be, and to this extent the flexibility obtained by conscious-ness expansion can serve to authenticate one's existence by freeing it from the past. On the other hand, because this expansion of one's being justifies the use of aspirin to relieve headache does not mean that it justifies the use of aspirin when there is no headache, any more than it justifies head-ache. Secondly, although landscape activities are immediately enjoyable, and anything enjoyable must be authentically human in some sense, they are nonterminating: the goal of getting "high," on dance, drink, or drug, is a state rather than an achievement. It is something one does immanently to oneself, as if one were worldless. This is its passivity. The "high" results in no action in the world and no realization of possibilities of being in the world. Because the pseudo-action is immanent, it is nonterminating: there is no point at which one achieves what he is "doing." The intent is to establish the state-of-being called "high," but then what? Just to be, as if this were separable from wide-awake action? As if the situationless-ness is a place to be? And after the "high," then what? Back to "reality"? Is not there always the hangover, in which the world is as dull as ever and being is more of a burden than before? Closely akin, but thirdly, the self-manipulation that is involved in "landscape activities" removes one from the actual landscape and hence from the values in the situation that can extend their requiredness to the person and demand something from him. The situationlessness of "landscape activities" signifies that the land-scape achieved therein is a pseudolandscape. But what is it to exist into a pseudolandscape but pseudoexistence? Hearing the call of being, wanting-

to-have-a-conscience, being someone himself by realizing authentic possibilities of being in the world, genuine historicizing in and with the world,
and genuine co-historicizing are impossible within this pseudolandscape,
but *these* are the structurations of authentic existing, of living life fully.

This can be corroborated by the formulation of the existential psychiatrist Viktor Frankl. Frankl suggested that the collective "neurosis" of
our time was an "existential vacuum," a pervasive sense of the meaninglessness of personal existence (loss of identity or the experience of the
absurd). He suggested that every age had its "collective neurosis" (such
as Freud diagnosed for the Victorian age), and that the twentieth-century
"neurosis" was a widespread boredom (everydayness) that developed
because traditions, mores, and instinctual life no longer exist to guide action (the loss of community). For evidence that the "existential vacuum"
was widespread, he listed the things usually claimed to be indicative of
cultural disintegration: conformity and other-direction; widespread alco-
holism; juvenile delinquency; the "nothing-butness" that says that human
existence is "nothing but" a result of bio-psycho-sociological conditions
and conditioning (which he called "neurotic fatalism"); the "Sunday
neurosis," or the inability to draw upon one's own resources during leisure
(which reveals the contentlessness of one's existence), and the practice
of filling this void that appears when the busywork is done by overorganiz-
ing even leisure time to ward off loneliness and depression; and the dis-
guised forms of the "existential vacuum" such as the will to power, the
will to money, the will to pleasure, and the will to sex.[17] These phenomena,
for Frankl, arise in conditions of existential frustration, when one is
unable to find significance in his life, and the "cure" is not to endure the
meaninglessness of life but to endure the inability to find or accept an
ultimate meaning for life in general that is allegedly objectively valid.[18]
The key to being able to endure this loss is to find the significance of one's
own life, which is as individual and unique as a move in chess. The "cure"
is not in asking for the meaning of one's life or in expecting things from
life (such as a meaningful existence), but rather in realizing that one is
questioned by life, by one's own life, for which one has to answer. Not
"What do I expect of life such that I will accept it as being meaningful?"
as if a person could dictate what life should be in some arrogant and
extravagant project, but "What does life expect of me?" as if one were
called to responsibility and being.

Frankl's theory of existential therapy focuses upon the restoral of
the sense of personal significance. For example, he often begins by asking
the "patient" quite bluntly, "Why haven't you committed suicide?" The
spluttered reply is often the key to the "cure," for it reveals the "patient's"
closest and most dearly held values, i.e., the core of the significance of
the "patient's" being: "But, but there's the children! They need me!"

"Ummm. Uh-huh." By expecting too much from life in search of some magic never-never land, the individual becomes disappointed and frustrated existentially, when all along, right under his nose, as it were, lies the true value of his being.[19]

Frankl's view, developed on the level of a concrete anthropology, is merely an ontic expression of what has already been stated ontologically. The question, "Why haven't you committed suicide?" restores the person to the origin of his being and enables him to hear the call of being through the concrete possibilities of his social-historical situation, which possibilities can then exert their demand to be realized upon him in his ontic realization that life expects something of him personally. This enables the person to take up his project of being and project from the null basis that he is to be somebody himself. The question brings the "patient" down from being up in the air, lost in geography, and restores him to earth and the leaping from it constituted by the personal significance appropriate to man's place between earth and sky, between the animals and the gods. The phenomena that Frankl includes as indicative of existential frustration manifest the falling away from one's self into the inauthentic existence of average everydayness wherein one is unable to project from the origin and is entrapped by the null basis that he is in the loss of freedom and courage to be that is manifested as the experience of one's own gratuitousness and lack of reason for being. These phenomena are also the concern of the conventional moralist, however, such that the educational program that takes the being of children and youth into account by allowing them to be someone themselves by maintaining their wanting-to-be-someone-too allows them to realize that life expects something of them, by letting them hear the call to being. This promotes the development of people who are able to live the way conventional morality describes, i.e., promotes the material aspects of the traditional aim of schooling that was formerly designated as "character."

AUTHENTIC EVERYDAY MORALITY

Within the context of schooling to develop character, within the context of an aim that has always been deemed as desirable and that still *is* desirable if the accomplishment of schooling is to be comprehensive, the ontological analysis can be transformed into a normative anthropology, into an ethical view of man. Having one's being to be, the factical description of human being, becomes the existential imperative that men ought to be themselves, that each person ought to be himself. Then, bearing in mind that there is no self other than the concrete possibilities that lie ahead of one, and that there is no "self-concept" in awareness when one is genuinely being himself by acting concretely with full attention upon the requirements of action in a complete "task-centeredness," it can be said that one ought to realize those concrete possibilities of being that belong to him alone. This means, rather strangely, that each person ought to find personal significance in life. Because this being oneself happens with others who also ought to be themselves, action that then occurs is authentic corporate action. To this authentic corporate action, "conformism" and "individualism" are both irrelevant, because these prevent the co-historicizing of corporate action. They prevent being authentically there in the situation and letting it disclose what it demands. Thus the structuration of authentic corporate action becomes a co-existential imperative to be with one another in the manner of authenic conventional morality.

There is a difference between inauthentic and authentic conventional morality that is easily overlooked. The Bohemian protest against inauthentic conventional morality is made in terms of what may easily be another mode of inauthentic existence, the price ordinarily paid for throwing out the baby with the dirty bathwater, as it were. It is necessary to ask the question properly. When is conventional morality inauthentic and when is it authentically human? The phenomenological critique can begin with the construct of character. Character, like psychological constructs, is something that exists only when seen from the outside. Within the bracketing of common-sense realism, another person's character can be seen, to be sure, but only within the mode of being that transcends the person's transcendence. To try to "have character" as a self-conscious project, then, means to fall into inauthentic existence, for it is to try to take the viewpoint of others toward oneself. It is to be a transcended-transcendence within having one's being for others, and is precisely opposed to what can establish personal continuity. For purified reflection there are only previous actions and alternatives chosen to reflect upon: looking within introspectively reveals no character. On the one hand, to look at another person and see his "character" alienates one from the other in his project of being because it supplants his being with a metaphysical entity. On the other hand, to look at oneself and see one's own character is to fall into shame in an alienation from the world and one's possibilities of being in it. Consciousness cannot become aware of its own character, for "it exists its character in pure indistinction non-thematically and non-thetically" because it cannot become conscious of itself, i.e., posit itself as an object for itself, except through shame.[20] This is precisely a loss of character. To be aware of another's character is to fail to meet him; to be aware of one's own character is to fail to go forward to meet oneself across concrete possibilities. In either case, "having character" is impossible: the construct of character would not exist where people had character. Perhaps it should be abolished that they may. Talk about developing the pupil's character as such participates in the forgetfulness of being; helping him to establish responsibility for his own being makes the existence of "character" possible.

Analogously with "conventional morality." Being with others is constitutive of one's own being, and this is so within both authentically being oneself and within average everydayness. Although it is characteristic of inauthentic existence to relate to others in modes of deficient solicitude, nevertheless even in everydayness there are variations in the kind of solicitude that modulates the being with one another: the considerateness that is involved in freeing the other for his possibilities and the inconsiderateness that attempts to transcend the other's being. Even in average, everyday existence, as between the clerk and the customer, there can be forbearance and overbearance, the former letting the other be and the latter ignoring that the other person exists. The former counts on others, the latter reckons with them.[21] In everydayness there is also the dwelling together in the common world embodied in the common language and in the socialized world of instrumental complexes, like sidewalks, that constitutes a being there in the other's presence that is a genuine being with one another, even though it occurs within average, mass existence.[22] Finally, even authentic existence "proximally and for the most part," as Heidegger suggests, appears (to the imaginary external observer) within average everyday existence.[23] The crucial distinction to be made is that within everyday existence there are two modes of being: authentic and inauthentic being. Walking on sidewalks, eating in restaurants, wearing clothes, using public transportation, etc., are done anonymously, as anyone, but these are not necessarily depersonalizing or inauthentic even though the "who" that does them is for the most part apparently undifferentiated. This existing factically with others, this everyday being with others, involves no necessary escape from responsibility for one's own being. Anonymous existence, the anyone, is positive and constitutive for human being; it becomes anthropologically negative only with the dispersion of the "self" into anonymity that disburdens the "anyone" from its responsibility for its being through the leveling down of publicness when the anybody becomes the nobody.[24] But the anybody can also be a covert somebody. Genuine average existence wherein the "self" is not dispersed into the social current is most readily seen in the use of the more basic social techniques, for one can still shave, eat, work, and so on, without losing responsibility for his being. Conventional morality, furthermore, not merely describes this genuine everydayness, it constitutes this moral facticity of "society."

Genuine everydayness and conventional morality describe the authentically human being, the person who is himself and wants to have a conscience, i.e., who is responsible for his being but who also accepts his societal facticity by committing himself to his thrownness into a world with others in his day-to-day life.[25] His morality, however, is nonthematic because the call of conscience is silent, coming as it does when it is heard authentically in the form of wanting-to-have-a-conscience.[26] The call to conscience comes silently, when authentically, because the person still has his being to be and he understands this.

The predominant mode of everydayness accompanied by deficient solicitude, however, occurs in the forgetfulness of being, of having one's being to be, and, of course, of responsibility for one's being. In this everydayness it is assumed that one has already achieved being and conscience is reified and speaks quite volubly. This anonymous, inauthentic existence, moreover, is susceptible to the state-of-mind of the crowd (making both demogoguery and social psychology possible), and this inconsiderate and overbearing everydayness exists conventional morality inauthentically. The possibility of falling into this inauthentic existence is ever present because it is tempting, tranquilizing and self-entangling. Its characteristics are idle talk, curiosity, and ambiguity.[27] The idle talk of inauthentic existence is characterized by an average understanding, gossip, and uprootedness corresponding to an alienation from the world. It is the world of opinions. Everydayness proceeds without evidence, without knowledge, and without being aware of the need for either upon which to base its opinions. It "thinks" it already understands everything, because it is so curious about everything that it takes it in at a glance and moves on. It also asserts that all opinions are equal and discourages and suppresses meaningful inquiry; it is already in the know. Idle talk is freefloating and gratuitous. When it includes moral language, then, its morality exists in the talk and only in the talk: what matters is what one says. That expressed ideals might guide action goes unnoticed. It appears to be hypocritical, but this is too facile, for in its alienation it goes *unnoticed* that its talk about morality could be reflexive: reflecting consciousness, in which idle talk occurs, becomes totally alienated from prereflective consciousness, in which action then occurs "unconsciously" (as the Freudians almost said). Although it is always "right," it does not exist in the truth of what it says; and although it spends its time in talk, it talks much more quickly than it acts, laboring under the impression that its talk about action is action. Action then becomes unimportant and is left unperformed. The reflection upon morality that occurs in inauthentic existence is not in the truth but in the know, which leads it to its certainty: verbal conformity to the "values" in the "culture" makes one assuredly right, the world is the best of all possible worlds, and the ethical problems are already all answered, except, of course, for those of "self-improvement" in the moralistic, introspective attempts that get one more self-entangled because they do not deal with concrete possibilities in the world.

Inauthentic conventional morality is inauthentic because the person is alienated from the world, existing inauthentically as an isolated subject. Within it, the person avoids concrete ethical decisions because he is situationless. He cannot see ethical decisions as such: they do not disclose themselves because being cannot clear a space for itself in this situationlessness. Its ethical concern becomes reduced to saying the right things and to owing things that it can calculate because it deals with possessions but avoids relating to people. Its responsibility is limited to the consequences of its actions in the sense that it is willing to pay for damages, which reduces it to its very own legalistic sense of existence that is right by calculation according to rules. Its ethical concern matches its technological mentality.[28] By confining itself to debts, claims, and obligations that can be made right through "bookkeeping" and through the shifting around of nonhuman entities, this inauthentic conventionality betrays itself: it is inauthentically human because it is nonhuman. Lest the baby be thrown out with the bath, however, it should be noted that one should pay his debts, return claims, etc., but that the ground of this obligation is that the "creditor" is a human being who helped in a time of need. "Paying-back," in a grounded morality, is the expression of gratitude. This is prephilosophically understood in the authentic verbal "Thank you." Inauthentic conventional morality, when it pays its debts, etc., is materially right but formally wrong because it is unaccompanied by guilt or solicitude in its being reduced to debts that anyone can repay, for its verbal "Thank you" is perfunctory and ceremonial. It may feel moral guilt ontically, but this is related to the nonhuman entities that are redistributed to obtain a good conscience, as if this were something one could have and as if life were a business that ran on independently of one's involvement in it.[29] This is deficient solicitude, because even while fulfilling obligations it reckons with others to obtain its own good conscience, using them as instrumentalities rather than counting on them. In using others as objects to achieve one's own righteousness, it becomes a transcending/transcendence, employing the maxims of morality within the arrogant pole of the conflict of being for others to judge them, at the same time that the very practice of using others to achieve one's own righteousness is an enslavement to the opinion of others in the shameful pole of being for others. It is because one is also a transcended-transcendence that he tries to become right with himself merely by paying his debts, for he is fearful of what "they" will think if he does not.

Within the arrogant pole of being for others, the primary project is to dominate the other. To disguise the crudity of the commanding, however, it clouds itself in the maxims of morality. Then to establish a semblance of validity, the maxims used to sit in "moral" judgment are claimed to be based upon some transcendent basis outside of one's own project of being in a flight into bad faith, i.e., in a flight from the anxiety that belongs to the realization that one's own "values" are chosen within one's project of being and require sustenance from one's own being in action in order to be values. This attempt to establish one's own values outside of one's own project of being indicates that it is ashamed of itself by ascribing objective status to subjective choices.[30] The attempt to transcend the other's transcendence is kept partially hidden from oneself in the lie to oneself that becomes cloaked in "morality," and this lie to oneself splits reflecting consciousness, and the "values" utilized in the project of transcending/transcendence, off from prereflective consciousness where they would have to be sustained by one's project of being in the world, i.e., in action, to have being. The choice of arrogance, then, is a flight from anxiety, and it is therefore ontologically impossible for the militant conventional moralist, who has reassessed his adolescent values in the crisis of practical experience in the fanatical way, to "practice what he preaches" because the anxiety he is fleeing would return were he to sustain the values of his reflective consciousness with his whole being. In trying to organize the other's project of being, the arrogant moralist forgets the question-worthiness of his own being; in the externalization of conscience, he forgets himself.

Within the shameful pole of being for others, on the other hand, the primary goal is to dominate the other through the project of "obeying." The shameful "conform" to the maxims of morality in the project of being transcended, but this is done merely to capture the freedom of the arrogant by forcing the favorable value judgment, not because the maxims are understood nor because the "values" implicated therein are chosen in one's project of being. This is also a flight into bad faith to flee ontological anxiety in a lie to oneself, as evidenced in the "moral holidays" and eruptions of the "irrational" that occur frequently to reveal the true values and the fact that one has not chosen to sustain the professed values in his project of being. It is also ontologically impossible for the "obedient conformer" to be "moral" when his being is not suppressed through some form of commanding, for he too forgets himself.

There are thus three ways of existing conventional morality inauthentically: in idle talk, arrogantly, shamefully. It is just talk, or it is applicable to the conduct of others, or it is ignored whenever one dares. These are not ontologically independent of each other, because the transcending/transcendence and transcended/transcendence modes of being for others slip and slide back and forth within the idle talk of inauthentic existence. To protest the "hypocrisy" is beside the point, because inauthentic existence is so completely alienated from itself: the Freudian psychoanalyst might as well protest the "resistance" of the "patient" whenever the crux of the "neurosis" is approached. To protest the "hypocrisy," furthermore, requires the assumption of a "value system." The protest would be beside the point unless it were that of authentic conventional morality, but then the clear and present danger is that of sliding into the arrogant manner of existing conventional morality inauthentically. If there is anything more tragic than throwing the baby out with the bathwater, it is throwing out the baby and saving the water.

The problem of authentic conventional morality is the problem of authentic coexistence within everyday existence. When people freely devote themselves to a common task, the achieving of the task reorients their individual existences. This is not so much a subsumption of self-interested, conflicting goals within a larger goal or a loss of personal identity in the acquisition of a group identity as it is a transformation of the being of each person to a genuine being with the others in a genuine co-historicizing. In this genuine being with one another, each person becomes liberated to contribute what he can, i.e., himself, to the common undertaking.[31] Team sports also illustrate how there is no necessary conflict between being oneself and being with others, for in football or baseball the "positions" are so different that each player is able, in favorable circumstances, to realize his own possibilities in complete harmony with the realization of the unique possibilities of each of the other players. Furthermore, he might be able to do so in no other way. There is no necessary conflict between individual and collective liberation, in other words, and it may be that each is a necessary condition of the other (as in the pedagogic paradox), as may be speculated from the difference between "good teams" and "bad teams." If individual and collective liberation proceed concomitantly, what form would this co-existential liberation take as an ontic project other than that of the collective ethic known as "conventional morality"? What form could it assume other than authentic conventional morality? If the schooling process is governed by the rule of the pedagogic paradox, i.e., if it proceeds as the continuous individual and collective liberation of the pupils, what would result from schooling other than the traditional aim of schooling, designated as character, interpreted as acting in the way described by conventional morality?

THE GROUND OF MORAL VALUE

In the adequate assessment of youthful ideals that permits authentic being as an adult, the person resolves to do what he can and does it. His operative values become those of honesty, reliability, faithfulness, keeping promises, and doing his job, whatever it may be. His values, in other words, become those that were always at the core of conventional morality: he has character and acts in the way conventional morality describes, but he does this authentically, i.e., without being conscious of it, without expecting rewards for doing so, without trying to impose his values on others, without justification, without excuse. It is absurd for him to be true (etc.) but he is, for no reason. If he were to look for reasons for being true, he would not only fall into the inauthentic existence that is "moral" only when it "pays," he would also fail to find sufficient reason, lose himself in reflection, and become alienated from the world around him. He therefore remains true without reason, retains responsibility for his existence, lets the situations in which he finds himself disclose their possibilities, and responds to their demands upon him. Because these situations include other people, the fulfillment of the possibilities disclosed exists "conventional morality." He experiences the claims of the being of other people with his whole being, which is the ground of any morality, but he can experience them only if he exists independently.

Before returning to the consideration of the traditional aims of education as a source of the desirable, it should be noted that this description of authentic everyday morality is neutral toward the conservative/liberal dichotomy. The Roman Catholic theologian Romano Guardini, the original formulator of the relation of values to life-phases, sought the ontological ground of "enduring values." The atheistic Jean-Paul Sartre, the original formulator of the relation of authentic values to revolt, sought the ontological ground of the values of the "true revolt." In either case the "values" are those of doing one's job, keeping one's word, remaining faithful, and maintaining personal sincerity.[32] For the former, embodying these in one's existence after the crisis of practical experience appears to ground the individual in the heart of the Western cultural heritage; for the latter, embodying these after the crisis of societal entrance appears to ground the individual in the world community. In either case the individual becomes grounded in the social-historical situation, struggling in and with his generation, acting in his everyday life the way conventional morality describes. Ascertaining whether these "values" really conserve the heritage or whether they really constitute a revolt is more philosophically than existentially or educatively interesting. The schooling preparation for authentic coexistence that occurs through maintaining the tension of the pedagogic paradox to let each life-phase be lived fully is neutral to the conservative/liberal interpretations of the authentic values to be realized in adult society, because that problematic is given to the individual for his decision in his reassessment of his youthful ideals. The adequate reassessment itself is open-ended toward the conservative and liberal alternatives. Both authentic conservatism and authentic liberalism embody the values of authentic everyday morality, and it is the latter that is the aim of schooling in respect to the development of "character."

The critique of inauthentic and authentic conventional morality indicates that anyone who desired to promote the development of character in schooling, who would also want to institutionalize the means to that end, would therefore prescribe grounding schooling in the pupil's being to turn schooling into existential education. Because the connection between description and prescription is not clear, the aim was imported from elsewhere to avoid an unconscious smuggling of the "ought" into the "is." It has not yet been said that authentic existence is better than inauthentic existence, nor that the development of character should be an aim of schooling. To avoid this issue, however, would be intellectually irresponsible. An attempt will be made to show why authentic existence is better than inauthentic existence as the first step in indicating that the development of "character" should be an aim of schooling.

In authentic coexistence each person relates to the other as the conscious/self-conscious being that he really is. Being authentically with one another in authentic solicitude has always been designated as *love* by prephilosophical understanding; *love*, not as romantic love but as in "Love thy neighbor," has always been central to conventional or everyday morality. It exists charity. In everyday morality, in the so-called conventional morality that belongs with authentic everyday existence, there is no disagreement with the judgment that one should help his "neighbor" in a time of need, that one should not quarrel with him, that a soft answer calms wrath, that one should ask permission before borrowing things, and so on. In this authentic morality of authentic everydayness the complications of ethical problems that become so philosophically interesting do not arise, nor do the noisy and jealous stipulations and constant one-up-manship of inauthentic conventionality arise. At the relatively undifferentiated, "low level" of everyday existence, it is quite clear, ontically, that love is better than hate. Ascertaining which of alternative actions is loving and which is hateful is a matter of situated practical wisdom, competence at which develops with experience. In spite of this difficulty, or, rather, because of it, there are ontic grounds for saying that authentic conventional morality is better than inauthentic conventionality, that love is better than hate, in each and every case. Ontically, there are grounds for saying that one should love his neighbor, even though one hastens to add that how this love will manifest itself depends entirely upon the situation and how its requirements disclose themselves. Ontologically, one can say that the modes of inauthentic existence as transcending/transcendence and transcended/transcendence are impossible projects: neither the other person nor oneself can really be turned into an object. Both still have their being to be such that the projects are necessarily unsuccessful and transmute themselves into each other, but one cannot say this is ontologically bad, only that they are ontologically impossible. Ontically, however, one can say that anyone who pursues impossible projects is a clown, and, more securely, that anyone who prefers hate to love is a knave, and, even more securely, that anyone who attempts to lie to himself is a fool. The strength of the forces of alienation make this conclusion somewhat simplistic, yet one can use the words in a denotative and non-emotive way if one is not seeking a basis for third-person moral judgment but is looking for modes of existence that are incongruous within themselves. There is a mode of human being that is so fragmented and at odds with itself that it can only be described as an attempt of part of one's being to lie to another part, and this attempt to lie to oneself, this project of bad faith with oneself, is an attempt to fool oneself. This mode of existence is that of the fool. There is a mode of human being that is so unable to tolerate its own question-worthiness that it continuously uses others as objects for its own selfish goals, and this attempt to live in a world wherein other people do not exist in their own right, this projection of a world of the nonbeing of other people, is that of the knave. There is a mode of human being that is so alienated from the world and others that it is unable to realize any genuine possibilities in the world with other people, and the self-understanding of this project of pursuing impossible goals is sufficiently aware of itself that this mode of existence is that of the clown. Then inauthentic conventional morality in the modes of being as a fool, knave, or clown is bad because it is not what it assumes itself to be and because it prevents one's own liberation from misconceptions of oneself in a project of becoming one's self. Ontically, it is bad to be as a fool, knave, or clown.

It is true that human being is without excuse, that all choices are ultimately arbitrary, and that the attempt to say that inauthentic morality is bad is itself in bad faith. It is also true that this is irrelevant to the formulation of a social ethic. The necessary presupposition for the being of social ethics is that existence is good; therefore, "Thou shalt not kill." This proves a major, representative maxim of conventional morality, but the proof is not even a syllogism and requires "unpacking." The choice to do social ethics is arbitrary, without excuse, but once it is under way, it is logically, ontologically, and existentially necessary to presuppose that human existence is good. Otherwise one stops doing social ethics. This presupposition does not imply that any society or state-of-being of society is good. It does imply a logical, ontological, and existential acceptance of society in its existing state as being factually there.

That others exist is a fact. If all human being is without excuse, then, subjectively, the other (any other, individually, or all others, collectively) has as much right to exist as I do. If I exist without justification, and if he exists without justification, then neither one of us has any "objective right" to exist, but nevertheless he has as much right to exist as I do. Therefore, "I shall not kill." This is not a logical conclusion of the argument but an existential promise I feel called upon to make immediately upon understanding the words, "He has as much right to exist as I do," even though I recognize the gratuity of both of our existences. These words simply say, "He exists," which draws forth my promise. The "I shall not kill" is not emotive, nor subjective, nor a choice: it is an existential promise that brings the "Thou shalt not kill" into being, even though I may not have heard those words. I can refuse to make the promise only through claiming more right to exist than I am willing to grant the other, which I cannot do without lying to myself about the worth of my existence. Though I could refuse to make the promise, I nevertheless ought not want to refuse to make it. I do not fully understand the source of this ought, I simply experience it coming from the other's being when I understand that he exists. Therefore, "Thou shalt not kill" is a valid norm among self-conscious human beings. This "maxim" is not emotive nor is it an imperative. It is a second-person paraphrase of a first-person promise. It is also a structure of the space between us after having made the promise. The burden of proof is thus shifted to whoever wishes to deny the validity of the structuration for his own being and conduct: the disprover has to claim for himself more right to exist than other people. He may be able to justify this right, but it is not clear how.

The injunction against murder is not dependent upon saying it is wrong or bad: existence is coexistence and one ought not murder. This is a unitary phenomenon, a moment in human being that alters the being of human being that should be hyphenated when designated in writing: existence-is-coexistence-and-murder-is-impossible. In this perspective the injunction against murder appears as a "natural" ought, an "ought" that is embodied in the essence of man as existence and coexistence, and where there is genuine coexistence, the verbal injunction disappears because there is no murder. To repeat, the person is not capable of this or that act because he has this or that "virtue," but because he is a social-moral being clearly aware of the conditions of human existence. Where there is genuine coexistence, murder becomes an impossibility. Other rules of conventional morality could be similarly "justified," *mutatis mutandis*, as describing the freely adopted spatializing of authentic coexistence.

If doing social ethics necessarily involves presupposing that existence is good, this is not to say that, objectively speaking, existence *is* good. To claim this would involve bad faith in the objectification of values. That existence is good can be said in another way, however, to meet the objections coming from those philosophers who would say that the phrase "existence is good" is not only meaningless but also commits the "naturalistic fallacy," by ascribing goodness to some "natural property." There are people who have come to the conclusion that life was not worth living, to whom existence was not good. They chose nonbeing by way of suicide. If any of the Christian martyrs, e.g., could have escaped burning through recanting, then their choice not to recant was a decision that life was not good under those circumstances. The Buddhist monk who uses gasoline to protest a regime decides that life under the circumstances is not good. In certain cases on one's own responsibility this choice can be an honest, rational, liberating movement. Those of us who have not committed suicide, to the contrary and to the point, are committing the "naturalistic fallacy" with our whole being simply by not choosing suicide, which, objectively, is an ever-present possibility. Human being is unique in that it constantly faces the forced option: commit either suicide or the naturalistic fallacy. One either values human being ("I find existence to be good thus far") on the prereflective level of awareness or one commits suicide at once. Refusal to do the latter implicates one in silently saying that being is better than nonbeing. This tacit saying that existence is good, furthermore, occurs within the phenomenon of being responsible for all men, as all action does. In any action one not only determines who he is but also what man is and who man can be. By not committing suicide, one not only says, "My existence, all things considered, is worth while," he also says, "Human existence, on the whole, is good," for each action, by choosing in one's own person who man is, chooses for mankind. Each action decides anew what humanity is. Doing social ethics, then, not only logically but also existentially presupposes that human existence is good; therefore, "Thou shalt not kill." One can choose not to do social ethics, but if one so chooses he cannot repudiate the validity of the norm, "Thou shalt not kill," without logical and existential inconsistency, for such attempts at repudiation fall within social ethics. If one chooses not to commit suicide, furthermore, he cannot evade doing social ethics, for the tacit choice that one makes for all men, "Human existence, on the whole, is good," merely by choosing to live actually constitutes a social ethic, albeit equally quietly. To avoid bad faith one merely has to remember that it is a perfectly gratuitous choice, an absolutely (i.e., objectively) groundless choice, to refuse to commit suicide. As long as one freely chooses to go on living he "buys the whole bag," as they say, and to make the choice lucidly in full awareness of the consequences is to commit oneself to the conditions of human existence and to exist in one's everyday life the way that everyday morality describes.

This still does not say authentic existence is better than inauthentic existence. It says that to be fully aware of one's existence really leaves no choice between authentic and inauthentic conventional morality, or between authentic everyday morality and something else. There is no distinction between authentic everydayness, authentic everyday morality, and simply morality, and there never was, is, or can be a choice between morality and immorality. To choose to exist is to choose as valid the norms of authentic everyday morality, at least for one's day-to-day conduct. It has not yet been said that it is good to be aware of the consequences of the choice or to be responsible for them, i.e., to exist authentically. This has to be claimed in some way in order to ground the assertion that the development of "character" should be an aim of schooling.

MORALITY AND LAW

The elucidation of the reason why the norms of conventional morality structure the being of the individual in his authentic everyday existence can be repeated at the societal level. "Society" qua "society" could commit suicide, but it does not. It remains an ever-present possibility for society, particularly within the conditions of the arms race, but at least "society" has not yet committed suicide. It thereby presupposes that its own existence is good. Its existence may be wholly gratuitous, but what is its reason for being once it makes the gratuitous choice to exist? Unless one reifies "society," the only reply one can give is to sustain its members as free beings, as authentically human beings.[33] Its very existence presupposes that coexistence is good, and that authentic coexistence is better. To promote coexistence "society" institutionalizes law. Laws are unnecessary unless the existence of society presupposes that authentic coexistence, commonly designated as *justice*, is better than inauthentic coexistence (commonly called *injustice*). Laws can only promote the justice of authentic everyday coexistence, rather than the justice of authentically individual existence, but nevertheless the existence of society presupposes that the coexistence promoted by laws is better than the inauthentic coexistence that would prevail were there nothing rather than laws. Society as such, moreover, is the space between people that is structured by authentic everyday morality. This authentic everyday society, however, is nothing in and of itself; it exists only as the societal aspect, the coexistential aspect, of authentic individual everyday existence. The very being of society, then, presupposes that authentic everyday individual existence is better than inauthentic everyday individual existence. Since "society" institutionalizes schools to sustain "society" in its being, the existence of schooling presupposes that development of "character" as the promotion of authentic everyday morality should be an aim of schooling. The very being of "society" presupposes that the very being of schooling presupposes promoting "character" as an aim of schooling. Because falling into inauthentic existence remains an ever-present possibility, so should "citizenship training" be an aim of schooling.

Authentic everyday existence is possible when one is fully aware of the potentiality for being of himself and others. Even though authentic existence is differentiated out of everydayness in a self-conscious modification of inauthentic being, nevertheless authentic everyday morality is a mode of authentic existence rather than a mode of ungenuine existence. The structuration of the space between people in *authentic* conventional morality, in other words, is freely spatialized into being by the project of authentic existence in open, anticipatory resolve and authentic solicitude. This is the necessary condition for the possibilities of the situation to disclose themselves and for authentic corporate action to co-historicize itself, for authentic existence to be authentic coexistence. Because authentic action involves one's whole being, the presence of "moral principles" in consciousness would close one off from the situation, and action that was decided "on principle" would be inauthentic action because it would miss the possibilities presenting themselves. Although authentic everyday morality *acts* in accordance with the principles of conventional morality, the only authentic "principles" are those that can arise within action without alienating premeditation and consequent concealment of the possibilities of situation. Hannah Arendt suggested that the "principles" that could arise within action were limited to two, forgiving/being forgiven and promising/keeping promises.[34] To these can be added love, truth-telling, and fidelity. These "principles" are in the moral realm what the admonition, request, appeal, and so on, are in the pedagogic realm, because they are *descriptive* of coexistence and thus become "prescriptive" for one's actions when he understands in an existential way that the other person exists as an openness to the world and future and when he then responds to the coexistential imperative. If human being has its being to be and is in question in its being, there is no assurance of who one will be tomorrow. The assurance that one makes to other people that he will in fact be the same person tomorrow is the promise. The verbal articulation of the promise is an implicit assurance that one will be the same person when the promise is due.[35] Promises, however, are gratuitous in "fair weather" and are made exclusively for "foul weather" when it hurts to keep them. If one kept his word "on principle" and justified it with reasons, he would abjure the principle and find other reasons if it hurt too much when the promise was due, unless he also recognized existentially that the person to whom the promise was made existed. To deliberate over whether or not the promise should be kept, furthermore, already betrays the other person. The authentic promise develops nonthematically within action as part of a larger vow to remain oneself in the wanting-to-have-a-conscience of the response to the call to being. Analogously, one remains faithful and forgives because no one deserves friendship. Friendship is not the kind of thing that can be either deserved or undeserved: friends are friends. To remain faithful, one "forgives" ahead of time. As for promises, one cannot remain faithful for reasons or reasons will fail when the friendship is tested, and to deliberate over whether one should or should not be faithful already betrays the friendship. To act upon a principle of fidelity, moreover, is to remain self-enclosed and to have no friends. Faithfulness authentically occurs within action and nonthematically as part of the structure of authentic coexistence in recognition of the other's existence in response to the call from being.

Analogously, one speaks truthfully to another person whom one understands to exist as a self-conscious being because a single lie makes friendship (and authentic coexistence) impossible. A single "white lie" gives both partners to the lie lives diminished by that friendship that remains impossible forever after. Even if undiscovered, and however "innocent," the one lie erects an insurmountable barrier and creates a fictional world for the other. This destroys his subjecticity in a moment of arrogance unless he sees through the lie, which also makes friendship impossible because of the awareness that the other put his own interest above friendship and showed in the lie a lack of trust indicative of the probable quality of his future speech and of the relationship itself. There seems little doubt that faithfulness, honesty, and promise-keeping are the keystones to both conventional morality and to authentic existence, that their realization requires the courage to be someone oneself, power over one's own existence, hearing the call of being, and responding to the existential and coexistential imperatives. There also seems little doubt that authentic everyday morality involves extraordinary expectations, that it is perfectly obvious why "conventional" morality is not very conventional, that "society" requires laws to establish the minimal conditions for justice that could not be obtained under everyday morality alone, and that schooling for "character" requires supplementation by schooling for citizenship to establish the minimal conditions of justice, i.e., of authentic everyday coexistence.

Because conventional morality is, like human existence itself, "proximally and for the most part" inauthentic, the existence of society presupposes the establishment of laws to structure the spatiality between people according to the minimal conditions of authentic, everyday coexistence, e.g., traffic laws. The stop sign can appear in human existence like the commandment "Thou shalt not kill" if the individual reads it that way; it can also serve to indicate how road space ought to be spatialized into by the individual who understands that other people also exist; it will serve to structure the spatializing and temporalizing of the authentically existing individual in his everyday driving. The illustration may be as trivial as most everyday concerns, yet it serves its purpose. The times that it may be proper to run the stop sign, e.g., going to the hospital in an emergency, are exceptional and do not contradict the day-to-day validity of the stop sign, even for "authentic existence," which is easily seen in this case to be achievable only by "going through the universal," as Kierke-gaard suggested. In conventional morality and in citizenship regarded as obedience to laws, it may very well be that the "maxims" and "laws" are too general to fit individual situations and that authentic individual existence goes far beyond the reach of custom and regulation, but none-theless the sphere of the unique situation is reached by going through the general situations in which universal maxims and laws do in fact describe the authentically human possibilities of being. Learning how to drive a car is primarily learning how to spatialize and temporalize (i.e., how to exist) into the spatiality structured by traffic laws in a gross, general way wherein the laws are universally valid. They require, for example, a stop for every stop sign. Only after the universal is achieved is one able to assume the responsibility for his actions that might justify a violation of the universal law for the sake of some more authentic pos-sibility (getting to the hospital to get the hemorrhage stopped) in a teleological suspension of the ethical. Because there are people who do not seem to recognize that others exist and who are unable to spatialize into the space of authentic everyday existence provided by laws, however, enforcement of laws can be justified to help people achieve the universal and the common world from which authentic individual existence can individualize itself later.

CITIZENSHIP: MATERIAL ASPECTS

These considerations concern the place of law in human exist-ence generally, but are particularly significant to the educational view that must be taken in respect to schooling, particularly in light of the analysis of life-phases. If childhood is principally an esthetic phase and if youth is principally an ethical phase, then the teleological suspension of the ethical that belongs to authentic existence could under no circumstances occur before the crisis of practical experience. If this is so, it would be societally, pedagogically, and existentially disastrous not to "teach" citizen-ship in the form of conformity to unexceptional laws during childhood and youth, just as the child learns the general concept first.[36] It would have to occur as the schooling half of the pedagogic paradox corresponding to the existential half, wherein among other things the pupil comes to an existential recognition of the existence of others; but nevertheless "citizen-ship training" as obedience to laws is an essential part of an existential education as well as being a desirable aim of schooling.

This requires careful articulation not to be misunderstood. For in-dividual existence after the crisis of practical experience, it is probably true that concrete situations are too complicated for the external application of maxims or laws; authentic action does not pause to reflect upon laws or maxims but chooses among concrete alternatives; maxims and laws are thematically irrelevant to authentic action; concrete awareness that other people exist is the ground of the being of all laws and maxims; maintaining awareness of this ground is existentially, ethically, and pedagogically superior to the reliance upon laws and maxims as guides to conduct; rules and laws provide handy tools for arrogant third-person judgment at the expense of the forgetfulness of one's own being; affirmations on the reflective, thematic level generate their own negation on the prereflective level of action, such that reflection upon laws and rules creates the illusion that he who says the maxims or laws is already righteous prior to action; people with social power are apt to tend to corrupt maxims and laws through applying them in an interpretation that defends injustices, which makes the only authentic and just actions those of revolt; particular laws can be unjust per se and in respect to a particular situation; and legalism is the greatest danger to moral consciousness, to authentic existence, and to genuine coexistence.

Nevertheless, legality is a necessary aspect of the moral facticity of society and is desirable for both individual and societal existence. To stop for a stop sign just because it is there, i.e., to spatialize and temporalize willingly into the space of law, is a nonthematic recognition that more traffic goes the other way. This is reducible to recognizing that other people exist. Driving on the road that other people built and paid for tacitly recognizes this coexistence, but not as lucidly as freely sharing the space of the road by stopping for the stop sign, as freely spatializing into the legalized space and having one's being in the law.

Being-in-the-law is constitutive of human existence and is equiprimordial with being-in-the-world and being-in-the-truth.[37] Because it is equiprimordial, there is no conflict between being-in-the-law and authentic individual existence. First, obeying traffic laws is a very small "restriction" compared to the freedom of choice they create. In return for the surrender of freedom of caprice is its transformation to the freedom of initiative and power to drive anywhere on the continent that one likes: the structuring of one's personal spatializing and temporalizing according to the space defined by traffic laws compares to the much broader spatializing and temporalizing thereby made possible as the restricting influence on the child's world that occurs through the learning a "native language" compares to the access to the human world that he thereby gains.

Traffic laws have been selected for illustrative purposes for the readiness of the spatial metaphor (like the wandering in the landscape of the German Youth Movement), but the same principle holds for other kinds of laws that disclose other modes of coexistence analogously to the way that other languages (of chemistry, of mathematics) disclose new regions of the human world. Far more possibilities of being are opened up than are denied. Traffic laws may be unique, however, in that they were developed in this century, are highly modifiable at local, situated levels, and are therefore likely to embody justice, i.e., authentic everyday coexistence, in their sphere of influence. But secondly, just as being-in-the-world is positively constitutive of authentic existence to the extent that disclosure of world is of authentic possibilities of being, so is being-in-the-law positively constitutive of authentic existence and authentic coexistence to the extent that the disclosure of the possibilities of coexistence that occurs through individual laws are of authentic possibilities of being and co-being.

The designation *being-in-the-law* concerns the externalization of one's projection in accordance to the space of law in the generic sense, which means into the space disclosed by particular laws that are absolutely just, but to none other. This sounds more metaphysical than it is, for particular laws are revised and repealed to come closer to providing justice. Laws are revised to accord with justice, to accord with law, to accord with the "natural law" that pertains to the essence of man as existence and coexistence.[38] When it is said that being-in-the-law is equiprimordial with being-in-the-world and being-in-the-truth, it merely means that authentic everyday morality is constitutive of human existence whether or not it becomes codified into laws. Because inauthentic existence is also inauthentic coexistence, there has to be the pressure of laws to maintain external conformity to the space of authentic everyday coexistence as the necessary condition for the being of society. Just as in authentic everyday morality one experiences an objective limit that he is unable to cross because it destroys the other's subjecticity (i.e., one simply is unable to lie to a friend whom one respects because one is unable to deceive him), so in inauthentic existence the pressure of laws has to come from without to establish the objective limit that cannot be crossed if laws are to establish the minimum space of justice: he who will not stop for stop signs has to undergo the pressure of law enforcement in order to obtain, at least, grumbling compliance to the demands of coexistential justice that other people might coexist authentically, and to obtain, at most, a wakening from being-in-the-world to being-in-the-law. Just as the pedagogic admonition can waken the pupil from not-being-obligated and being-in-the-world to being-obligated and being-in-the-truth, i.e., to being-in-the-truth-of-one's-own-being, so can the enforcement of laws waken the guilty offender from not-being-obligated and being-in-the-world to being-obligated and being-in-the-law, i.e., to being-in-the-truth-of-others.

That is, laws do not exist in books, courts, or out in social space: they become grounded ontologically only in individual existence through the individual's projection into the space they define. He who does not see that the laws are to be "obeyed" needs not legal instruction but an existential conversion from being-in-the-world to being-in-the-law that is not unlike the conversion from being-in-the-world to being-in-the-truth that is constitutive of educating. Both conversions are from a state of not-being-obligated to one of being-obligated, the difference being that the former depends upon the validity of the coexistential imperative and the latter upon the existential imperative. The authenticity of being-in-the-law depends upon the co-primordiality of existence and coexistence and the unitary having-to-be-one's-self-with-others. Although law enforcement at the level of adult existence is necessary and desirable for the maintenance of the limit between people to awaken the arrogant to the conditions of coexistence, to the conditions of society, it is not the model for the primary educational way to promote citizenship because it embodies, after all, the violent and corrective use of force, the commanding-obeying that allows no room for disobedience and is unlikely to obtain genuine obedience. In civil affairs this is tolerable; educationally the person has to commit himself to his facticity in society, to being thrown into existence with others, which constitutes being-in-the-law and fulfills the laws. How to get the pupil to commit himself to the moral facticity of society as this is codified and defined in the laws in force is the phenomenological formulation of the problem of schooling for citizenship, for the desirability of promoting citizenship as an aim of schooling is the desirability of transforming political power into the education to freedom that renders the violent use of power in law enforcement unnecessary.

The rules and regulations of schooling are the laws in force in the pupil's existence. This is not to say that they are analogous to the legal order of adult society, nor that they resemble that legal order, nor that they are a microcosm of the macrocosm. They *are* the legal order, and represent the moral facticity of schooling. Just as the laws in force in society embody the law, when they are just, so do schooling rules and regulations embody the law when they are just. Children and youth are rightly judged to be not legally responsible for their actions when they are "under age," which means they are legally estimated to be incompetent in understanding the laws in force in society. When schooling rules and regulations are absolutely just, however, they are the legal order belonging to the life-phase of the child and youth. For the pupil to be in the truth of the rules and regulations of schooling is for him to be committed to the moral facticity of the society within his horizon, to the truth of his coexistence with other pupils and with teachers, and constitutes the being-in-the-law that neither forgets the meaning of the being of the pupil for educating nor the meaning of education for the being of the pupil.

Education for citizenship, then, first of all requires that the rules and regulations of schooling be absolutely just, i.e., that they be revised as necessary according to the justice of authentic coexistence so that they establish the space of authentic everyday existence of schooling in the way that permits the pupil to spatialize and temporalize as he would if he were existing authentically and relating to others in authentic solicitude. When schooling rules and regulations do structure the space of schooling according to the demands of genuine, everyday coexistence, then their enforcement exists *schooling* for citizenship. If they are to be in force to establish the moral facticity of schooling, they have to be enforced absolutely, in each and every case, with no exceptions, just like laws. If what constitutes enforcement in schooling, however, is appropriate to the life-phase of the pupil and occurs within the pedagogic paradox governed by authentic solicitude, then enforcement of schooling rules and regulations exists *educating* for citizenship.

In adult law enforcement the judge judges the amount of enforcement that is necessary to fit the exigencies of the particular case. Within the limits of legal statute, he estimates the appropriate fine and/or length of imprisonment, issues a warning, suspends sentence, etc. The universal enforcement of universal laws occurs through the further attempt to achieve justice by trying to fit the punishment to the demands of the particular case. Although these kinds of enforcement are inappropriate to schooling, the distinctly educative enforcement is also appropriate to the particular case. The fact that schooling rules and regulations are universally enforced is demanded by schooling for citizenship and justice; the way in which they are enforced is modified according to the individual case to meet the demands of educating for citizenship and justice. What constitutes a just enforcement not only has to be decided anew in each particular case, but the possibility of disobedience has to be retained for an enforcement to be educative. There is no reason why the various modulations of the request, the admonition, the appeal, the challenge, etc., cannot constitute a form of enforcement that, on the one hand, exerts a very slight pressure of the moral facticity of schooling and that, on the other hand, lets room for disobedience in waiting for the pupil's growth so that he might be in the law and also in the truth. The request, the appeal, etc., not only can be used to sustain the "pressure" of law, they can forgive ahead of time, let room for disobedience, evoke the pupil's awareness of the existence of other people, and rely upon the power of co-being. This reliance upon the power of being changes schooling for citizenship to educating for citizenship and fulfills not only the letter of laws but also the spirit of law.

The most important of the reasons for attempting to fulfill the spirit of the law is that morality and citizenship are not equiprimordial: laws exist merely to supplement the more primordial everyday morality. Educating for citizenship as obedience to laws, accordingly, is merely a supplement to the more primordial educating for "character" as the promotion of authentic everyday morality. It is merely a supplement, desirable only when necessary due to the readiness of human being to fall into inauthentic existence. Then insofar as citizenship is an aim of educating, schooling rules and regulations have to be enforced universally, but insofar as this is supplementary, it should occur within the pedagogic arena through the use of the request, appeal, admonition, etc., in order to disclose the reason for the rule (or, better, the ground of the rule), rather than to promulgate the rule. The intent is not to get the pupil to conform to rules, but to be committed to the moral facticity of schooling. As the concept of "character" does not exist where people "have character," and probably should be abolished that they might "have character," so would the explicit formulation of rules and regulations disappear where children and youth respond to the coexistential imperative. Perhaps they should be abolished that they might so respond.

One full illustration will suffice. School could start any time of day and classes could meet anywhere. They could begin at sunrise or noon and could meet in the teacher's home, the library, or the park. For the greatest convenience to all, however, there are schools, and classes begin at a regular time. A given pupil, e.g., has to be in Room 121 at nine a.m. It might be said the rule is to be on time, that this is necessary for the efficient operation of the school or to "run the institution," or that it is good to develop habits of punctuality or to be punctual; but all of this misses the point, the ground of the "rule." If there is to be educating in mass society, there has to be schooling to bring pupils and teachers together. The class starts at nine o'clock in Room 121 so that the pupils and teacher can be with one another. The authentic reason why a given pupil ought to be in Room 121 at nine o'clock, then, is that the others are there. At the risk of laboring the obvious in order to establish the total context and make the obvious obvious, the time and place are ultimately arbitrary and unjustifiable, but once the logistics are decided upon administratively, the reason it is important to be on time is simply because that is when the others are there, i.e., because they exist. If a given pupil is tardy, or habitually tardy, he needs not to learn a school rule or a moral maxim about punctuality—these are too verbal and alienate the pupil from the real reason. If he is to become able to come on time, if he is to become clearer about his situation and remain someone himself, he has to become aware of the being of the other children and the teacher. He may appear to know that they exist, but he has not recognized with his whole being that they exist as self-conscious beings whose very being as pupils and as a teacher places claims upon his very being as a pupil. He needs a reversal of his being if he is to be able to respond to the demands of his situation, if his situation is to extend its demands to him. What can the teacher say to enforce the "schooling regulation" and to awaken the pupil to the truth of his coexistence that he might be in the law? The request: "Could you come five minutes earlier tomorrow so that we can begin together?" The invitation: "We'd be able to start together if you'd be a bit earlier." The appeal: "Would you *please* be here when the other children arrive?" The challenge: "You live a block further from school and have to hurry to get here when they do, don't you?" The provocation: "Well, here's our ten o'clock scholar." The admonition: "You know you ought to be here when everyone else arrives so we don't have to wait for you."

Of course these sayings would have to be heard by the pupil as a request, invitation, appeal, etc., for them to be constituted as such, which would mean that within them the teacher would have to speak directly to the pupil, without irony, sarcasm, etc., but this merely means that she has to enforce the rule about arriving on time appropriately by respond-ing to the demands of the immediate situation: she has to understand the particular pupil well enough to speak authentically to him, to disclose the truth of his coexistence to him, and to waken him to his obligation for co-being. Because these sayings allow room for disobedience, they allow the pupil to be someone himself and also permit genuine obedience, for genuine being-in-the-law, and thus occur within the authentic solicitude that takes the being of the pupil into account. To enforce all school rules and regulations by an appropriate request, appeal, admonition, etc., is to take the significance of the being of children and youth into account in educating to citizenship as well as to take account of the desirability of educating for citizenship for the being of the pupil.

CITIZENSHIP: FORMAL ASPECTS

If schooling occurs under the rule of the pedagogic paradox, half of which is concerned with the authentic everydayness of schooling, then the traditional aim of education to promote citizenship in respect to its material aspects is fulfilled. This was the conclusion reached earlier concerning both the material and formal aspects of character as an aim of education. The formal aspects of education to citizenship, i.e., education for democratic living, requires explicit consideration at this point. Educat-ing for a democracy signifies educating for a life embodying democratic ideals. Democratic ideals can be considered from two aspects. The great, stirring democratic ideals are, in the battle cry of the French Revolution, liberty, equality, and fraternity. But what is freedom other than the liberated, authentic existence of the independently functioning adult who has adequately reassessed his adolescent ideals? And what is brotherhood other than the genuine coexistence achieved by this adult? And how could freedom and fraternity be implemented in the life-phases of childhood and youth in school other than through the pedagogic paradox that exists the co-primordiality of authentic individual existence (liberty) and authentic coexistence (fraternity)? How could they be promoted in schooling other than through the search for identity and community, the concomitant projects of individual and collective liberation that exist the paradox? The second aspect of democratic ideals concerns their implementation in the maintenance of civil liberties, the resolution of public problems through the use of reason in their public discussion, and the central belief in the worth, dignity, and integrity of the individual person.[39] But how could one implement the belief in civil liberties and adoption of the rule of reason other than by allowing the room for behavioral and intellectual disobedience that exists the pedagogic paradox in schooling? And how could one implement the ideals of equality and the ultimate value of the individual other than by relying upon the nonviolent power of being to establish the pedagogic relation? How could one begin to implement the beliefs in the equality of the worth and dignity of people other than by asking the questions concerning the significance of the being of children and youth for educating and the significance of education for their being?

Any society that professes allegiance to democratic ideals and also wishes to implement those ideals through schooling would find it desirable to ground educating in the being of the pupil. This brief treatment does not adequately deal with the vast number of issues raised in the large body of literature that has developed since educating for democracy replaced citizenship as an aim of schooling, but perhaps the concepts of democracy do not exist where people are democratic. Perhaps they should be abolished that they might so be. Be this as it may, from the viewpoint of the desirability of the traditional aims of education for character and citizenship, in both the formal and material aspects of each, it is desirable to promote authentic individual and authentic coexistence in educating. It is desirable to ground educating in the being of the pupil and to ground his being in the being of the world.

VOCATION

It stands otherwise with vocation, the third member of the venerable trinity, at least at first glance. The eclipse of the first two aims in the post-Sputnik era is due to the overwhelming emphasis that has come to be placed upon schooling as vocational preparation. This is part of the mobilization of the planet and the dominance of the worker in the technologizing of the world in the general alienation of man and forgetfulness of being. Because it is precisely from the aim of schooling as vocational preparation that the greatest alienation of the pupil occurs in the forgetfulness of his being, the direction of approach must be reversed in order to fulfill the ontological and societal functions of philosophy of education by indicating how the grounding of education in the pupil's being is desirable from the point of view of this traditional aim of education. What is called for is a delimitation of the scope of vocational preparation within schooling to allow room for the authentic individual existence and authentic coexistence found to be desirable in the consideration of the other aims of schooling. This delimitation will also ground schooling as vocational preparation in the being of youth.

The content of the curriculum in the schooling aspect of the pedagogic paradox has been specified only in the very general terms becoming to this inquiry. It has been assumed that its content should be largely determined by the teacher, who herself is presumably sufficiently educated to be able to do this without the assistance of the curriculum packages that insufficiently take the being of the pupil into account, and who herself has in view the general requirements of vocational and college preparation in societal context. The content of schooling is the intellectual-historical world of the youth's explorations, but this is the academic and utilitarian emphasis that is balanced by educating in the "life-adjustment" emphasis of the other half of the paradox. To identify schooling with vocational and college preparation in this way indicates the lack of an ontological distinction between the two: college preparation is a form of vocational preparation, and the appropriate vocational preparation is akin to college preparation. Although college preparation is sometimes distinguished from vocational preparation, this has to be interpreted as signifying that the specific vocational choice is deferred until the choice of a major subject in college must be irrevocably made. Although this choice may be deferred until the second or third year of college, it does not signify that all that has gone before is not vocational preparation. It indicates that the deferment establishes as broad a basis as possible for the inevitable choice and subsequent specialization. This suggests that perhaps the vocational choice cannot be grounded in the being of the pupil as a first-person, existential choice until he is considerably well along into youth as a life-phase.

As a life-phase, youth can be considered as comprised of two subphases, "separated" by the decisive event of the vocational choice. If the person lives his childhood and youth fully, then as his life-possibilities come into view, as he recognizes, accepts, and wants to be an economically independent adult and sees the place in society that he wants to occupy, he is enabled to make the choice of occupation with his whole being. If the being of youth is to be taken into account in educating and the aims of educating for character and citizenship be attained, then he has to be allowed to make this choice authentically. The attestation of the pre-philosophical understanding of the possibility of the authenticity of this choice is to be found in the etymology of the word *vocation*: a calling. To choose an occupation authentically is to choose it as a place to occupy, to dwell in, to which dwelling place one is called in accordance with his understanding of what life expects from him. The authentic vocational choice is made in response to a call from being. As this call comes to one from one's future self only through concrete situations, it is only when youth has sufficiently explored the intellectual-historical world that he is able to see the situation of adult existence as an extension of his own situation and is able to receive this call to being and make a vocational choice with his whole being. To look at a "profile" derived from a battery of standardized tests is to look backwards to where he has been, and constitutes a fixation in the past as well as a diversion of attention. It constitutes a distraction and fragmentation of his being and an alienation from the situations in which he is to find himself. If his education has been grounded in his being, he already understands anything important that such a "profile" could tell him because it merely organizes the answers he submits to test items, and if he is not alienated from himself he has already put these together for himself. Where such a "profile" seems to be needed, educating has not been occurring, and what is really needed is educating. If he has lived childhood fully and is living youth fully, he will respond to the call of being and make a vocational choice as an existential choice when he is ready. To push him to it earlier through the organization of schooling, mechanical logistics, and the structure of the curriculum participates in the oblivion of being.

The significance of the being of youth for educating for vocation is that they require common education until they can make their own vocational choices with their whole being. The significance of vocational education for the being of youth is that when they make this choice, they are then ready to explore with great vigor the particular, specialized curriculum that is ordinarily designated a vocational preparation. This curriculum completes their schooling by situating them directly in the social-historical world, for its last phase is some form of apprenticeship, on-the-job training, internship, or the like. If something is to be done about the "loss of identity" and the "loss of community," then specialized vocational preparation will be deferred, the way it is for the overprivileged, until the youth is able to choose his vocation existentially so that he can live both subphases of youth fully.

To recover from inauthentic individual existence, the youth has to be able to answer the call to being through an authentic vocational choice. To recover from inauthentic coexistence, equal facilities have to be available for all youth. This means that post-secondary schools have to be available for the vocational preparation of each alike.[40] All such "training" belongs at the post-secondary level to promote the development of the authentic choice, and it belongs to everyone the way tax-supported higher education is now supplied for the elect. Schooling in tax-supported junior colleges, state colleges, and land-grant universities is vocational preparation at public expense for the "chosen few" who are able to defer the vocational choice until they are ready, and sooner or later the equivalent public money ought to be available to furnish the equivalent post-secondary vocational preparation for all that all might be able to live their youth fully and get it over with. Sooner or later it ought to be recognized that for some youth to be allowed to defer the vocational choice until the college years while other youth are forced into making it in the junior high school before their youth has even begun, i.e., while they are still children, is the grossest inequality and that it ought to be declared unconstitutional for the public schools to sort and select for vocational purposes at the elementary and secondary levels. Until post-secondary vocational schooling is available for everyone, there is no way to overcome the general forgetfulness of being. When is the youth old enough to choose an occupation as a vocation? What is the significance of the being of youth? Why are there youth?

If all vocational preparation were deferred until the post-secondary level of schooling, then the common curriculum of the elementary and secondary levels would establish the common world, the condition necessary for authentic coexistence (Chapter 8). If the latter were governed by the pedagogic paradox, it would also establish the conditions for authentic individual existence (Chapters 9 and 10). This is what is now demanded by citizenship and character as aims of education. It is also demanded by authentic vocational education, for the vocational training that occurs before the authentic vocational choice occurs remains ungrounded and contributes to the alienation of the youth from the world, himself, and others. If it is desirable to have vocational preparation as an aim of schooling at the elementary and secondary levels as it now is, then it is not desirable to ground education in the being of the pupil, child or youth. In the larger perspective, however, vocational training can become grounded in the being of the pupil and become vocational education. Then in regard to the total process of possible schooling (including post-secondary schooling, some of which does not yet exist), it is desirable to ground educating in the being of the pupil to the exact extent that it is desirable for people to exist authentically at work.

If it is desirable for people to exist authentically at work through working willingly, eagerly, and happily at that to which they are called, then it is desirable to subordinate the aim of vocational preparation to the aims of character and citizenship as herein defined and grounded in the being of children and youth. If it is not subordinated to education for individual and collective liberation, not only do the efforts toward the latter go astray but the alienation from the world in the world of work is thereby increased even with the most advanced curriculums. If vocation is not subordinated to the other traditional aims, then these aims might as well be forgotten, as they mostly are, but then one should also forget the problems that are manifestations of the loss of identity and the loss of community, such as personal and societal disintegration, poverty, racial discrimination, increased crime rates, the destruction of the earth, famine, and war, because one should willingly accept the consequences of this refusal to transform political power into the nonviolent power of being and this forgetfulness of the being of children and youth and the consequences of the broader, all-encompassing oblivion of being of which this forgetfulness is a sign. If one forgets the being of children and youth in educating he should willingly go through the zone of nihilism that the technologizing of the world is bringing about on the planetary level through the dominance of inauthentic work. The phrase "go through," however, is too optimistic, for the consequence of the general loss of being is to enter the zone of nihilism with no assurance whatsoever that it is a "zone" from which a recovery of being is subsequently possible. But what is the significance of this nothingness for education? Why is there educating and why not rather nothing?

Notes

CHAPTER 1

1. Erwin Straus, *The Primary World of the Senses*, trans. J. Needleman (New York: Free Press, 1963), pp. 285–87.
2. Alfred Schuetz, "On Multiple Realities," *Philosophy and Phenomenological Research*, 5 (June 1945), 537–38, 569; and Martin Heidegger, *Being and Time*, trans. J. Macquarrie and E. Robinson (New York: Harper & Row, 1962), section 69b.
3. Martinus Langeveld, *Studien zur Anthropologie des Kindes* (Tübingen: Max Niemeyer Verlag, 1956), p. 34.
4. Heidegger, *Being and Time*, sections 9 and 10.
5. *Ibid.*, pp. 255, 437; also Jean-Paul Sartre, *Being and Nothingness*, trans. H. E. Barnes (New York: Philosophical Library, 1956), p. 171.
6. See John Wild's "Reply to Father Adelman and Professor Schrag," *Philosophy and Phenomenological Research*, 32 (March 1962), 413.
7. Ulrich Sonnemann, *Existence and Therapy* (New York: Grune & Stratton, 1954), pp. 14–15.
8. The attempt to be objective, i.e., to live in an objective time through the use of objective concepts in one's thinking, the attempt to live in a "present without a future, or an eternal present, is precisely the definition of death," so that the "ideal of objective thought is both based upon and ruined by temporality." Maurice Merleau-Ponty, *Phenomenology of Perception*, trans. C. Smith (London: Routledge & Kegan Paul, 1962), p. 333. By permission of Routledge & Kegan Paul and Humanities Press, New York.
9. Schuetz, "On Multiple Realities," pp. 551–55.
10. Carl Rogers, "The Loneliness of Contemporary Man as Seen in 'The Case of Ellen West,'" *Review of Existential Psychology and Psychiatry*, 1 (Spring 1961), 101.
11. Konrad Mohr, *"Die Pädagogik Herman Nohls,"* Erziehung und Leben (Heidelberg: Quelle und Meyer, 1960), ed. Otto Bollnow, p. 87.
12. Schuetz, "On Multiple Realities," pp. 570–72; Sonnemann, *Existence and Therapy*, pp. 16, 30. See Heinz Hartmann's *Psychoanalysis and Moral Values* (New York: International Universities Press, 1962), pp. 9–13, for indications that most applications of psychoanalytic ideas are regarded by orthodox Freudians as misapplications.
13. Sonnemann, *Existence and Therapy*, pp. 14–15.
14. Edmund Husserl, "The Crisis of European Humanity and Science," *The Search for Being* (New York: The Noonday Press, 1962), pp. 404–13. When Skinner, for example, suggests that he has merely formulated the theory that has reinforced him, he psychologizes the truth and validity of his own theory away.
15. Martinus Langeveld, *Einführung in die Pädagogik* (Stuttgart: Ernst Klett

Verlag, 1963), p. 104; and Gustav Würtenberg, *Existenz und Eriziehung* (Dusseldorf: Schwann, 1949), p. 43.

16. Langeveld, *Studien*, p. 15–16.
17. *Ibid.*, p. 23.
18. Alfred Schuetz, *The Problem of Social Reality* (The Hague: Martinus Nijhoff, 1962), p. 116.
19. If the variables are isolated by the statistical analysis, a very peculiar form of platonizing occurs. If they are isolated beforehand, it is ordinarily done by an external arrangement of the problem investigated. M. Langeveld, *"Theoretische und empirische Forschung in der Erziehungswissenshaft," Zeitschrift für Pädagogik*, 4 (August 1964), 384; and John Wild's "Rejoinder to Thornton Read's Reply," *Philosophy and Phenomenological Research*, 1 (June 1940), 410–13.
20. Langeveld, *Studien*, p. 111.
21. Mohr, "Herman Nohls," p. 74.
22. Langeveld, *Studien*, pp. 30, 40.
23. Langeveld, *Einführung*, p. 90.
24. Sartre, *Search for a Method*, trans. H. E. Barnes (New York: Knopf, 1963), p. 96.
25. Sonnemann, *Existence and Therapy*, p. 16; and Paul Tillich, "Existentialism and Therapy," *Review of Existential Psychology and Psychiatry*, 1 (Winter 1961), 15.
26. William Luijpen, *Existential Phenomenology* (Pittsburgh: Duquesne University Press, 1960), p. 285.

CHAPTER 2

1. That is, by pragmatism in the United States, by the various forms of analytic philosophy among English-speaking philosophers in general, by Russian philosophers operating within some form of Marxism, and by existentialists and phenomenologists on the European continent.
2. See the annotated bibliography in Section F, *Philosophy of Education; An Organization of Topics and Selected Sources* (Urbana: University of Illinois Press, 1967), compiled by Harry Broudy, et al.; and the anthology devoted exclusively to the matter, *What is Philosophy of Education?* J. C. Lucas, ed. (New York: Macmillan, 1969).
3. For Herbart, see Adolph Meyer, *The Development of Education in the Twentieth Century* (Englewood Cliffs, N. J.: Prentice-Hall, 1949), pp. 19, 21–22; John Childs, *Education and Morals* (New York: Wiley, 1967), Science Editions, pp. 17–20; William O. Stanley, *Education and Social Integration* (New York: Bureau of Publications, Teachers College, Columbia University, 1953), pp. 13, 119–24.

CHAPTER 3

1. For development of the idea that Husserl, Heidegger, Sartre, and Merleau-Ponty are the central figures in the broader movement in existential phenomenology, see James M. Edie, "Transcendental Phenomenology and Existential-

ism," *Philosophy and Phenomenological Research,* 25 (September 1964), 52–63. For the demonstration of the unity of the movement, see William A. Luijpen, *Existential Phenomenology.*

2. Husserl dealt with the phenomenological reductions throughout his writings. That he set aside the viewpoint of naïve realism, the natural sciences, formal logic, and the existence of the phenomenon can be seen in Edmund Husserl, *Ideas; General Introduction to Pure Phenomenology,* trans. W. R. Boyce Gibson (New York: Macmillan, 1951), pp. 11, 110–11, 150–53, 171, 176. See also the third of the 1907 lectures published as *The Idea of Phenomenology,* trans. Wm. P. Alston and George Nakhnikian (The Hague: Martinus Nijhoff, 1964), pp. 32–42. *Cf.* Aron Gurwitsch, *The Field of Consciousness* (Pittsburgh: Duquesne University Press, 1964), pp. 164–68, for one of the briefest and most accurate accounts of the reductions. For a longer introductory explanation of the reductions, see Quentin Lauer, "Basic Phenomenological Techniques," *Phenomenology: Its Genesis and Prospect* (New York: Harper & Row, 1965), pp. 46–64; originally published as *The Triumph of Subjectivity* (New York: Fordham University Press, 1958).

3. The reference is to Snygg and Combs, Lewin, Rogers, and so on. The general point was indicated to me by Harry Broudy in conversation.

4. Husserl, *Ideas,* pp. 119–21.

5. Edie, "Transcendental Phenomenology," pp. 57–59.

6. *Ibid.,* p. 62.

7. John Dewey, *Democracy and Education* (New York: Macmillan, 1916), p. 386.

8. Harry Broudy, "How Philosophical Can Philosophy of Education Be?" *Journal of Philosophy,* 52 (October 1955), pp. 612–22; and *Building a Philosophy of Education* (Englewood Cliffs, N. J.: Prentice-Hall, 1960), Preface and Chapter 1.

9. This needs to be qualified because much of the speculative framework of *Building a Philosophy* is dropped in *Democracy and Excellence in the American Secondary School* (Chicago: Rand McNally, 1964), which Broudy co-authored with B. Othanel Smith and Joe R. Burnett. Whether or not it is still presupposed in this book, however, is an interesting question.

10. By "first generation" I mean Dewey, Kilpatrick, and Bode; and by "second generation" I mean Childs, Raup, Counts, Hullfish, and Rugg.

11. By "third generation" I mean Axtelle, Benne, Brameld, Smith, Stanley, and Thomas; and by fourth and fifth I mean others too numerous to mention.

12. William O. Stanley, *Education and Social Integration,* pp. 128–30, and Chapter 8.

13. R. Bruce Raup, Kenneth Benne, George Axtelle, and B. Othanel Smith, *The Improvement of Practical Intelligence* (New York: Teachers College Press, 1962), originally 1943.

14. Kenneth Benne, *Education in the Quest for Identity and Community* (Columbus: Ohio State University Press, 1962), p. 4.

CHAPTER 4

1. And, of course, the smaller the phases and the more the detail the less generally valid is the interpretation.

2. Romano Guardini, *Die Lebensalter; Ihre Ethische und Pädagogische Bedeutung,* number six in the series, *Weltbild und Erziehung,* 5th Ed. (Würzburg: Werkbund-Verlag, 1959), p. 15.

3. *Ibid.,* pp. 16, 25.

4. *Ibid.*, pp. 26, 70.
5. *Ibid.*, p. 30.
6. *Ibid.*, p. 22.
7. *Ibid.*, pp. 23, 35.
8. *Ibid.*, p. 24.
9. *Ibid.*
10. *Ibid.*, p. 31.
11. *Ibid.*, p. 35.
12. *Ibid.*, p. 36.
13. *Ibid.*
14. *Ibid.*, p. 37.
15. *Ibid.*, p. 38.
16. *Ibid.*
17. *Ibid.*, p. 39.
18. *Ibid.*, pp. 41–44.
19. *Ibid.*, pp. 44–45.
20. *Ibid.*, pp. 49–50.
21. *Ibid.*, p. 55.
22. Martin Heidegger, *Being and Time*, sections 74–75.

CHAPTER 5

1. Kenneth D. Benne, *A Conception of Authority* (New York: Bureau of Publications, Teachers College, Columbia University, 1943).
2. It should be apparent why calling the nipple a "stimulus" omits that which is specifically human. After indicating that the theory of reflexes replaced natural movements by artificially isolated elements, Langeveld suggested that the newborn infant had many "reflexes" of *no* biological significance, indicating that to explain some action as reflexive was inadequate if there were other "reflexes" that extinguished themselves through disuse. Martinus J. Langeveld, *Studien zur Anthropologie des Kindes*, p. 76. The mother's pushing the nipple into the baby's mouth may be the first pedagogic act.
3. *Cf.* Langeveld, *Studien*, p. 61.
4. *Ibid.*, p. 80.
5. That the "senses" function together in experiencing can be demonstrated. If the sound is turned off on television, and just the visual part of dancing is observed, the dance appears extremely ungraceful. Seeing the movement of the dance may be inseparable from hearing the music, at least for inferior performance. Then music does not accompany the dance but constitutes it, even for the spectator. That the various "senses" are "going on" at the same time and experienced as united, that their separation is an artificial and theoretically induced phenomenon, is clear when the natural synesthesia of the child is noted.
6. Langeveld, *Studien*, pp. 58, 84.
7. *Ibid.*, pp. 93–94.
8. Maurice Merleau-Ponty, *The Structure of Behavior*, trans., A. L. Fisher (Boston: Beacon Press, 1963), p. 167.
9. Langeveld, *Studien*, p. 58.

10. *Ibid.*, p. 60.
11. *Ibid.*, p. 49.
12. Rudolph Allers, *Existentialism and Psychiatry* (Springfield; Charles C. Thomas, 1961), p. 63.
13. Langeveld, *Studien*, p. 92.
14. *Ibid.*, p. 14.
15. Martinus Langeveld, *Einführung in die Pädagogik*, p. 102.
16. *Ibid.*, p. 85.
17. *Ibid.*, p. 165.
18. *Ibid.*, p. 102.
19. *Ibid.*, p. 49.
20. *Ibid.*, p. 95.
21. Maurice Merleau-Ponty, *Phenomenology of Perception* (London: Routledge & Kegan Paul, 1962), p. 178. By permission of Routledge & Kegan Paul and Humanities Press, New York.
22. Merleau-Ponty, *Structure of Behavior*, p. 222.
23. The following is somewhat derived from F.J.J. Buytendijk's "Experienced Freedom and Moral Freedom in the Child's Consciousness," *Educational Theory*, 3 (January, 1953), pp. 1–13, but more in principle than in detail. I have retained the names of some of the stages, but the descriptions are corrected where necessary. For example, Buytendijk suggested that the first stage of experienced freedom is that of caprice and revolt, but he sees this as projecting the world of refusal or as a result of encountering obstacles. The child revolts against obstacles to experience his freedom. My difference with Buytendijk is that this presupposes a previous experience of freedom that was blocked by the obstacle so that the reaction to the obstacle is a second and more sophisticated level than he imagined. The phase of "negativism" therefore is not the first experiencing of freedom by the child: his negating obstacles would be pointless unless this were to regain a lost freedom that I wish to call freedom of caprice. This of course suggests that freedom of refusal and revolt is more meaningful than caprice but not as meaningful as choice, which is precisely the point. My difference with Buytendijk, that is, is that his descriptions do not seem to stay sufficiently within the phenomenological reduction.
24. Langeveld, *Einführung*, p. 42.
25. Heidegger, *Being and Time*, p. 440.

CHAPTER 6

1. See Frank W. Lutz and Laurence Innaccone, *Understanding Educational Organizations: A Field Study Approach* (Columbus: Merrill, 1969) for good reasons for the superiority of field method over others.
2. This mostly follows the interpretation of Arnold Stenzel in *"Die anthropologische Function des Wanderns und ihre pädagogische Bedeutung," Erziehung und Leben*, ed. Otto F. Bollnow (Heidelberg: Quelle und Meyer, 1960), pp. 96–99.
3. *Ibid.*, p. 104.
4. Martin Heidegger, *Being and Time*, p. 173.
5. *Primary optimism* is distinguished from secondary optimism in that the latter

is a matter of temporary exuberance, an explicit *Weltanschauung*, self-conscious confidence, or "positive thinking," any of which may be superficial and dis-junctive with the underlying state-of-being. The distinction is Binswanger's. Stenzel, *"Die Function des Wanderns,"* p. 105.

6. *Ibid.*, p. 106.
7. *Ibid.*, pp. 107–8.
8. *Ibid.*, pp. 108–9.
9. *Ibid.*, p. 110.
10. Heidegger, "Remembrance of the Poet," *Existence and Being* (Chicago: Reg-nery, 1949), pp. 260–61.
11. Heidegger, "What is Metaphysics?" *Existence and Being*, p. 358.
12. Heidegger, "Hölderlin and the Essence of Poetry," *Existence and Being*, p. 274.
13. *Cf.* Erwin Straus, *The Primary World of the Senses*, pp. 327–28.
14. Maurice Merleau-Ponty, *Phenomenology of Perception* (London: Routledge & Kegan Paul, 1962), p. 184. By permission of Routledge & Kegan Paul and Humanities Press. See also Georges Gusdorf, *Speaking*, trans. P. Brockelman (Evanston: Northwestern University Press, 1965), p. 49.
15. Straus, *World of the Senses*, p. 328.
16. *Ibid.*, pp. 318, 388.
17. Jean-Paul Sartre, *Being and Nothingness*, pp. 318–19.
18. *Ibid.*, pp. 124–29.
19. *Ibid.*, p. 145.
20. Jean-Paul Sartre, *Being and Nothingness*, tr. Hazel Barnes (New York: Philo-sophical Library, 1956), p. 32. By permission of Philosophical Library, Inc.
21. *Ibid.*, pp. 29–30.

CHAPTER 7

1. Romano Guardini, *Die Lebensalter*, p. 34.
2. See Straus, *The Primary World of the Senses*, p. 324 for a brief phenomenology of gypsy music.
3. Heidegger, *Being and Time*, pp. 217–19; Sartre, *Being and Nothingness*, p. 170.
4. Stenzel, *"Die Function des Wandern,"* p. 119.
5. John Dewey, *Democracy and Education*, p. 344. Emphasis his.
6. James E. McClellan, "The Logical and the Psychological: An Untenable Dualism?" *Language and Concepts in Education*, ed. B. O. Smith and R. H. Ennis, pp. 144–60. An example of what I mean by the "emotive" element in his "logical" analyses is his question: "Were educators really so stupid in 1902 that this perfectly obvious difference had to be pointed out?" McClellan must mean, in context, that if the distinction is new to the reader, it is not to Dewey's honor to have articulated it. It is one's own stupidity that makes it seem as though Dewey said something. Because one hesitates to confess to stupidity for not having noticed such a "perfectly obvious" difference, he ac-quiesces to the point. But see McClellan for a masterly historical account of the distinction.
7. Stenzel, *"Die Function des Wandern,"* pp. 119–20.
8. *Ibid.*, p. 120.
9. *Ibid.*, p. 105.
10. *Ibid.*, p. 120.

11. Heidegger, *Being and Time*, sections 33, 44; also his essay, "On the Essence of Truth," *Existence and Being*, esp. pp. 299–302.
12. Stenzel, *"Die Function des Wandern,"* p. 123.
13. *Ibid.*
14. Gustav Würtenberg, *Existenz und Erziehung*, pp. 30–31.

CHAPTER 8

1. Jean-Paul Sartre, *Search for a Method*, p. 96.
2. *Ibid.*, p. 95.
3. The reader can decide for himself whether it is too strong to refer to the practice of destroying children's and youth's possibilities of being by the designation *murder* to be descriptively accurate or whether its use is justified.

CHAPTER 9

1. Paul Ricoeur, *Fallible Man*, trans. Charles Kelbley (Chicago: Regnery, 1965), pp. 180, 182.
2. This, of course, is Sartre's phenomenology of being-for-others but herein, moralistically if you will, clearly designated as an inauthentically human interrelation because both projects, both the transcending-transcendence and the transcended-transcendence, presuppose that neither the other nor oneself is a being that is open to the world and in question in its having its being to be. *Being and Nothingness*, Part Three.
3. Paul Tillich, *Love, Power and Justice* (New York: Oxford University Press, 1954), pp. 48–49.
4. Hannah Arendt, *The Human Condition* (Chicago: University of Chicago Press, 1958), pp. 179–80, 186.
5. Martin Heidegger, "Hölderlin and the Essence of Poetry," *Existence and Being* (Chicago: Regnery, 1949), p. 276.
6. This appears to be close to what Arendt meant when she indicated how the development of the *polis,* the space of appearance that develops when people are able to disclose themselves, establishes political power (within her distinction of political power from force or strength), except it is transposed into the educational realm and it includes the intentionality of human existence. *The Human Condition*, pp. 198–200.
7. *Cf.* Heidegger, *Existence and Being*, "But the gods can acquire a name only by addressing and, as it were, claiming us. The word which names the gods is always a response to such a claim." P. 279.
8. Paul Tillich, *The Courage to Be* (New Haven: Yale University Press, 1952), pp. 81, 88–89.
9. Tillich, *Love, Power, and Justice*, p. 37.
10. Theodore Brameld, *Education as Power* (New York: Holt, Rinehart, & Winston, 1966), pp. 3–5.

11. These are the propaganda techniques through which societal interest groups achieve and maintain their memberships and consequently their power, and propaganda is a form of commanding, i.e., violent power. *Cf.* Brameld's last chapter, especially pp. 109–12.

CHAPTER 10

1. By the teacher's teachers and their teachers I refer to all "researchers" who who have made some contribution to knowledge (i.e., some disclosure of being) and added to the heritage.
2. Otto Friedrich Bollnow, *Existenzphilosophie und Pädagogik* (Stuttgart: Kohlhammer, 1959), pp. 19, 47.
3. *Ibid.*, p. 60.
4. *Ibid.*, pp. 60, 74–75.
5. This relies not only on Sartre's descriptions of being-for-others but also upon Heidegger's analysis of deficient and authentic solicitude in *Being and Time*, Section 26.
6. Bollnow, *Existenzphilosophie*, p. 75.
7. *Ibid.*, pp. 62–63.
8. *Ibid.*, p. 63.
9. *Ibid.*, p. 64.
10. *Ibid.*, p. 74.
11. Heidegger, *Being and Time*, pp. 329–34.
12. Bollnow, *Existenzphilosophie*, p. 74.
13. *Ibid.*, p. 65.
14. *Ibid.*, p. 66; and Heidegger, *Being and Time*, Section 57.
15. Bollnow, *Existenzphilosophie*, p. 66–68.
16. *Ibid.*, p. 62.
17. *Ibid.*, p. 112.
18. *Ibid.*, pp. 110–12.
19. *Ibid.*, pp. 93–103, 110.
20. *Ibid.*, p. 93.
21. *Ibid.*, pp. 105–7; and Heidegger, *Being and Time*, Section 69.
22. Bollnow, *Existenzphilosophie*, p. 120.
23. F. J. J. Buytendijk, "Experienced Freedom and Moral Freedom in the Child's Consciousness," *Educational Theory*, 3 (January 1953), 10–12.
24. If it is possible to measure the safety of the child's world so that a fair sample could be selected, this would be open to empirical confirmation/disconfirmation.
25. Bollnow, *Existenzphilosophie*, p. 132.
26. *Ibid.*, p. 134.

CHAPTER 11

1. Heinz Hartmann, *Psychoanalysis and Moral Values* (New York: International Universities Press, 1960), pp. 68–78.
2. See Harry S. Broudy, B. Othanel Smith, and Joe R. Burnett, *Democracy and*

Excellence in American Secondary Education (Chicago: Rand-McNally, 1964), Chapter Two, for an attempt to define these in a relevant way.

3. Martinus Langeveld, *Einführung in die Pädagogik*, p. 74.
4. Maurice Mandelbaum, *The Phenomenology of Moral Experience* (Glencoe: The Free Press, 1955), p. 177.
5. Erwin Straus, *On Obsession; A Clinical and Methodological Study* (New York: Coolidge Foundation, 1948), Nervous and Mental Disease Monographs, number 73, p. v.
6. Rudolph Allers, *Existentialism and Psychiatry*, (Springfield, Ill.: Charles C. Thomas, 1961), p. 45.
7. *Idem.*
8. Jan H. van den Berg, *The Phenomenological Approach to Psychiatry* (Springfield, Ill.: Charles C. Thomas, 1955), pp. 68–71.
9. Ludwig Binswanger, *Being-in-the-World*, tr. Jacob Needleman (New York: Basic Books, 1963), p. 218.
10. This is based mostly upon Sartre's thesis in *Transcendence of the Ego*, tr. F. Williams & R. Kirkpatrick (New York: Noonday, 1957) that became the foundation of his later work. See also Aron Gurwitsch, "A Non-egological Conception of Consciousness," *Philosophy and Phenomenological Research*, 1 (March 1940), 325–38.
11. Allers, *Existentialism and Psychiatry*, p. 47.
12. Reprinted from Jean-Paul Sartre, *Being and Nothingness*, tr. Hazel Barnes (New York: Philosophical Library, 1956), p. 376, by permission of Philosophical Library, Inc.
13. *Ibid.*, pp. 335–39, 342.
14. *Ibid.*, pp. 457, 508.
15. Heinz Lichtenstein, rev. of Sartre's *The Age of Reason*, in *Philosophy and Phenomenological Research*, 9 (September 1948), 150.
16. Reprinted from Heinz Lichtenstein, review of Jean-Paul Sartre's *The Age of Reason, Philosophy and Phenomenological Research*, 9 (September 1948), 151–53, by permission of the author and the editor of *Philosophy and Phenomenological Research*.
17. Viktor Frankl, *Man's Search For Meaning*, tr. Ilse Lasch (Boston: Beacon Press, 1962), pp. 108–10, 131. E.g., 'the sexual libido becomes rampant in the existential vacuum," p. 109.
18. *Ibid.*, p. 102.
19. *Ibid.*, pp. 98–110, 120, and Preface (by Gordon Allport).
20. Sartre, *Being and Nothingness*, p. 349.
21. Heidegger, *Being and Time*, pp. 159–63.
22. Sartre, *Being and Nothingness*, pp. 511–12.
23. *Cf.* "In anticipatory resoluteness, Dasein *holds* itself open for its constant lostness in the irresoluteness of the 'they.' " "In our analyses we have often used the expression 'proximally and for the most part.' 'Proximally' signifies the way in which Dasein is 'manifest' in the 'with-one-another' of publicness, even if 'at bottom' everydayness is precisely something which, in an existentiell manner, it has 'surmounted.' . . . Everydayness is determinative for Dasein even when it has not chosen the 'they' for its 'hero.' " Martin Heidegger, *Being and Time*, tr. J. Macquarrie and E. Robinson (New York: Harper & Row, 1962), pp. 356, 422. Reprinted by permission of Harper & Row, Publishers.
24. *Ibid.*, Section 27.
25. William A. Luijpen, *Existential Phenomenology*, p. 291.
26. Heidegger, *Being and Time*, Section 59.
27. Most of what follows in this paragraph is based on Heidegger, *Being and Time*, Sections 35–38.
28. *Ibid.*, pp. 327–28.
29. *Ibid.*, p. 340.
30. Sartre, *Being and Nothingness*, p. 626.

220 Being and Education

31. Heidegger, *Being and Time*, p. 159.
32. Jean-Paul Sartre, *Literary and Philosophical Essays*, tr. A. Michelson (London: Rider, 1955), p. 167.
33. John Wild, "A Reply to Mr. Gale," *Philosophy and Phenomenological Research*, 3 (Sept. 1942), 383.
34. Hannah Arendt, *The Human Condition*, p. 245.
35. *Ibid.*
36. I.e., at first every man is "Dadda," then every man not Daddy is man, then every man not Daddy or Uncle is man, and so on. Straus, *The Primary World*, pp. 93–94.
37. Werner Maihofer, *Recht und Sein; Prolegomena zu einen Rechtsontologie* (Frankfurt: Klostermann, 1959), p. 83. The indebtedness to Maihofer on the place of law in human existence is greater than I am able to document in the context of the text.
38. Luijpen, *Existential Phenomenology*, pp. 232ff.
39. Stanley, *Education and Social Integration*, p. 163.
40. See Broudy, *Building a Philosophy of Education*, pp. 362–71, and Broudy, Smith, and Burnett, *Democracy and Excellence in American Secondary Education*, pp. 31–41, for other reasons for the same recommendation.

Index